AF760085

PSYCHOLOGY OF EMOTIONS, MOTIVATIONS AND ACTIONS

SUICIDE FROM A GLOBAL PERSPECTIVE

PSYCHIATRIC APPROACHES

PSYCHOLOGY OF EMOTIONS, MOTIVATIONS AND ACTIONS

Additional books in this series can be found on Nova's website under the Series tab.

Additional e-books in this series can be found on Nova's website under the e-book tab.

PSYCHOLOGY OF EMOTIONS, MOTIVATIONS AND ACTIONS

SUICIDE FROM A GLOBAL PERSPECTIVE

PSYCHIATRIC APPROACHES

AMRESH SHRIVASTAVA
MEGAN KIMBRELL
AND
DAVID LESTER
EDITORS

nova publishers
New York

Copyright © 2012 by Nova Science Publishers, Inc.

All rights reserved. No part of this book may be reproduced, stored in a retrieval system or transmitted in any form or by any means: electronic, electrostatic, magnetic, tape, mechanical photocopying, recording or otherwise without the written permission of the Publisher.

For permission to use material from this book please contact us:
Telephone 631-231-7269; Fax 631-231-8175
Web Site: http://www.novapublishers.com

NOTICE TO THE READER

The Publisher has taken reasonable care in the preparation of this book, but makes no expressed or implied warranty of any kind and assumes no responsibility for any errors or omissions. No liability is assumed for incidental or consequential damages in connection with or arising out of information contained in this book. The Publisher shall not be liable for any special, consequential, or exemplary damages resulting, in whole or in part, from the readers' use of, or reliance upon, this material. Any parts of this book based on government reports are so indicated and copyright is claimed for those parts to the extent applicable to compilations of such works.

Independent verification should be sought for any data, advice or recommendations contained in this book. In addition, no responsibility is assumed by the publisher for any injury and/or damage to persons or property arising from any methods, products, instructions, ideas or otherwise contained in this publication.

This publication is designed to provide accurate and authoritative information with regard to the subject matter covered herein. It is sold with the clear understanding that the Publisher is not engaged in rendering legal or any other professional services. If legal or any other expert assistance is required, the services of a competent person should be sought. FROM A DECLARATION OF PARTICIPANTS JOINTLY ADOPTED BY A COMMITTEE OF THE AMERICAN BAR ASSOCIATION AND A COMMITTEE OF PUBLISHERS.

Additional color graphics may be available in the e-book version of this book.

Library of Congress Cataloging-in-Publication Data

Suicide from a global perspective : public health approaches / editors, Amresh Shrivastava, Megan Kimbrell and David Lester.
p. cm.
Includes index.
ISBN 978-1-61942-267-4 (hardcover)
1. Suicide--Prevention. I. Shrivastava, Amresh. II. Kimbrell, Megan. III. Lester, David.
RC569.S93434 2011
362.28--dc23

2011045820

Published by Nova Science Publishers, Inc. + New York

CONTENTS

FOREWORD

Suicide is the cause of death for nearly one million people a year. Death by suicide is often reported as being due to other causes to avoid stigmatization and other negative consequences of suicide for the family. It can, therefore, be assumed that the number of people who commit suicide is much higher than this number. Attempts at suicide, estimated to be ten times more frequent than completed suicide, often cause permanent impairment and disability. Suicide can stigmatize families across generations. The loss of life caused by suicide presents a significant loss for the communities in which it occurs – socially, economically and by blocking progress towards the creation of a civic society.

The aging of populations and the high prevalence of chronic diseases, both of which are risk factors for suicide and both of which characterize an increasing number of countries, as well as the increasing prevalence of several mental disorders (for example, depressive disorders) and the continuing growth of several other risk factors for suicide, make it possible to predict an increase in suicide rates worldwide unless resolute action is undertaken to prevent suicidal behavior. A major problem in that respect is that, in many countries, suicide is not seen as a major public health problem despite its frequency and the severity of its consequences. In part this is so because of a vicious circle. Methods of suicide prevention have not been sufficiently widely and vigorously applied, so that public health authorities, until now, have only a very limited number of compelling examples of successful suicide prevention programs. Therefore, these do not provide the resources for such programs, which in turn limits the possibility of producing successful programs that would convince them to continue their investment in this area of public health. In part, however, the absence of resolute action against suicide is due to the insufficient awareness of the magnitude and severity of the problem (and of the possibilities of effective intervention to reduce the problem) by the general population, by health and social service decision makers and by health professionals.

A textbook bringing together current knowledge about suicide, its causes and its prevention is a precious tool for public health efforts and for clinicians' daily work. The availability of an assembly of carefully and critically presented facts in the form of chapters responding to specific problems can help in the education of health professionals and provide them with data that they can use in developing proposals for action. It can draw attention to methods of work that have been tried elsewhere and found useful. It can provide a better understanding of the genesis of problem and its progression. When such a textbook is produced by an international group of experts from some thirty countries – developing and developed, North and South, East and West, characterized by different religions, traditions and cultures – it becomes even more useful because it presents knowledge seen through the eyes of professionals with rich experience gathered in dealing with the same problem under different circumstances prevailing in different parts of the world. These experts represent several disciplines that are involved in research and in practical work with people who may be at risk of suicide, and this multidisciplinary approach is another asset of this voluminous work.

It is, therefore, a pleasure to congratulate the authors of this work and to express the hope that the book will be read and used by many. The application of the knowledge that is assembled – in conducting further research, in education of different categories of personnel, and in providing care – will be the most significant reward for those who produced this book and, given the quality of their work and the efforts that they have made to make it such, they richly deserve it.

Professor N. Sartorius

PREFACE

This series of five volumes surveys the field of suicidology with two goals. As well as inviting well-known scholars from the field of suicidology to present their latest thoughts on the topics that they study, we have invited other scholars to apply the insights from their disciplines and their fields of study to the problem of understanding and preventing suicide.

Second, we have made an effort to invite scholars from the non-Western regions of the world to contribute their perspectives about suicidal behavior, thereby enriching our understanding of suicide. As a result, this volume has chapters from scholars whose work is not typically found in other edited books on suicidal behavior. For example, chapters cover the role of the environment and ecology in suicide, suicide in those with intellectual disabilities, and hidden suicide in the developing world, to name a few.

With these two goals, we have endeavored both to present contemporary thought about suicide and to break new boundaries in the ongoing efforts to understand this perplexing behavior.

Suicide is a multi-factorial problem, arising in a complex way from biological, psychological, sociological, cultural, environmental and geographical factors. An attempt has been made to bring in all of these factors into this survey. The present volume focuses on psychiatric perspectives.

Contributors

Editors

Amresh Shrivastava, MD
University of Western Ontario, Canada
dr.amresh@gmail.com

Megan Kimbrell, MA
The University of Akron
megan@justmegan.com

David Lester, PhD
The Richard Stockton College of New Jersey
lesterd@stockton.edu

Corresponding Authors

Ajit Avasthi, MD
Postgraduate Institute of Medical Education & Research,
Chandigarh, India
drajitavasthi@yahoo.co.in

Jayanti Chotai, MD
Umeå University, Sweden
jayanti.chotai@psychiat.umu.se

Ida F. Dancyger, PhD
New York University School of Medicine
ida.dancyger@gmail.com

Donald M. Dougherty, PhD
University ofTexas Health Science Center,
San Antonio, Texas
doughertyd@uthscsa.edu

Carl Ernst, PhD
Harvard Medical School, Massachusetts
ernst@chgr.mgh.harvard.edu

Jess G. Fiedorowicz, MD
University of Iowa
jess-fiedorowicz@uiowa.edu

Ian Storm Lewis, MD
Groote Schuur Hospital, South Africa
Ian.Lewis@uct.ac.za

Merete Nordentoft, PhD
University of Copenhagen
mn@dadlnet.dk

Maurizio Pompili, MD
Sant'Andrea Hosptial, Rome, Italy
Maurizio.Pompili@uniroma1.it

Annamaria Pusztai, PhD
University of Debrecen, Hungary
pusztaia@med.unideb.hu

Zoltan Rihmer, MD
Semmelweis University, Hungary
rihmerz@kut.sote.hu

Alec Roy, MD
VA Healthcare System, New Jersey
Alec.Roy@med.va.gov

Randy A. Sansone, MD
Wright State University ,
Boonshoft School of Medicine, Ohio
Randy.Sansone@khnetwork.org

Stig Söderberg, MD
Umeå University, Sweden
Stig.Soderberg@vll.se

J. K. Trivedi, MD
C.S.M. Medical University, Lucknow, India
jitendra.trivedi@gmail.com

Airi Värnik, MD
Tallinn University, Estonia
airiv@online.ee

Gil Zalsman, MD
Geha Mental Health Center, Israel
zalsman@post.tau.ac.il

PeterZill, PhD
University of Munich, Germany
peter.zill@psy.med.uni-muenchen.de

PART 1: THE PHENOMENOLOGY OF SUICIDE

In: Suicide from a Global Perspective
Editors: A. Shrivastava, M. Kimbrell, and D. Lester ISBN: 978-1-61942-267-4
© 2012 Nova Science Publishers, Inc.

Chapter 1

ATTEMPTED SUICIDE

Maurizio Pompili, Eleonora De Pisa, Marco Innamorati, Paolo Girardi, Roberto Tatarelli, and David Lester

INTRODUCTION

Suicide is one of the leading causes of death in the world, especially in those aged 15-35. A history of suicide attempts has been considered to be a significant risk factor for future suicidal behavior including completed suicide (Rudd, 2006). Although the exact number of people killing themselves, attempting suicide or thinking of ending their lives worldwide is still a matter of discussion, there is general agreement that the risk of repeated non-fatal suicidal acts seems to be growing. More and more suicide attempters repeat their suicidal acts, not only once, but often several times, with increasing risk of an eventual fatal outcome. Lester (1987) reported that those who make repeated suicide attempts are more socially deviant in general than other suicidal persons. Those who perform such repeated behavior seem to belong to a separate category compared with those who complete suicide or attempt suicide only once or a few times.

In the year 2000 approximately one million people died by suicide. For every completed suicide, there are somewhere between 10 and 40 attempted suicides (World Health Organization, 1999; World Health Organization, 2002). Other sources estimate that there are ten to 25 non-fatal suicide attempts for every suicide completion, and these numbers rise to 100–200 for adolescents (Maris, 2002). The Youth Risk Behavior Survey, conducted by the Centers for Disease Control and Prevention (CDC) biennially (Centers for Disease Control and Prevention, 2004) consistently reports that a large number of youth in grades 9-12 consider or attempt suicide (Brener, Krug and Simon, 2000). However, no reliable data exist on the real dimension of the burden of suicide attempts worldwide.

Suicidal behavior ranges from ideation, to non-fatal attempts, to completions, all of which have their own different subtypes and levels of seriousness or lethality. It is important to decide whether we are trying to assess an individual's suicide risk or a population's suicide risk, and over what time frame (this weekend, in several weeks, this year or over a lifetime) (Maris, 2002).

Women attempt suicide more than men do, and one of the most obvious reasons why this is so is that they choose different methods for suicide. Men are more likely to use firearms and hanging whereas women are more likely to use poisons and medication. The methods used by men are more lethal than those used by women and, therefore, women are more easily saved when treated in an emergency department. However, as Lester (1984) pointed out, even within any one method for suicide, men are still more likely to die than women and, thus, differences in choice of method cannot be the sole explanation for sex differences in the outcome of suicidal actions.

In the 1960s, Erwin Stengel (1964) stated that people completing suicide and people unsuccessfully attempting suicide constituted two different groups if only because the age and sex distributions were so different. Suicide is more common among elderly people and among men, whereas younger people and women predominate among those who make nonfatal attempts. Beautrais (2001) also concluded that attempted and completed suicide are two overlapping populations that share common psychiatric diagnoses and historical features with the distinction between them again gender (males are more likely to kill themselves) and the type of psychiatric disorder (attempters were more likely than those dying by suicide to have a current diagnosis of anxiety disorder and to be socially isolated). Arguing that the two groups also differ in intent and motives, Kreitman, et al. (1969) proposed the term parasuicide to replace the label "attempted suicide," thereby stressing that the differences between those completing and those attempting suicide is not simply a question of the outcome of the self-destructive act (Bille-Brahe, Schmidtke, Kerkhof, et al., 1995). More recently, the terms self-injurious behavior or self-poisoning (depending on which method is used to injure the self) have become more common.

A World Health Organization Working Group (Working Group on Preventive Practices in Suicide and Attempted Suicide, 1986) defined attempted suicide as follows: Attempted suicide (parasuicide) is an act with a non-fatal outcome, in which an individual deliberately initiates a non-habitual behavior that, without intervention from others, will cause self-harm, or deliberately ingests a substance in excess of the prescribed or generally recognized therapeutic dose, and which is aimed at realizing changes which the subject desired via the actual or expected physical consequences. This definition of attempted suicide includes acts interrupted by others before the actual self-harm occurs (for example, a person removed from a railway track before the train arrives), but excludes, as in the case of completed suicide, self-harmful acts by people who do not understand the meaning or consequences of their act (for example, because of developmental disability or severe mental illness).

Non-fatal suicidal behavior has often been considered to be a manipulative act. In 1961, Farberow and Shneidman's book, entitled *The Cry for Help*, noted the desire of attempted suicides to get attention from others. Lester (1987) stressed that, even if the suicidal act results in punishment, the person may still find it rewarding, especially if a previous attempt was ignored by others. Sifneos (1966) studied a group of attempted suicides and found that the manipulative aspect of the behavior was a common feature in the sample. The majority of his patients were satisfied with the results of their manipulative behavior and were not motivated to receive psychotherapy. Anxiety was lacking in these patients, and they appeared apathetic and fatalistic. They were more introspective and self-centered, had few but rather intense relationships, had difficulty expressing their emotions and had exaggerated expectations for themselves.

THE TROUBLE WITH NOMENCLATURE

One problem in studying nonlethal suicidal behavior is the lack of consensus about what terms should be used to refer to these types of behaviors (O'Carroll, Berman, Maris, et al., 1996). Self-injurious behavior exists on a continuum from actions without conscious intent to die, to actions with lethal intent that do not result in death (suicide attempts), to intentional, self-inflicted death (completed suicide). Often it is difficult to identify a person's intent to die, and thus it is difficult to differentiate attempted suicide from self-injurious behavior in which there was no intent to die. The label "attempted suicide" should be used only in cases of individuals who want to die and who survive by chance, that is, they are rescued and taken to an emergency department and the lethality of the gesture was high. A more precise classification of suicide attempts would be one that included lethality as well as a measure of the intent to kill oneself. This would allow for the distinction to be made between a superficial cut made by an individual who wanted to solve an interpersonal conflict and a firearm shot in the head of an individual who survived following a complicated neurosurgical operation. At the present time, both individuals are labeled as suicide attempters by some researchers.

A major clarification of the nomenclature in suicidology was suggested by O'Carroll, et al. (1996; Silverman, Berman, Sanddal, et al., 2007a; Silverman, Berman, Sanddal, et al., 2007b) but researchers continue to use rival nomenclatures, and it is not unusual to encounter researchers using inappropriate terms for suicidal individuals.

Attempted suicide should be distinguished from suicidal gestures. A suicidal gesture occurs when a person, for example, swallows some aspirins or increases by three-four fold the dosage of benzodiazepines that he or she takes regularly each day. Although there is a small chance of dying in this way, these are low-lethality methods for attempting suicide. Such individuals may be psychologically distressed, but they are not planning to die. They should, however, be taken seriously and receive psychiatric treatment (Lester, 1989).

According to the revised nomenclature (Silverman, Berman, Sanddal, et al., 2007a; Silverman, Berman, Sanddal, et al., 2007b), a suicide attempt is now defined as self-inflicted, potentially injurious behavior with a nonfatal outcome for which there is evidence (either explicit or implicit) of intent to die. A suicide attempt may result in no injuries, injuries, or death. If there is some degree of suicidal intent, then it is labeled suicide attempt, type I (no injury), or suicide attempt, type II (with injury) regardless of the degree of injury or lethality of method. It is, therefore, considered an act with intent to die, and in this way is distinguished from self-harm or self-injurious behavior.

Self-reports of suicide attempts also have limited validity due to inconsistent definition and problem with recall bias (Kjoller, Norlev and Davidsen, 2004). Freeman, et al. (1974) reported that most of the people included in their study of the intention to kill oneself after self-injurious behavior called their suicidal behavior a suicide attempt when in fact their intention to die was minimal. In the CDC's Youth Risk Behavior Survey (2005) only one in three adolescents who reported a suicide attempt required any medical attention. Meehan, et al. (1992) reported that for every ten self-reported attempts only one resulted in hospitalization. This indicates that the term is used to describe other forms of distress or self-injury. We share O'Carroll, et al.'s (1996) opinion who stated that, "Because the term 'attempted suicide' potentially mean so many different things, it runs the risk of meaning almost nothing at all' (p. 238).

ATTEMPTED SUICIDE AMONG YOUTHS

Suicide attempts and other acts of self-harm that result in nonfatal injuries take a heavy toll on the health of younger persons. In 2002, an estimated 124,409 visits to USA emergency departments were made after attempted suicides or other self-harm incidents by persons aged 10–24 years (Centers for Disease Control and Prevention, 2004).

The CDC analyzed self-report data from the 2001 nationally representative sample of high school students in the United States and found that students who reported attempting suicide during the preceding 12 months were nearly four times more likely to report fighting than those who reported not attempting suicide. The observed association between suicide attempts and fighting suggests that violence prevention programs directed at reducing both suicide and fighting are appropriate for youths. However, although the mechanisms linking suicidal behavior and interpersonal violence are unclear, aggressiveness, impulsivity, substance abuse, depression and hopelessness appear to increase the risk for both suicidal and violent behaviors (Plutchik, 1995; Pompili, Innamorati, Lester, et al., 2007; Trezza and Popp, 2000).

Stigma

Not only does the stigma of mental illness prevent people from seeking treatment, which in turn exposes them to a greater risk of suicide, but also suicide can appear to be the best solution for a stigmatized individual. Following a suicide attempt, many individuals feel isolated or ignored by health professionals (McGaughey, Long and Harrisson, 1995). In addition, suicide is, itself, a source of stigma, and those with suicidal ideation are considered weak, sinful and selfish, which may prevent those individuals from seeking treatment early in the suicidal process.

Pompili, et al. (2005) reviewed research on the attitudes of emergency staff towards suicidal and self-harming patients and found an overall negative attitude towards these patients, a factor that has been associated with negative outcomes. Negative attitudes of emergency staff toward completed suicide and attempted suicide were also reported in some earlier studies (Ghodse, 1978; Goldney and Bottrill, 1980; Patel, 1975). Explanations for these negative attitudes focus on the stigma of suicidal behavior. Medical staff prefer to work with patients who have not caused their own self-injury, and they consider working with attempted suicides a "nuisance."

Nurses have a key role in working with suicidal patients, but it appears that suicidal patients evoke negative attitudes in some nurses (McLaughlin, 1995). Their attitudes toward suicidal patients may influence the outcome of the suicide crisis, and nurses should be able to recognize risk factors for suicide and work empathically with suicidal patients.

ATTEMPTED SUICIDE AMONG SOME PSYCHIATRIC DISORDERS

Attempted suicide is a common feature of most psychiatric disorders.

Schizophrenia

Suicide attempts among those with schizophrenia are serious and typically require medical attention. Intent is generally strong, and the majority of those who attempt suicide have made attempts in the past. The methods used by schizophrenics to attempt suicide are usually more lethal than those used by attempters in the general population (Pompili, Amador, Girardi, et al., 2007).

Gupta and colleagues (1998) reported that attempted suicide in schizophrenic patients was associated with the number of lifetime depressive episodes, and depression has been recognized as a major risk factor among persons with schizophrenia who have attempted suicide. Roy, et al. (1984) found that significantly more of their patients with schizophrenia who had attempted suicide had suffered from a major depressive episode at some time during their illness. Great caution is required in the period after hospital discharge, because patients with schizophrenia usually experience hopelessness and demoralization after discharge. For these patients, discharge often means losing the hospital environment and the people who in some way have become central in their life. The number of psychiatric admissions, which is usually higher among schizophrenics who have attempted suicide, may be indicative of a severe relapsing illness.

Drake (2007) stressed that, in terms of suicidal history, schizophrenics who complete suicide had made more previous suicide attempts than those who had attempted suicide, but the differences were not statistically significant. Only a history of explicit suicide threats statistically differentiated the two groups. Remarkably, most of the explicit threats were based on an awareness of the illness and fears regarding the course of the illness. For example, several patients stated quite explicitly that they planned to kill themselves if they continued to have relapses of the illness and an inability to function. Patients who subsequently completed suicide also expressed higher performance expectations, consistent with their awareness of their illness and accurate perceptions of their functional status.

The completed suicides were also more depressed. During hospitalization they reported feeling depressed, inadequate, hopeless, worthless and suicidal. Psychological symptoms of depression, rather than biological symptoms of depression, differentiated the completed suicides from the attempted suicides. Behaviors during hospitalization, such as being impulsive, demanding, and agitated, failed to discriminate between completed suicides and attempted suicides. The only hospital-based behavior that did discriminate between the two groups was that the completed suicides were more likely to be rated as "improved" at the time of discharge.

Bipolar Disorder

Suicide attempts are common in bipolar disorder (BPD) patients and are often related to substance abuse, a family history of affective disorders and severe depressive episodes. Patients hospitalized during depressive episodes also have a significantly higher frequency of prior suicide attempts (Lopez, Mosquera, de Leon, et al., 2001). Moreover, BPD is associated more frequently with a history of suicide or suicide attempts than are most DSM-IV psychiatric disorders, other than major depressive disorders (MDD) (Chen and Dilsaver, 1996). Kuo, et al. (2001), and Goldsmith, et al. (2002) suggested that a history of suicide attempts is a strong predictor of future attempts. Fagiolini, et al. (2004) investigated suicide attempts and ideation in patients with Type I BPD and reported that severity of BPD and higher body mass index (BMI) were correlated with a history of attempted suicide. They noted that suicide risk may be a transient event preceded by severe suicidal ideation lasting only a few minutes or hours. Michaelis, et al. (2003) reported that BPD patients who made a single suicide attempt were more likely than those who made multiple suicide attempts to demonstrate high suicidal intent in their first attempt.

There is disagreement on whether the risk of suicide is the same in Type I and Type II BPD (Valtonen, Suominen, Mantere, et al., 2005) or higher in Type II BPD (Rihmer and Kiss, 2002; Baldessarini, Pompili, and Tondo, 2006a).

In an investigation of 60 reports based on suicide attempts in more than 70,000 subjects, Baldessarini, et al. (2006a) found an annual risk of 2.13% per year vs. 2.86% per year in BPD patients and major affective disorder (MAD) patients, respectively, whereas the attempt risk was 26.1% vs. 21.8%, respectively. The male: female ratio was 1.37 in BPD and 0.85 in MAD patients.

Baldessarini, et al. (2006b) suggested using the ratio of attempted suicide/completed suicide (A/S) as a measure of the lethality of suicidal behavior in different groups of patients. In the general population, the proportion of attempted to completed suicides (about 25:1) is four to six times higher than in major affective disorder patients, in whom the A/S ratio averages only about 5:1 or less, suggesting that suicidal behavior in patients with mood disorders has a higher lethality. The A/S ratio was 2.5 times greater among lithium-treated subjects than among those not treated with lithium, suggesting a reduction in lethality attributable to lithium treatment, with fewer fatalities per attempt.

Eating Disorders

Pryor, et al. (1996) reported that binge/purging anorexics were more likely than restricters to have attempted suicide. Favaro and Santonastaso (1997) found that anorexia nervosa participants were more likely to engage in suicidal ideation than bulimia nervosa participants.

Viesselman and Roig (1985) investigated 95 patients suffering from bulimia (binge eating only), bulimarexia (binging and purging), and anorexia nervosa (food restriction only) and found that 20% of their bulimic patients who had attempted suicide also had a diagnosis of major depressive disorder, and 11% of these individuals were drug and alcohol abusers. A higher frequency of attempted suicide has been reported in bulimic women with alcohol dependency (Bulik, Sullivan, Carter, et al., 1997; Suzuki, Higuchi, Yamada, et al., 1994).

Shearer, et al. (1988) found that suicide attempts were more serious in those patients who had a borderline personality disorder comorbid with the eating disorder.

Favaro and Santonastaso (1997) found that 25% of bulimic patients who had attempted suicide had at least one prior suicide attempt. Corcos, et al. (2002) found that bulimics who had attempted suicide reported suicidal ideation more often during adolescence and had made their first attempt during this period.

Franko, et al. (2004) reported that a history of drug use disorder at intake and laxative abuse predicted suicide attempts in bulimic subjects, whereas depression was not found to predict suicide attempts.

Personality Disorders

Garvey and Spoden (1980) found that 72% of their patients with antisocial personality disorder had attempted suicide. Woodruff and colleagues (1971) reported suicide attempts in 23% of outpatients diagnosed with antisocial personality disorder, while Robins (1966) found 11% of a group of sociopaths had attempted suicide. It is possible that some suicide attempts occur whose true purpose is some secondary gain (such as hospital admission). If this were true, one would expect a difference between those patients admitted to the hospital and those seeking outpatient treatment.

Garvey and Spoden (1980) found that most nonserious suicide attempts were almost exclusively related to problems with a significant other. It is interesting to note that, for most suicide attempts, drug overdose was used most frequently (71% of attempters). The finding that male sociopaths use nonviolent suicide methods (e.g., drugs) almost twice as frequently as a diagnostically heterogeneous group of psychiatrically-ill male suicide attempters, suggests that sociopaths prefer the apparent "safety" of drugs as opposed to more violent and dangerous methods. The almost total lack of seriousness of their attempts further suggests that sociopaths have no real intention of killing themselves. The findings of this study support the notion that sociopaths use suicide attempts to manipulate others or to act out their frustration.

Oloff, et al. (1994) found that patients with borderline personality disorder or comorbid disorders attempted suicide for the first time earlier in life than depressed patients. The suicide intent of the patients with borderline personality disorder was greater than that of depressed patients. The patients with borderline personality disorder differed from the depressed patients in having an earlier onset of suicidal behavior and a higher lifetime number of attempts. Comorbidity of personality disorder and major depressive episodes was associated with an increased number of suicide attempts. Among patients with borderline personality disorder, impulsivity was associated with the number of suicide attempts independent of comorbid depression or substance use disorder. In this study, hopelessness predicted the lifetime number of suicide attempts and the degree of serious intent to die. Hopelessness may contribute to the seriousness of suicidal behavior in borderline personality disorder, especially in patients with comorbid depression, by increasing the number of attempts, the level of subjective intent, and the degree of objective planning. A diagnosis of borderline personality disorder, with or without a major depressive episode, predicted the number of suicide attempts but not the specific attempt characteristics. Similarly, a diagnosis of major depression episode did not predict attempt characteristics.

Suominen, et al. (2000) found that suicide attempts among subjects with or without personality disorders did not differ significantly in suicide intent as measured by the Suicidal Intent Scale (SIS), hopelessness as measured by the Beck Hopelessness Scale (BHS), somatic severity (lethality) of the index attempt, or impulsiveness. In that study, the suicide attempts of patients with personality disorders were associated with current Axis I depressive syndromes, psychoactive drug use disorders or both in 98% of the cases. Suicide attempts of those with personality disorders were more commonly associated with psychoactive drug use disorders and depressive disorders not otherwise specified and, less commonly, with a major depressive disorder than suicide attempts among those without personality disorders. According to Soloff, et al. (1994), risk factors for attempted or completed suicide in borderline personality disorder derived from clinical reports and longitudinal follow-up studies include: (1) comorbidity with affective disorder; (2) alcohol and substance abuse; (3) impulsivity, aggression, and hostility; (4) repeated attempts; (5) antisocial traits; and (6) severity of borderline personality disorder.

Interventions

Certain interventions, such as providing lithium for manic depressive illness or strengthening social support in the community (Baldessarini, Tondo and Hennen, 1999), have been found to reduce the risk of attempted suicide. Risk factors that cannot be changed (such as a previous suicide attempt) can alert others to the heightened risk of suicide during periods of the recurrence of a psychiatric illness or a substance abuse disorder or following a significant stressful life event (Oquendo, Malone, Ellis, et al, 1999). Protective factors are quite varied and include an individual's attitudinal and behavioral characteristics, as well as attributes of the environment and culture (Plutchik and van Praag, 1994). Information about risk and protective factors for attempted suicide is more limited than that for suicide, possibly because of the lack of consensus about what actually constitutes suicidal behavior (see the discussion above). This lack of agreement makes reliable research difficult to conduct and, as a result, it is not yet possible to know with certainty whether the risk and protective factors for suicide and non-lethal forms of self-injury are the same. Some authors argue that they are, whereas others accentuate differences (Duberstein, Conwell, Seidlitz, et al., 2000; Linehan, 1986).

Despite the fact that effective treatments exist for these disorders and conditions, the stigma associated with psychiatric illness, suicide and substance abuse prevents many persons from seeking assistance since they fear encountering prejudice and discrimination. About two thirds of people with mental disorders do not seek treatment (Kessler, Nelson, McGonagle, et al., 1996). The stigma of suicide, while deterring some from attempting suicide, is also a barrier to treatment for many persons who have suicidal thoughts or who have attempted suicide.

Family members of suicide attempters often hide their behavior from friends and relatives since they may believe that it reflects badly on their own relationship with the suicide attempter or they believe that suicidal behavior itself is shameful or sinful. Studies have found that over 70% of persons attempting suicide never seek health services (Crosby, Cheltenham and Sacks, 1999). Fewer than 50% of adolescent attempters are referred for treatment following an emergency department visit (Piacentini, Rotheram-Borus, Gillis, et al., 1995; Spirito, Brown, Overholser, et al., 1989), and a large proportion of those who are referred fail to attend their initial appointment. It is important to train emergency department staff to treat suicide attempts with seriousness and to emphasize to the adolescent's family members the dangers of ignoring suicide attempts and the benefits of follow-up treatment in order to reduce the reoccurrence of attempted suicide. Such staff training has been associated with greater completion of treatment on the part of persons who sought care in emergency departments (Rotheram-Borus, Piacentini, Cantwell, et al., 2000). From a health care perspective, both the patient and the healthcare delivery system benefit from better linkages between emergency and appropriate follow-up care.

Hospitals should also handle suicides more effectively. Specifically, immediate acceptance of the patient and treatment should be the first duty of hospitals. Occasionally, hospitals in some countries do not accept patients with suicidal ideation or after an attempted suicide, an unacceptable policy. Some of the common reasons for refusing registration and admission include a non-accepting attitude on the part of the hospital staff, considering suicide emergencies as increasing the workload, thinking that suicidal patients are merely seeking attention, and medico-legal fears (such as lawsuits). The unsympathetic attitude of some hospital staff discourages people from seeking help. Publicity should be provided about first-aid measures and the location of emergency help centres, especially for handling poisoning and burn injuries. Many common household first-aid practices can, in fact, be dangerous, and there should be no delay in taking the affected person to a hospital.

Meehan, et al. (1992) stressed the need to assess suicide attempts better through precise protocols in the emergency room aimed at describing what really happened, determining if hospitalization is needed and, above all, assessing whether the injuries were intended to cause death. A partnership between medical staff working in the emergency department and mental health professionals would thus, also be of great help in the assessment of suicide attempts (Pompili, Girardi, Ruberto, et al., 2005).

Conclusion

This chapter has reviewed some of the issues surrounding attempted suicide and provided a selective review of the topic. Nevertheless, even a comprehensive analysis of this ambiguous behavior would find it difficult to draw definitive conclusions. Despite common usage of the term, attempted suicide may be confused with other self-harm behaviors. The term "attempted suicide" should be used only when there is clear intention to die but, for some reason, the individual is rescued. Even among genuine suicide attempters, the lethality of the action should be taken into account. Lethality, which is the probability that death will occur (or the medical seriousness of the injury), may help to classify suicide attempters and design effective treatments. An attempted suicide is also a cry for help, but we should bear in mind that focusing on this aspect of the suicide attempt can result in undertreatment of these individuals. Clinicians should assess the suicidal intent and lethality of attempted suicides and provide clear treatment plans for them. Their behavior carries a high probability of repetition, and attempted suicide is a major risk factor for subsequent completed suicide.

References

Baldessarini, R. J., Pompili, M. and Tondo, L. (2006a). Suicide in bipolar disorder: risks and management. *CNS Spectrums*, 11, 465-471.

Baldessarini, R. J., Tondo, L., Davis, P. et al. (2006b). Decreased risk of suicides and attempts during long-term lithium treatment: a meta-analytic review. *Bipolar Disorders*, 8, 625- 639.

Baldessarini, R. J., Tondo, L. and Hennen, J. (1999). Effects of lithium treatment and its discontinuation on suicidal behavior in bipolar manic-depressive disorders. *Journal of Clinical Psychiatry*, 60 (Suppl. 2), 77-84.

Beautrais, A. L. (2001). Suicides and serious suicide attempts: two populations or one? *Psychological Medicine*, 31, 837-845.

Bille-Brahe, U., Schmidtke, A., Kerkhof, A. J. et al. (1995). Background and introduction to the WHO/EURO Multicentre Study on Parasuicide. *Crisis*, 16, 72-78, 84.

Brener, N. D., Krug, E. G. and Simon, T. R. (2000). Trends in suicide ideation and suicidal behaviour among high school students in the United States, 1991-1997. *Suicide and Life-Threatening Behavior*, 30, 304-312.

Bulik, C. M., Sullivan, P. F., Carter, F. A. et al. (1997). Lifetime comorbidity of alcohol dependence in women with bulimia nervosa. *Addictive Behaviors*, 22, 437-446.

Centers for Disease Control and Prevention (2004). Morbidity and Mortality Weekly Report.

Centers for Disease Control and Prevention. 2005). *Youth risk behaviour surveillance system.* Centers for Disease Control and Prevention.

Chen, Y. W. and Dilsaver, S. C. (1996). Lifetime rates of suicide attempts among subjects with bipolar and unipolar disorders relative to subjects with other Axis I disorders. *Biological Psychiatry*, 39, 896-899.

Corcos, M., Taieb, O., Benoit-Lamy, S. et al. (2002). Suicide attempts in women with bulimia nervosa: frequency and characteristics. *Acta Psychiatrica Scandinavica*, 106, 381-386.

Crosby, A. E., Cheltenham, M. P. and Sacks, J. J. (1999). Incidence of suicidal ideation and behavior in the United States, 1994. *Suicide and Life-Threatening Behavior*, 29, 131-140.

Drake, R. E. (2007). Suicide attempts and completed suicides among schizophrenia patients. In R. Tatarelli, M. Pompili, and P. Girardi (Eds.) *Suicide in schizophrenia,* pp. 77-81. New York: Nova Science Publishers.

Duberstein, P. R., Conwell, Y., Seidlitz, L. et al. (2000). Personality traits and suicidal behaviour and ideation in depressed inpatients 50 years of age and older. *Journals of Gerontology Series B: Psychological Sciences and Social Sciences*, 55, P18-26.

Fagiolini, A., Kupfer, D. J., Rucci, P. et al. (2004) Suicide attempts and ideation in patients with bipolar I disorder. *Journal of Clinical Psychiatry*, 65, 509-514.

Favaro, A. and Santonastaso, P. (1997). Suicidality in eating disorders: clinical and psychological correlates. *Acta Psychiatrica Scandinavica*, 95, 508-514.

Franko, D. L., Keel, P. K., Dorer, D. J. et al. (2004). What predicts suicide attempts in women with eating disorders? *Psychological Medicine*, 34, 843-853.

Freeman, D. J., Wilson, K., Thigpen, J. D. et al. (1974). Assessing intention to die in self-injury behavior. In C. Neuringer (Ed.) *Psychological assessment of suicide risk,* pp. 18–42. Springfield: Charles C. Thomas.

Garvey, M. J. and Spoden, F. (1980). Suicide attempts in antisocial personality disorder. *Comprehensive Psychiatry*, 21, 146-149.

Ghodse, A. H. (1978). The attitudes of casualty staff and ambulance personnel towards patients who take drug overdoses. *Social Science and Medicine*, 12, 341-346.

Goldney, R. D. and Bottrill, A. (1980). Attitudes to patients who attempt suicide. *Medical Journal of Australia*, 2, 717-720.

Goldsmith, S. K., Pellmar, T. C., Kleinman, A. M. et al. (Eds.) (2002). *Reducing suicide: a national imperative*. Washington, D.C.: Joseph Henry Press.

Gupta, S., Black, D. W., Arndt, S. et al. (1998). Factors associated with suicide attempts among patients with schizophrenia. *Psychiatric Services*, 49, 1353-1355.

Kessler, R. C., Nelson, C. B., McGonagle, K. A. et al. (1996). The epidemiology of co-occurring addictive and mental disorders: implications for prevention and service utilization. *American Journal of Orthopsychiatry*, 66, 17-31.

Kjoller, M., Norlev, J. and Davidsen, M. (2004). Recall bias and suicidal behaviour in a six year follow-up study. In *10th European Symposium on Suicide and Suicidal Behaviour*, pp. 118. Copenhagen, Denmark: National Institute of Public Health.

Kreitman, N., Philip, A. E., Greer, S. et al. (1969). Parasuicide. *British Journal of Psychiatry*, 115, 746-747.

Kuo, W. H., Gallo, J. J. and Tien, A. Y. (2001). Incidence of suicide ideation and attempts in adults: the 13-year follow-up of a community sample in Baltimore, Maryland. *Psychological Medicine*, 31, 1181-1191.

Lester, D. (1984) Suicide. In C. S. Widon *(Ed.) Sex roles and psychopathology*, pp. 145-156. New York, NY: Plenum.

Lester, D. (1987) *Suicide as a learned behavior*. Springfield: Thomas.

Lester, D. (1989) *Questions and answers about suicide*. Philadelphia: Charles Press.

Linehan, M. M. (1986). Suicidal people: one population or two? *Annals of the New York Academy of Science*, 487, 16-33.

Lopez, P., Mosquera, F., De Leon, J. et al. (2001). Suicide attempts in bipolar patients. *Journal of Clinical Psychiatry*, 62, 963-966.

Maris, R. W. (2002). Suicide. *Lancet*, 360, 319-326.

McGaughey, J., Long, A. and Harrisson, S. (1995). Suicide and parasuicide: a selected review of the literature. *Journal of Psychiatric and Mental Health Nursing*, 2, 199-206.

McLaughlin, C. (1995). Counselling the overdose patient in casualty. *British Journal of Nursing*, 4, 688-690, 707-688.

Meehan, P. J., Lamb, J. A., Saltzman, L. E. et al. (1992). Attempted suicide among young adults: progress toward a meaningful estimate of prevalence. *American Journal of Psychiatry*, 149, 41- 44.

Michaelis, B. H., Goldberg, J. F., Singer, T. M. et al. (2003). Characteristics of first suicide attempts in single versus multiple suicide attempters with bipolar disorder. *Comprehensive Psychiatry*, 44, 15-20.

O'Carroll, P. W., Berman, A. L., Maris, R. W. et al. (1996). Beyond the Tower of Babel: a nomenclature for suicidology. *Suicide and Life-Threatening Behavior*, 26, 237-252.

Oquendo, M. A., Malone, K. M., Ellis, S. P. et al. (1999). Inadequacy of antidepressant treatment for patients with major depression who are at risk for suicidal behavior. *American Journal of Psychiatry*, 156, 190-194.

Patel, A. R. (1975). Attitudes towards self-poisoning. *British Medical Journal*, 2, 426-429.

Piacentini, J., Rotheram-Borus, M. J., Gillis, J. R. et al. (1995). Demographic predictors of treatment attendance among adolescent suicide attempters. *Journal of Counsulting and Clinical Psychology,* 63, 469-473.

Plutchik, R. (1995). Outward and inward directed aggressiveness: the interaction between violence and suicidality. *Pharmacopsychiatry*, 28 (Suppl. 2), 47-57.

Plutchik, R. and Van Praag, H. M. (1994). Suicide risk: amplifiers and attenuators. In M. Hillbrand and N. J. Pallone (Eds.) *The psychobiology of aggression,* pp. 173-186. Binghamton: Haworth Press.

Pompili, M., Amador, X. F., Girardi, P. et al. (2007). Suicide risk in schizophrenia: learning from the past to change the future. *Annals of General Psychiatry*, 6, 10.

Pompili, M., Girardi, P., Ruberto, A. et al. (2005). Emergency staff reactions to suicidal and self-harming patients. *European Journal of Emergency Medicine*, 12, 169-178.

Pompili, M., Innamorati, M., Lester, D. et al. (2007). Gender effects among undergraduates relating to suicide risk, impulsivity, aggression and self-efficacy. *Personality and Individual Differences*, 43, 2047-2056.

Pryor, T., Wiederman, M. W. and McGilley, B. (1996). Clinical correlates of anorexia nervosa subtypes. *International Journal of Eating Disorders*, 19, 371-379.

Rihmer, Z. and Kiss, K. (2002). Bipolar disorders and suicidal behavior. *Bipolar Disorders*, 4 (Suppl. 1), 21-25.

Robins, L. N. (1966) *Deviant children grown up*. Baltimore, MD: Williams and Wilkins.

Rosenberg, M. L., Gelles, R. J., Holinger, P. C. et al. (1987). Violence: homicide, assault, and suicide. In R. W. Amler and H. B. Dull (Eds.) *Closing the gap: the burden of unnecessary illness,* pp. 164-178. New York: Oxford University Press.

Rotheram-Borus, M. J., Piacentini, J., Cantwell, C. et al. (2000). The 18-month impact of an emergency room intervention for adolescent female suicide attempters. *Journal of Consulting and Clinical Psychology*, 68, 1081-1093.

Roy, A., Mazonson, A. and Pickar, D. (1984). Attempted suicide in chronic schizophrenia. *British Journal of Psychiatry*, 144, 303-306.

Rudd, M. D. (2006). Suicidality in clinical practice: anxieties and answers. *Journal of Clinical Psychology*, 62, 157-159.

Shearer, S. L., Peters, C. P., Quaytman, M. S. et al. (1988). Intent and lethality of suicide attempts among female borderline inpatients. *American Journal of Psychiatry*, 145, 1424-1427.

Sifneos, P. E. (1966). Manipulative suicide. *Psychiatric Quarterly*, 40, 525-537.

Silverman, M. M., Berman, A. L., Sanddal, N. D. et al. (2007a). Rebuilding the tower of Babel: a revised nomenclature for the study of suicide and suicidal behaviours. Part 1: Background, rationale, and methodology. *Suicide and Life-Threatening Behavior*, 37, 248-263.

Silverman, M. M., Berman, A. L., Sanddal, N. D. et al. (2007b) Rebuilding the tower of Babel: a revised nomenclature for the study of suicide and suicidal behaviours. Part 2: suicide-related ideations, communications, and behaviors. *Suicide and Life-Threatening Behavior*, 37, 264-277.

Soloff, P. H., Lis, J. A., Kelly, T. et al. (1994). Risk factors for suicidal behavior in borderline personality disorder. *American Journal of Psychiatry*, 151, 1316-1323.

Spirito, A., Brown, L., Overholser, J. et al. (1989). Attempted suicide in adolescence: a review and critique of the literature. *Clinical Psychology Review*, 9, 335-363.

Stengel, E. (1964). *Suicide and attempted suicide*. London, England: Penguin Books.

Suominen, K. H., Isometsa, E. T., Henriksson, M. M. et al. (2000). Suicide attempts and personality disorder. *Acta Psychiatrica Scandinavica*, 102, 118-125.

Suzuki, K., Higuchi, S., Yamada, K. et al. (1994). Bulimia nervosa with and without alcoholism: a comparative study in Japan. *International Journal of Eating Disorders*, 16, 137-146.

Trezza, G. R. and Popp, S. M. (2000). The substance user at risk of harm to self or others: assessment and treatment issues. *Journal of Clinical Psychology*, 56, 1193-1205.

Valtonen, H., Suominen, K., Mantere, O. et al. (2005). Suicidal ideation and attempts in bipolar I and II disorders. *Journal of Clinical Psychiatry*, 66, 1456-1462.

Viesselman, J. O. and Roig, M. (1985). Depression and suicidality in eating disorders. *Journal of Clinical Psychiatry*, 46, 118-124.

Woodruff, R. A., Jr., Guze, S. B. and Clayton, P. J. (1971). The medical and psychiatric implications of antisocial personality (sociopathy). *Diseases of the Nervous System*, 32, 712-714.

Working Group on Preventive Practices in Suicide and Attempted Suicide (1986). Copenhagen: WHO Regional Office for Europe.

World Health Organization (1999). *Figures and facts about suicide*. Geneva: WHO.

World Health Organization (2002). *Suicide prevention in Europe*. Geneva: WHO.

In: Suicide from a Global Perspective
Editors: A. Shrivastava, M. Kimbrell, and D. Lester
ISBN: 978-1-61942-267-4
© 2012 Nova Science Publishers, Inc.

Chapter 2

Completed Suicide

Annamaria Pusztai

Introduction

According to WHO data in 1998, suicide accounted for 1.8 % of the global number of deaths. This rate is expected to increase to 2.4% by 2020 (Bertolote, 2002). The highest rate of suicide occurs in Eastern-Europe (Lithuania 41.1; Slovenia 31.0; Hungary 24.5; Estonia 23.7 per 100,000 per year in 2003). The lowest rates can be found in Latin America and in Muslim countries where the rate is 6.5 or lower.

Globally the number of males completing suicide is four times higher than the number of females. A reverse trend is observed only in China. Suicide rates tend to increase with age, with the suicide rate being six to eight times higher for the elderly than for the young, although more youngsters commit suicide globally than old people. People commit more suicides (55%) between the ages of 5 and 44 than above the age of 45 and, in both sexes, those between 35 and 44 are the most endangered group. The most common methods of completed suicides are violent, including firearm and self-hanging. In Europe, hanging is the most common method.

Attempted and Completed Suicide

Worldwide, 10 to 20 times more people attempt suicide than complete suicide (Bertolote, 2002). The rate of attempted suicides is very difficult to estimate since the number of unreported cases is high. Some 10%-15% of suicide attempters eventually complete suicide while 85%-90% of them die a natural death. The typically completed suicide is male and uses a violent method. The typical attempted suicide is female and uses a nonviolent method.

Psychiatric disorders are less frequently present in attempted suicides while more serious psychiatric disorders, such as schizophrenia, are characteristic of completed suicides. In both groups, depression is common, and drug users and those suffering from personality disorders are also common.

Causes of Suicide

Biological Bases

The findings of twin and adoption research suggest the influence of genes on suicide. Roy (1992) and others report that the concordance rate for suicide in monozygotic twins (13.2%) is much higher than that in dizygotic twins (0.7%). Genes may not influence suicidal tendencies directly, but they may pose a danger via genetically-determined characteristics such as a vulnerability to distress, neuroticism and impulsivity. Suicidal behavior is also controlled in part by the serotonergic system.

Clinical Factors

The incidence of psychiatric disorder in suicides is not clear. Several researchers diagnose 90% of completed suicides as having a psychiatric disease at the time of death (Arsenault-Lapierre, 2004). Others find that only one fourth or one third of suicides have a psychiatric disorder.

Depression

The most common psychiatric disorder in completed suicides is depression. The incidence of mood disorders in suicides is 35.8% (Bertolote, 2002). The most dangerous time is not at the lowest point of the depression but during the six weeks after the onset of treatment when the motivation to act increases and low spirits continue. Depressed individuals who complete suicide have more serious subjective depression, more pervasive suicidal thoughts and fewer reasons to live (Mann, 1999). Other symptoms of suicidal depression include hopelessness, feelings of guilt, loss of interest in habitual activities and low self-esteem. On the basis of the findings of NIMH Collaborative Depression study (Fawcett, 2000), anhedonia, hopelessness, serious distress, agitation, panic attacks, aggression and impulsivity increase the risk of suicide.

Schizophrenia

Suicide is more common in patients with schizophrenia, especially the paranoid form and especially during the first three months after returning home from the hospital (Roy, 1982). Kaplan and Harrow (1999) found that impaired functioning after hospitalization was a significant risk factor. The danger of suicide is also increased in schizophrenic patients with permanent auditory hallucinations and with post-psychotic depressions (Krupinski, 1998).

Alcohol Dependency

Alcoholism is a significant factor in predicting suicide. In the short term, alcohol dependency may protect against self-aggression but, in the long term, it is a risk factor. Alcohol dependency is often viewed as masked suicide. The profile of a typical alcoholic suicide is a white, unmarried, middle-aged male with a long history of drinking and alcohol abuse, who makes a violent suicide act after an interpersonal break-up or loss of support. He is unemployed, and his social support system is poor. The presence of alcohol abuse leads to disruptions in his social and family relationships and causes problems in daily living.

Neurosis

Research indicates that panic disorders are significantly related to suicide, especially when mood disorders and drug use are also present (Maris, et al., 2000; Schmidt, 2000). Suicide is also more common in patients with post-traumatic stress disorder.

Personality Disorders

Psychological autopsy studies suggest that 31%-37% of completed suicides have Axis II personality disorders (Maris, et al., 2000). The most common personality disorders are Cluster B (antisocial, borderline, histrionic and narcissistic) and Cluster C (avoidance, dependent and compulsive). Patients with borderline personality disorder make an average of 3.4 suicide attempts during their lifetime, and their rate of completed suicide is high, mostly committed before age of 40 (Kuritárné, 2005).

Isometsa (1996) found that 95% of patients with Cluster B personality disorders have a comorbid depression or chronic drug use, and this increases the risk of suicide. In patients with borderline personality disorder, mood instability, isolation and impulsivity are also risk factors.

Comorbidity

The significance of comorbid diagnoses in increasing the risk of suicide has been confirmed by many research studies. Several authors have stated that secondary affective conditions are more likely than primary ones to result in completed suicides (e.g., Henriksson, 1993).

Psychological Dimensions

Brent (1994) found that two types of temperament are closely related to the risk of suicide: impulsive/aggressive and depressive/reticent, especially when present along with personality disorders. Research on temperament has also found correlations between suicidal behavior and reward dependency and seeking novelty (Fekete, 2004).

Hopelessness (Beck, 2001) and a low level of self-efficacy are common in suicidal individuals, as is an inadequate ability to solve interpersonal problems and a negative estimation of one's problem-solving capacity. A negative attribution style and perfectionism are also significant components of suicidal cognition. Suicides tend to be immature personalities who are inclined to passive and avoidance coping (Goldsmith, 2002).

Social Factors

Social isolation increases the likelihood of suicidal acts. Inadequate social relationships and a lack of social support also play a role. In terms of marital status, being "unmarried" poses the highest risk factor for suicide. Members of religious congregations, especially women, are more protected and, the stronger a person's religion is, the more protected he/she is against suicide (Goldsmith, 2002). Work and a productive life protect against suicide, whereas unemployment is associated with an increased rate of suicide. Roy (1983) found that suicide in other family members significantly increased the risk of suicidal behavior and other serious mental disorders.

Cultural Factors

To some extent, cultures pass on the possibility of suicide as a potential solution for some life situations. Members of the given culture preserve these models even after emigration, which emphasizes the importance of the cultural aspects of suicide. Among the Japanese and in the Muslim world, altruistic suicide and suicide on behalf of the nation are common. Sick Eskimos may commit suicide in the interest of their community, and Indian widows are sometimes expected to die after their husband's death.

Goldsmith (2002) emphasised the role of culture in influencing aspects of suicidal behavior. For example, culture can determine attitudes towards suicide. If these are accepting, then a common reaction is likely to be one of approval of suicide. Stigma toward the suicidal individual and the availability and acceptability of treatment is culturally determined. The preferred method for suicide is also culturally determined.

Goldsmith (2002) and Takahashi (1997) have noted that the reliability of international suicide rates is limited. There are different classifications and different meanings for suicidal act, as well as differences in the availability and effectiveness of emergency healthcare, all of which can influence the officially reported rate of suicide in a country. Occasionally there is no adequate infrastructure to register suicide acts precisely

Prevention

In 2004 experts from 15 countries met and identified the five following priority areas of prevention (Mann, 2005):

Educational Programs for the Population and for Specialists

The objective here is to awaken the general public to suicide and to help them understand the reasons for suicide. This would facilitate reducing the stigma associated with suicide. Education for healthcare workers, family doctors, gate-keepers in the community (priests, pharmacists, etc.) is important as these individuals can help recognize and treat those with depression and other psychiatric diseases.

Treatment for Patients with Risk Factors

Applying better and more widespread assessment procedures, cases of depression could be diagnosed in the adult population, which could in turn improve treatment and reduce suicide rates. Teaching coping strategies and a better handling of interpersonal situations may assist individuals to cope with stress. Vulnerable groups should also be made aware of the availability of services.

Treatment of Psychiatric Disorders

The most effective treatment for psychiatric conditions is pharmacotherapy combined with psychotherapy. Cognitive therapy, problem-solving therapy and interpersonal psychotherapy are especially effective. Poor adherence with treatment plans is common, and follow-up is helpful in these cases.

Tighter Restrictions on Access to Lethal Methods

In some regions, the number of suicides committed with firearms decreases after regulating their possession. In 1984-1988, the purchase of alcoholic drinks was restricted in the Soviet Union, resulting in a 34% decline in completed suicide (Goldney, 2000). In England, paracetamol is sold in restricted quantities and in appropriate packaging, which has had a protective effect on suicidal acts using impulsive drug overdosing.

The Role of the Media

The media can both help and hinder suicide prevention. Suicides committed by celebrities can increase the number of suicide acts, and sensationalization in the reporting of such acts can worsen the situation. On the other hand, the media can also be used to educate the public about suicide prevention. Suicide chat rooms on the Internet are common these days, and the Internet can have both preventive and destructive impacts.

Evaluating Suicide Prevention Programs

As a result of educational programs for family doctors on the island of Gotland, the rate of suicide decreased significantly. Unfortunately, when more than half of the trained family doctors left their positions, the number of suicides increased. As a result of a prevention program in Maryland targeting youngsters, suicidal acts decreased among 15-24 year-olds. Emergency telephone crisis intervention services help thousands of suicidal individuals each day. A suicide prevention program implemented by the American Air Force resulted in a significant decrease in suicide. After a national program for suicide prevention was initiated in Norway, the rate of suicide dropped by 20% as compared to the peak in 1989 and, after the first ten years of the Finnish national program, the number of suicides decreased by 9%. Prevention programs are effective and capable of decreasing suicide rates.

CONCLUSION

Coordinated multi-national research is needed to measure the phenomenon of suicide using a common classification system and methodology. This would help highlight real differences between nations and cultures. The next step is converting this information into primary and secondary prevention programs. Developing programs for the general population and for groups at high risk is important. In developing countries changes in attitudes and cooperation are required, especially for professionals. Large-scale education programs should be organized to disperse myths, stigma and taboos associated with suicide. Every doctor's office should become a center for suicide prevention. Last but not least, the significance of psychotherapy is important to highlight as it can provide some of the most effective help for individuals.

REFERENCES

Arsenault-Lapierre, G., Kim, C. and Turecki, G. (2004). Psychiatric diagnoses in 3275 suicides: a meta-analysis. *BMC Psychiatry*, 4 [No pagination].

Beck, A. T., Rush, A., Shaw, B. (2001). *A depresszió kognitív terápiája*. Budapest, Hungary.

Bertolote, J. and Fleischmann, A. (2002). Suicide and psychiatric diagnosis: a worldwide perspective. *World Psychiatry*, 1, 181-185.

Brent, D. A., Johnson B. A., Perper J., et al. (1994). Personality disorder, personality traits, impulsive violence, and completed suicide in adolescents. *Journal of the American Academy of Child and Adolescent Psychiatry*, 33, 1080–1086.

Fawcett, J., Busch, K., Jacobs, D., et al. (2000). Suicide: a four-pathway clinical biochemical model. In R. Maris, A. Berman, and M. Silverman (Eds.), *Comprehensive textbook of suicidology*. New York: Guilford.

Fekete, S. (2004). *Az öngyilkosság. Az öröklődéstől a kultúráig*. Pécs, Hungary.

Goldney, R. (2000). The privilege and responsibility of suicide prevention. *Crisis*, 21, 8-15.

Goldsmith, S., Pellmar, T., Kleinman, A., et al. (2002). *Reducing suicide: National imperative*. Washington, DC: National Academies Press.

Henriksson, H., Aro, H., Marttunen, M., et al. (1993). Mental disorders and comorbidity in suicide. *American Journal of Psychiatry*, 150, 935-940.

Isometsa, E., Henriksson, M., Heikkinen, M., et al. (1996). Suicide among subjects with personality disorders. *American Journal of Psychiatry*, 153, 667-673.

Kaplan, K. and Harrow, M. (1999). Psychosis and functioning as risk factors for later suicidal activity among schizophrenia and schizoaffective patients: a disease-based interactive model. *Suicide and Life-Threatening Behavior*, 29, 10-24.

Krupinski, M., Fischer, A., Grohmann, R., et al. (1998). Risk factors for suicides of inpatients with depressive psychoses. *European Archives of Psychiatry and Clinical Neuroscience*, 248, 141-147.

Kuritárné, I. (2005). *A borderline személyiségzavar*. PhD disszertáció, Debrecen, Hungary.

Mann, J., Waternaux, C., Haas, G., et al. (1999). Toward a clinical model of suicidal behavior psychiatric patients. *American Journal of Psychiatry*, 156, 181-189.

Mann, J., Apter, A., Bertolote, J., et al. (2005). Suicide prevention strategies. *Journal of the American Medical Association*, 294, 2064-2074.

Maris, R., Berman, A., Maltsberger, J., et al. (1992). *Assessment and prediction of suicide.* New York: Guilford.

Maris, R., Berman, A. and Silverman, M. (2000). *Comprehensive textbook of suicidology.* New York: Guilford.

Roy, A. (2000). Risk factors for suicide in psychiatric patient. In R. O'Connor and N. Sheehy, (Eds.), *Understanding suicidal behaviour.* Leicester, UK: BPS Books.

Roy, A. (1983). Family history of suicide. *Archives of General Psychiatry*, 40, 971-974.

Roy, A. (2000). Genetics, biology, and suicide in the family. In R. Maris, A. Berman, and M. Silverman (Eds.), *Comprehensive textbook of suicidology.* New York: Guilford.

Schmidt N., Woolaway-Bickel K. and Bates M. (2002). Suicide and panic disorder: integration of the literature and new findings. In S. Goldsmith, T. Pellmar, A. Kleinman, et al. (Eds.), *Reducing Suicide: National imperative.* Washington, DC: National Academies Press.

Takahashi, Y. (1997). Culture and suicide: from a Japanese psychiatrist's perspective. *Suicide and Life-Threatening Behavior*, 27, 137-147

In: Suicide from a Global Perspective
Editors: A. Shrivastava, M. Kimbrell, and D. Lester
ISBN: 978-1-61942-267-4
© 2012 Nova Science Publishers, Inc.

Chapter 3

SUICIDE: THE PROCESS FROM SUICIDAL IDEATION TO SUICIDE ATTEMPT

Marco Sarchiapone, Vladimir Carli, and Alec Roy

INTRODUCTION

When we discuss suicidality, we refer to different psychopathological phenomena. The idea of suicide as a process consisting of various elements is not new in psychiatry. In 1961 Farberow and Shneidman described the "cry for help," which presupposes a process before death by suicide that is determined by "the messages of suffering and anguish and the pleas for response that are expressed by and accontained within suicidal behaviors." Ringel (1976) described the *presuicidal syndrome*, related to that specific psychic state of mind that leads to suicidal acts. He discussed an alarm signal indicative of a tendency towards suicide and outlined three principal components: constriction; inhibited aggression turned toward the self; and suicidal fantasies. More recently Michel (1997) interpreted suicide as a goal-directed action as he described suicidal behavior similarly to any other human behavior, by focusing on developmental processes. He described a "suicide carrier" that included goal, intention, plans, strategies, decision, evaluation, choice, success, and failure.

The concept of the suicide carrier was previously presented by Maris (1981), who used path analysis and showed that salient failures for male suicides tended to be work, achievement and sex-related; while for female suicides they tended to be marriage, family and sex-related. Starting from a different point of view, Van Heeringen (2003) used the concept of the *suicidal process* to describe the onset and development of suicidality as a process within the individual and in interaction with surrounding people. He described the suicidal process as "starting with suicidal ideation and implying a progression of suicidality which can evolve through ideation, plans about taking one's life and communication regarding suicidal behavior, and growing through often recurrent suicide attempts, with increasing lethality and suicide intent, and ends with fatal suicide." The trait-dependent predisposition to suicide would be determined by the perception of "defeat," "no escape," and "no rescue," with each feature lying upon a phenomenological, neuropsychological, neuroanatomical, temperamental and neurobiological foundation.

The existence of a suicidal process is also confirmed by the presence of a temporality in suicidal behavior which, for instance, may be different among suicidal individuals with different psychiatric diagnoses. Portzky (2005) focused attention on the duration of the suicidal process and studied the psychological autopsies of nineteen adolescent suicides. His work suggests that the suicidal process in young suicides with adjustment disorder, compared to other psychiatric diagnosis, is triggered by the experience of an adverse life event. This resulted in a rapidly evolving suicidal process ending in a fatal suicide. Here the suicidal intent is as strong as compared to those suicides diagnosed with other psychiatric disorders who have a more prolonged and slowly evolving suicidal process.

In an attempt to analyze factors associated with temporal sequencing of suicide, Kaplan, et al. (2006) performed a population based prospective study on the US National Health Interview Survey (NHIS). Six hundred and fifty-three completed suicides were identified and differences in risk factors for suicides who died within one year from the interview were assessed in comparison with those who died more than one year after the interview. The authors reported that earlier suicides were more likely to be white, less educated, unemployed and to use firearms than other methods compared with later decedents.

Recent genetic studies of suicidal behavior have used the concept of the suicidal process in their design. After the well-established finding about suicide running in families (Roy, et al. 1997), research on the genetics of suicidal behavior focused its attention on suicidal endophenotypes, thus separating the different suicidal phenomena that compose the suicidal process. Rujescu (2003) reported an association between a COMT functional single nucleotide polymorphism and aggression in suicidal behavior. Aggression has in turn been associated with early onset suicidal behavior (Brent, et el., 2002). Roy and Janal (2005), in a study of over 1,800 patients with substance dependence, reported that female sex and childhood trauma are independent risk factors for both an early onset of first attempting suicide and for making more attempts. These data also confirm a temporal sequencing of suicidal behavior, with genetically susceptible subjects developing a faster suicidal process.

Our research group on suicidal behaviors has tried to identify correlations between suicidal thoughts and the presence of suicidal acts in a sample of approximately 150 depressed patients with suicidal ideation. We found significant correlations between suicide attempt, childhood trauma, a history of aggression, severity of depression and some features of suicidal ideation. In particular, expression to others of suicidal ideation (the tendency to spontaneously convey one's suicidal thoughts) represented a protective factor, as well as resilience. In the same individuals, the presence of childhood trauma was also associated with a history of aggression and, together with the severity of depressive symptoms, with a low tendency to express one's suicidal thoughts to others. Aggressiveness and low resilience correlated also with the presence of a suicide attempt or a suicidal plan, but were unrelated to non-specific thoughts about death, such as "life is not worth living" or "I was better off dead." These results suggest rather clearly the complexity of interactions among the vulnerability factors previously described. They allow us to suggest a model of suicidality in which non-specific death thoughts could be linked to distal factors such as the presence of a psychiatric diagnosis, or to proximal risk factors such as a stressful event. Aggressiveness or low resilience could be seen as contributing to the transition from these non-specific ideas to suicidal ideas, and ultimately to the elaboration of a suicidal plan and making a suicide attempt. Childhood trauma can be seen as linked to specific personality traits such as introversion and, therefore, to difficulty in conveying one's suicidal ideation, or impulsivity, which can both facilitate transition to act.

The common thread running through these perspectives is the assumption that suicidal behaviour covers a wide spectrum of thoughts, communications and acts. These range from the least common (completed suicide), to the more frequently occurring attempted suicide and suicidal communications, to the most common (suicidal ideation and verbalizations). They also include the assumption of the existence of a path that leads from temperament traits and life stressors to suicidal ideation and suicide attempts. It should be noted that the variables under consideration have different dimensions. Suicidal ideation may be considered a continuous variable. Suicidal ideation can encompass a wide variety of thoughts ranging from non-specific wishes to die or thinking that life is not worth living, to more specific ideas of death by suicide, to the construction of a more or less articulated suicidal plan. Thinking about suicide is by far the most common form of suicidality and may have different levels: from a symptom of a severe psychiatric illness, such as a bipolar disorder or schizophrenia, to a comforting thought ("If things get worse I may still kill myself").

There are specific tools that may be used to measure suicidal ideation which focus on its frequency, its intensity and its characteristics. General population studies show that up to 20% of people admit moderate suicidal ideation, involving a structured suicidal plan, at least once in their lives. Another 20% reported suicidal thoughts with no formation of a suicidal plan.

A suicide attempt is an on/off event, as it may or may not occur. An evaluation can be done to examine its severity, its lethality and the intent to die, but the presence of a suicide attempt, defined as "a self-destructive act with some intent to end one's life that is not self-mutilatory in nature" has to be considered as a categorical variable. Acting does not necessarily overlap with that psychopathological dimension that we call suicidality. For instance, there could be several self-destructive behaviors without a basic conscious wish to die. For example, some degree of suicidal intent has been reported in single-car accident drivers suggesting the presence of unconscious suicidal motivations in single accidents (Peck and Warner, 1995). At the same time, some patients with an explicit suicidal ideation will never act upon it. Additionally, patients who repeatedly attempt suicide in their life may eventually die by other unrelated causes while individuals with a mild degree of suicidal ideation can make many impulsive suicide attempts, rendering their survival a matter of chance.

The theme evident from the discussion thus far is the extreme complexity of trying to understand the path from suicidal ideation to suicide attempt. This argument of complexity is true when taking into account any human behavior, but it is even clearer if we consider a dysfunctional and anti-conservative behavior such as a suicidal act. The path which ultimately leads from suicidal ideation to suicide attempts and even completed suicide, therefore, not only is complex, but also does not exist on a continuum.

The link between a continuous measure of suicidal ideation and the occurrence of a categorical suicide attempt may be explored by introducing the concepts of suicidal threshold and suicidal vulnerability. Each and every discourse on the vulnerability to suicidal behavior should take into account the multifactorial basis of suicide. Thus, it can be imagined that every individual has his own specific vulnerability to suicidal behavior and that this vulnerability may originate from a number of risk factors such as certain psychopathological traits, stressful events and biological, genetic and social factors. In the medical literature there are plenty of reports of risk factors that are associated with suicide, ranging from genetic susceptibility to life stressors, biochemical impairment in the brain neurotransmitters, sociodemographic conditions, neurocognitive peculiarities such as poor problem solving and decision making, to impulsive aggression and childhood trauma.

These risk factors coexist with a series of protective factors against suicide. In particular, resilience, religious beliefs and a functioning support group all have their function in lowering the suicidal risk. Wasserman (2001) pointed out that, "what makes the difference between life and death however, is not only the presence of risk factors, but also access to protective factors that strengthen the suicidal person's coping strategies." These risk and protective factors determine each individual's risk for suicide and, only when a determined threshold is reached, that is, the suicidal threshold, will an individual accomplish a suicidal act. The suicidal process may also be defined then as the path that leads an individual to reach the suicidal threshold, with risk factors accelerating the process and protective factors simultaneously slowing down the process.

Even if the knowledge about the many risk factors for suicide can be useful for identifying people at high risk for suicide, the huge number of risk and protective factors and their unpredictable interactions make it difficult to establish the risk in a single individual. This is especially true while we still do not know how these factors fit into the suicidal process. Ultimately, a better knowledge of the suicidal process will help mental health professionals to improve their skills in recognizing, assessing and treating suicidal patients.

REFERENCES

Brent, D., A., Oquendo, M., Birmaher, B. et al. (2002). Familial pathways to early-onset suicide attempt: risk for suicidal behavior in offspring of mood disordered suicide attempters. *Archives of General Psychiatry*, 59, 801-807.

Farberow, N. L. and Shneidman, E. S. (1961). *The cry for help.* New York: McGraw-Hill.

Kaplan, M. S., McFarland, B. H., Huguet, N., and Newsom, J. T. (2006). Sooner versus later: factors associated with temporal sequencing of suicide. *Suicide and Life-Threatening Behavior*, 36, 377-385.

Maris, R. W. (1981). *Pathways to suicide.* Baltimore, MD: Johns Hopkins University Press.

Michel, K. and Valach, L. (1997). Suicide as goal-directed action. *Archives of Suicide Research,* 3, 213–221.

Peck, D. L. and Warner, K. (1995). Accident or suicide? Single-vehicle car accidents and the intent hypothesis. *Adolescence,* 30, 463-472.

Portzky, G., Audenaert, K. and Van Heeringen, K. (2005).Suicide among adolescents: a psychological autopsy study of psychiatric, psychosocial and personality-related risk factors. *Social Psychiatry and Psychiatric Epidemiology*, 40, 922-930.

Ringel, E. (1969). *Selbstmor, dverhu¨tung*. Bern-Stuttgart: H. Huber.

Roy, A. and Janal, M. (2005). Family history of suicide, female sex, and childhood trauma: separate or interacting risk factors for attempts at suicide? *Acta Psychiatrica Scandinavica,* 112, 367-371.

Roy, A., Rylander, G. and Sarchiapone, M. (1997). Genetic studies of suicidal behavior. *Psychiatric Clinics of North America,* 20, 595-611.

Rujescu, D., Giegling, I., Gietl, A. et al. (2003). A functional single nucleotide polymorphism (V158M) in the COMT gene is associated with aggressive personality traits. *Biological Psychiatry,* 54, 34-39.

Van Heeringen, K. (2001). The suicidal process and related concepts. In K. Van Heeringen (Eds.) *Understanding suicidal behaviour: the suicidal process approach to research, treatment and prevention,* pp. 3-15. Chichester, UK: Wiley.

Wasserman, D. (2001). *Suicide: an unnecessary death.* London, UK: Martin Dunitz.

In: Suicide from a Global Perspective
Editors: A. Shrivastava, M. Kimbrell, and D. Lester
ISBN: 978-1-61942-267-4
© 2012 Nova Science Publishers, Inc.

Chapter 4

THE SUICIDE PATHWAY

Alan J. Flisher and Ian Storm Lewis

INTRODUCTION

A large amount is known about the causes of suicide, but the application of this knowledge to clinical scenarios is hampered by a number of factors. First, suicide is a complex phenomenon with many interacting causes at the cultural, community, economic, family and individual levels. The identification of individual causes of suicide, or even a set of causes, is difficult to apply clinically as even the most comprehensive and thorough studies confine themselves to a limited set of these interacting causes (Rihmer, 2007). Second, suicide is a relatively rare event, compared to the prevalence of risk factors for suicide. Third, suicide risk is a fluid construct, affected by many factors which may change dramatically from moment to moment. Factors which may be predictive of suicide on one day may be absent the next. This makes accurate assessment a significant challenge and prediction of future behavior a near impossibility (Gutierrez, 2006). Finally, each suicide, and each suicidal individual, is unique. There is no single pathway, or even set of pathways, that can be applied to individuals with suicidality. Thus, each individual requires a unique etiological model.

Despite these challenges, it is essential to have an approach to understanding the causes of suicide to inform both clinical and public health approaches to addressing the challenges inherent in suicidality. We propose to resolve this dilemma by positing a heuristic suicide pathway (Figure 4-1) (Flisher, 1999). According to this pathway, suicidal behavior occurs in individuals who are predisposed to suicide. Thus, certain individuals are exposed to increased risk from one or more of the following *predisposing factors* in one or more of the following domains: demography, biology, psychopathology, physical illness, cognition, religion, and suicidal history (Table 4-1). It takes a precipitating event to change a state of being predisposed to suicidal behavior to actual behavior (Table 4-2). The precipitating event can be accompanied by the additional psychological *precipitating factors* of an altered state of mind, or social precipitating factors such as suicides in the community, reports of suicide in the media, or the season of spring. Finally, the *opportunity* needs to be present to make a suicide attempt, such as access to a means of suicide and privacy.

Each of the predisposing and precipitating factors will not be considered separately. Some of the risk factors have received attention in other chapters in this volume, and will thus receive more cursory attention here.

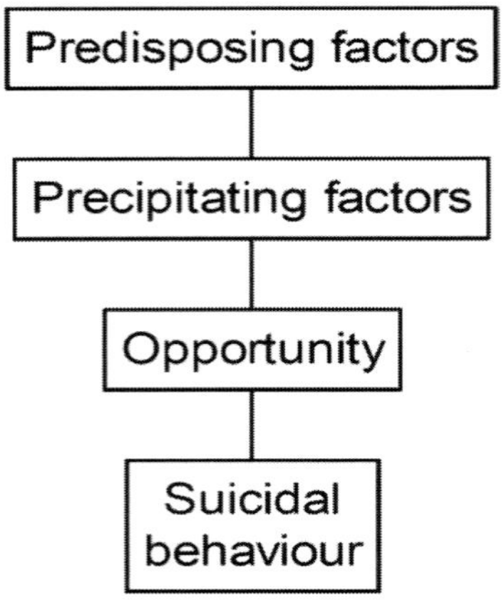

Figure 4-1. The suicide pathway.

Table 4-1. Predisposing factors for suicide

Demography
Gender
Age
Socio-economic status
Biology
Genetic factors
Biochemical factors
Psychopathology
Medical and surgical conditions
Cognitive distortions
Religion and culture
History of suicide
Family history
Personal history

Table 4-2. Precipitating factors for suicide

Social factors	Psychological factors
Clusters	Stressful life events
Media exposure to reports of suicides	Altered states of mind
Seasonal variation	

Predisposing Factors: Demography

Gender

In most settings where gender has been examined as a risk factor for completed or attempted suicide, it has been found that male gender is a risk factor for the former, while female gender is a risk factor for the latter. However, in China, the suicide rate is higher among rural young women than their male counterparts which is attributed to easy access to pesticides and rat poison (Yip and Liu, 2006).

Age

Generally speaking, the rates of suicide rise in adolescence, remain stable during adulthood, and rise in old age. It has recently been reported that suicide is a leading cause of death among young people in the two giant developing countries of China (Phillips, et al., 2002) and India (Aaron, et al., 2004).

Socioeconomic Status

A systematic review of the literature by Rehkopf and Buka (2006) found widely divergent findings regarding the direction of the association between area socioeconomic characteristics and area suicide rates. However, as one would anticipate, their analysis supported an increased risk of suicide in regions with high levels of poverty and deprivation and high unemployment rates. Differences in the suicide rate between different racial and ethnic groups are not due to racial or ethnic factors *per se*, but rather to other factors with which race/ethnicity is correlated, of which culture and socioeconomic status are the most obvious (Flisher, et al., 1994; Burrows, et al., 2007).

Biology

Biochemical Factors

Mann and Currier (2007) reviewed prospective studies of suicidal behavior and serotonergic, noradrenergic, dopaminergic and hypothalamic-pituitary-adrenocortical (HPA) axis function in mood disorders.

They concluded that the most promising biologic predictors of suicide were low levels of 5-HIAA in the cerebrospinal fluid and HPA axis dysfunction (as demonstrated by dexamethasone non-suppression).

Each of these predictors was associated with about a 4.5-fold increased risk of suicide.

Genetic Factors

There is growing evidence that genetic factors contribute to suicidal behavior. Molecular genetic studies have focused particularly on the serotonergic pathway. In a review, Bondy and colleagues (2006) noted that two genes have emerged so far as being involved in the vulnerability for suicidality: the polymorphisms of the tryptophan hydroxylase 1 (TPH1) gene, which was suggested as a quantitative risk factor for suicidal behavior; and the insertion/deletion polymorphism of the serotonin transporter gene (5-HTTLPR), which does not seem to be involved in general suicidal behavior, but in violent and repeated suicide attempts.

PSYCHOPATHOLOGY

Harris and Barraclough (1994) identified 235 reports of mortality studies of medical or psychiatric disorders with two years or more of follow-up, less than 10% loss of subjects, observed numbers of suicides given and either the expected number of suicides or the facts from which to derive this. They tested whether the ratio of the observed number of suicides to the expected number (standardised mortality ratio (SMR)) was significantly different to the expected ratio using the Poisson distribution. The psychiatric disorders with significantly increased suicide mortality (with the SMR) were as follows: eating disorders (23.1), alcohol dependence (5.9), schizophrenia (8.5), major depressive disorder (20.3), bipolar affective disorder (15.1), dysthymic disorder (12.1), anxiety disorders (10.0) and personality disorders (7.1).

Flisher (1999) identified seven psychological autopsy studies involving child and adolescent suicides. The studies were consistent in the conclusion that almost all children and adolescents dying by suicide were suffering from a psychiatric disorder (most commonly mood disorders) at the time of their death, with the proportion being more than 90% in all but one study. Furthermore, all three studies with non-clinical control groups found that the prevalence rates of any diagnosis, any mood disorder and major depression were significantly higher in those committing suicide than in controls. In the study with the strongest design in terms of sample size, ascertainment procedures, and characteristics of control group (Shaffer et al., 1996), it was found that 91% suffered from any disorder; 61% from any mood disorder; and 32% from major depressive disorder, 13% from dysthymic disorder, 3% from bipolar disorder, 3% from depression not otherwise specified or atypical depression, and 6% from adjustment disorder with depressed mood.

Psychological autopsy studies involving adult suicides report similar conclusions. For example, Seguin et al. (2006) investigated all suicides in New Brunswick in a 14-month period in 2002-2003. They were able to investigate 102 of the 109 suicide deaths occurring in this period. Of these, 65% had a mood disorder, 59% had a substance-related disorder and 42% had both a mood and substance-related disorder. They also found that 52% of the suicides had a personality disorder, half of which were Cluster B personality disorders such as borderline personality disorder.

Medical and Surgical Conditions

The review mentioned above by Harris and Barraclough (1994) that addressed psychopathology and suicide also included medical and surgical conditions. The following conditions were found to be associated with an increased risk of suicide (with the SMR's): HIV (6.7), HIV and haemophilia (3.8), Huntington's Disease (2.9), malignancies (1.8), multiple sclerosis (2.4), peptic ulcer (2.1), renal dialysis (14.5), renal transplantation (3.8), spinal cord injuries (3.8), and systemic lupus erythematosis (4.3). However, there are a number of illnesses where there was inconclusive evidence of increased suicide mortality. These include amputation, selected intestinal diseases (Crohn's Disease and ulcerative colitis), alcoholic liver disease, neurofibromatosis, Parkinson's Disease and systemic sclerosis. Thus, it would appear that it is not the presence of a disease *per se* that contributes to risk for suicide. Rather, certain diseases display characteristics that confer a heightened risk of suicide.

Cognitive Distortions

The presence of cognitive distortions (such as negative cognitive bias and perfectionism) may serve as a predisposing factor for suicidal behavior (Beevers and Miller, 2004).

Religion and Culture

The religious and cultural context is relevant for the etiology of suicide in two ways. First, the presence of religious and cultural proscriptions may reduce the probability of suicide in a predisposed individual (Dervic, et al., 1996). Suicide is strongly proscribed in Catholicism, Islam and Judaism, and adherents of these religions are indeed less likely to commit suicide than matched controls. Second, there may be culture-specific factors that make suicide more likely. For example, suicide rates are relatively high among young Indian women and girls in South Africa (Flisher and Parry, 1994). One explanation that has been offered for this observation is that there is parental prohibition of such young women and girls engaging in romantic relationships. They are thus not in a position to disclose or discuss these relationships with their parents or other significant adults. When these relationships break up, the young women and girls feel particularly unsupported in their social networks. Not having people to turn to for support, they feel hopeless and lonely, and resort to suicide.

History of Suicide

Family History

There is consensus that a family history of suicide is associated with suicidal behavior (Kim, et al., 2005). Other aspects of family history are also relevant. In a review of the literature describing the risk factors for suicidal behavior among young people, Beautrias

(2000) found evidence for a wide array of adverse family factors, including parental separation or divorce, parental discord, impaired parent–child relationships, parental psychopathology, and exposure to childhood physical and/or sexual abuse, that appear to be associated with increased risk of suicidal behavior.

Personal History

Individuals with a history of suicide attempts form a well-defined high-risk group for suicide. For example, Shaffer, et al. (1996) found in their psychological autopsy study conducted in New York that the presence of a previous suicide attempt in males increased the odds of suicide by a factor of 19. Christiansen and Jensen (2007) extracted data from the Danish suicide register and concluded on the basis of survival analysis that death from suicide occurred four times more often among those that had previously attempted suicide compared to those who had not done so. The National Comorbidity Survey Replication (NCS-R), a household survey of adults aged 18 years and over in the USA, assessed the 12-month occurrence of suicide ideation, plans and attempts in a sub-sample of 5,692 respondents. A history of prior attempts is the strongest correlate of a suicide attempt in the previous 12 months (Borges, et al., 2006).

Precipitating Factors: Psychological Factors

Stressful Life Events

Almost any life event can serve as a precipitating factor for suicidal behavior, including childhood abuse (especially physical abuse and violent sexual abuse), school stress from academic failure or difficulties, problems in romantic relationships, family disruptions and discord (for example, arguments, divorce, deteriorating family relationships due to the presence of psychopathology in family members), and parent-child conflict (Brezo, et al., 2007; Chiou, et al., 2006; Joiner, et al., 2007).

These stressful life events, some of which are relatively common, are generally not the sole cause of suicidal behavior. However, in individuals who are at heightened risk due to exposure to one or more predisposing factors, experiencing a life event can serve as the "final straw," especially if they do not possess the social or problem-solving skills to address the life event in an adaptive manner.

Altered States of Mind

Suicidal behavior may take place when the individual is not able to think in their normal manner due to experiencing an altered state of mind, for example from panic, intoxication and dread (Goodwin and Roy-Byrne, 2006).

Social Factors

Clusters

Gould has provided evidence that suicides can occur in space-time clusters, where an unusually large number of suicides occur in a circumscribed geographical area in a short period of time (Gould, et al., 1990a, 1990b). It would appear that the existence of other suicides over a short period of time among people to whom one is in proximity can lower the threshold for suicide in predisposed individuals. However, such clusters are much more common among adolescents and young adults, with almost no clusters being observed involving people over the age of 24 years.

Media Exposure to Reports of Suicides

Studies on the influence of media on suicidal behaviors have tended to draw a consistent conclusion, namely that media reporting of suicide can lead to copycat behaviors, particularly if the coverage is extensive, prominent, sensationalist and/or explicitly describes the method (Pirkis, et al., 2007). In a meta-analysis of 55 studies on the effect of suicide stories in the media on suicide, Stack (2005) determined that studies measuring the presence of either an entertainment or political celebrity were more than five times more likely to find a copycat effect, whereas studies focusing on stories that stressed negative definitions of suicide were 99% less likely to report a copycat effect (Stack, 2005).

Seasonal Variation

Durkheim observed that there was seasonal variation in suicide, with a peak in spring or summer and a trough in winter (Durkheim, 1897). This finding has been repeatedly replicated in the northern (Massing and Angermeyer, 1985; Fruehwald, et al., 2004) and southern (Flisher, et al., 1997) hemispheres. Two explanations have been offered for this pattern. First, it could be due to circannual rhythms in biochemical processes that are associated with vulnerability or resistance to stressors (Maes, et al., 1993). Second, it could be due to changes in social activity, with those who are socially isolated being adversely affected when others in their community become more socially active in spring (Durkheim, 1897).

Opportunity Factors

If an individual is exposed to one or more predisposing and precipitating factors for suicide, s/he can proceed to attempt suicide only if they have the opportunity to do so. This opportunity can involve access to firearms (Miller, et al., 2007), lethal substances as occurs with health workers (Agerbo, et al, 2007), or pesticides (London, et al., 2005).

CONCLUSION

We hope that the suicide pathway can be used both for clinical and preventive purposes. In clinical situations it is important to understand the suicide pathway for each suicidal patient. This will suggest what interventions are indicated and ensure that the patient is approached in a comprehensive manner. When developing preventive interventions (which are addressed in other chapters in this book), the suicide pathway suggests suitable targets for programming.

REFERENCES

Aaron, R., Joseph, A., Abraham, J. (2004). Suicide in young people in rural South India. *Lancet,* 363, 1117-1118.

Agerbo, E., Gunnell, D., Bonde, J. P., Mortensen, P. et al.. (2007). Suicide and occupation: the impact of socio-economic, demographic and psychiatric differences. *Psychological Medicine,* 37, 1131-1140.

Beautrais, A. L. (2000). Risk factors for suicide and attempted suicide among young people. *The Australian and New Zealand Journal of Psychiatry*, 34, 420-436.

Bondy, B., Buettner, A., Zill, P. (2006) Genetics of suicide. *Molecular Psychiatry,* 11, 336-351.

Borges, G., Angst, J., Nock, M. K., Ruscio, A. M. et al. (2006). A risk index for 12-month suicide attempts in the National Comorbidity Survey Replication (NCS-R). *Psychological Medicine,* 36, 1747-1757.

Brezo, J., Paris, J., Tremblay, R., Vitaro, F. et al. (2007). Identifying correlates of suicide attempts in suicidal ideators: a population-based study. *Psychological Medicine,* 37. 1551-1562.

Burrows, S., Vaez, M. and Laflamme, L. (2007). Sex-specific suicide mortality in the South African urban context: the role of age, race, and geographical location. *Scandinavian Journal of Public Health,* 35, 133-139.

Chiou, P. N., Chen, Y. S., Lee, Y. C. (2006). Characteristics of adolescent suicide attempters admitted to an acute psychiatric ward in Taiwan. *Journal of the Chinese Medical Association,* 69, 428-435.

Christiansen, E. and Jensen, B. F. (2007). Risk of repetition of suicide attempt, suicide or all deaths after an episode of attempted suicide: a register-based survival analysis. *Australian and New Zealand Journal of Psychiatry,* 41, 257-265.

Dervic, K., Oquendo, M. A., Currier, D., Grunebaum, M. F. et al. (2006). Moral objections to suicide: can they counteract suicidality in patients with cluster B psychopathology? *Journal of Clinical Psychiatry,* 67, 620-625.

Durkheim, E. (1897). *Le suicide*. Paris: Felix Alcan.

Flisher, A. J. (1999). The management of suicidal behaviour in adolescents. *Specialist Medicine,* 21, 418-423.

Flisher, A. J. (1999). Mood disorder in suicidal children and adolescents: recent developments. *Journal of Child Psychology and Psychiatry,* 40, 315-324.

Flisher, A. J. and Parry C. D. (1994). Suicide in South Africa: an analysis of nationally registered mortality data for 1984-1986. *Acta Psychiatrica Scandinavica,* 90, 348-353.

Flisher, A. J., Parry, C. D. H., Bradshaw, D., and Juritz, J. M. (1997). Seasonal variation of suicide in South Africa. *Psychiatry Research,* 66, 13-22.

Fruehwald, S., Frottier, P., Matschnig, T., Koenig, F. et al. (2004). Do monthly or seasonal variations exist in suicides in a high-risk setting? *Psychiatry Research,* 121, 263-269.

Goodwin, R. D. and Roy-Byrne P. (2006). Panic and suicidal ideation and suicide attempts: results from the National Comorbidity Survey. *Depression and Anxiety,* 23, 124-132.

Gould, M., Wallenstein, S. and Kleinman, M. H. (1990a). Time-space clustering of teenage suicide. *American Journal of Epidemiology,* 131, 71-78.

Gould, M., Wallenstein, S., Kleinman, M. H., O'Carroll, P. et al. (1990b). Suicide clusters: an examination of age-specific effects. *American Journal of Public Health,* 80, 211-212.

Gutierrez, P. M. (2006). 2005 Shneidman Award Address. Integratively assessing risk and protective factors for adolescent suicide. *Suicide and Life-Threatening Behavior,* 36, 129-35.

Harris, E. C., Barraclough, B. M. (1994). Suicide as an outcome for medical disorders. *Psychological Medicine,* 73, 297-298.

Joiner, T. E. Jr., Sachs-Ericsson, N. J., Wingate, L. R., Brown, J.S. et al. (2007). Childhood physical and sexual abuse and lifetime number of suicide attempts: a persistent and theoretically important relationship. *Behavior Research and Therapy,* 45, 539-47.

Kim, C. D., Seguin, M., Therrien, N., Riopel, G. et al. (2005). Familial aggregation of suicidal behavior: a family study of male suicide completers from the general population. *American Journal of Psychiatry,* 162, 1017-1019.

London, L., Flisher, A. J., Wesseling, C., Mergler, D. et al. (2005). Suicide and exposure to organophosphate insecticides: cause or effect? *American Journal of Industrial Medicine,* 47, 308 – 321.

Maes, M., Cosyns, P., Meltzer, H. Y., De Meyer, F. et al. (1993). Seasonality in violent suicide but not in non-violent suicide or homicide. *American Journal of Psychiatry,* 150, 1380-1385.

Mann, J. J. and Currier D. (2007). A review of prospective studies of biologic predictors of suicidal behaviour in mood disorders. *Archives of Suicide Research,* 11, 3-16.

Massing, W. and Angermeyer, M. C. (1985). The monthly and weekly distribution of suicide. *Social Science and Medicine,* 21, 433-441.

Miller, M., Lippmann, S. J., Azrael, D., and Hemenway, D. (2007). Household firearm ownership and rates of suicide across the 50 United States. *Journal of Trauma,* 62, 1029-1035.

Palmer, B. A., Pankratz, V. S. and Bostwick, J. M. (2005). The lifetime risk of suicide in schizophrenia: a reexamination. *Archives of General Psychiatry,* 62, 247-253.

Pirkis, J., Burgess, P. Blood, R. W., and Francis, C. (2007). The newsworthiness of suicide. *Suicide and Life-Threatening Behavior,* 37, 278-283.

Rehkopf, D. H. and Buka, S. L. (2006). The association between suicide and the socio-economic characteristics of geographical areas: a systematic review. *Psychological Medicine,* 36, 145-157.

Rihmer, Z. (2007). Suicide risk in mood disorders. *Current Opinion in Psychiatry,* 20, 17-22.

Seguin, M. and Lesage, A. (2006). Suicide cases in New Brunswick from April 2002 to

May 2003: the importance of better recognizing substance and mood disorder comorbidity. *Canadian Journal of Psychiatry,* 51, 581-586.

Shaffer, D., Gould, M., Fisher, P., Trautman, P. et al. (1996). Psychiatric diagnosis in child and adolescent suicide. *Archives of General Psychiatry,* 53, 339-348.

Smith, J. M., Alloy, L. B., Abramson, L. Y. (2006). Cognitive vulnerability to depression, rumination, hopelessness, and suicidal ideation: multiple pathways to self-injurious thinking. *Suicide and Life-Threatening Behavior,* 36, 443-454.

Stack, S. (2005). Suicide in the media: a quantitative review of studies based on non-fictional stories. *Suicide and Life-Threatening Behavior,* 35, 121-133.

Yip, P. S. and Liu, K. Y. (2006). The ecological fallacy and the gender ratio of suicide in China. *British Journal of Psychiatry,* 189, 465-456.

In: Suicide from a Global Perspective
Editors: A. Shrivastava, M. Kimbrell, and D. Lester
ISBN: 978-1-61942-267-4
© 2012 Nova Science Publishers, Inc.

Chapter 5

DELIBERATE SELF HARM, PARASUICIDE AND NON-FATAL SUICIDAL BEHAVIOR: FROM DEFINITIONS TO EMPOWERING PRACTICES

Inger Ekman and Stig Söderberg

INTRODUCTION

Deliberate acts of self-harm have been a growing clinical problem in the Western world for the last three decades, and is also an emerging problem in urbanized parts of developing countries. During the last few decades, young women have predominated, but current clinical observations indicate deliberate acts of self-harm are also a growing problem among young men in Western society.

DEFINITIONS IN RESEARCH ON NON-FATAL SUICIDAL BEHAVIOR

In reading the scientific literature, the terminology and definitions of the problem are quite varied and need some clarification. Three different concepts are being widely used: attempted suicide/suicide attempt, parasuicide and deliberate self-harm. These concepts define somewhat different groups of behaviors which complicate comparisons between studies. Attempted suicide/suicide attempt is the most limited concept. It usually implies a wish to die and a potential lethality of the act. The other two concepts, parasuicide and deliberate self-harm, are akin to each other in their definition, but have different connotations.

Deliberate self-harm (DSH) is the broadest concept, including all non-fatal deliberate acts intended to cause harm. A definition of deliberate self-harm developed by the Child and Adolescent Self-harm in Europe (CASE) group reads as follows:

> "An act with a non-fatal outcome in which an individual deliberately did one or more of the following: Initiated behavior (for example, self-cutting, jumping from a height), which they intended to cause self-harm; ingested a substance in excess of the prescribed or generally recognised therapeutic dose; ingested a recreational or illicit drug that was an act that the person regarded as self-harm; ingested a non-ingestible substance or object" (Hawton, et al., 2002).

The concept of parasuicide was introduced to avoid problems inherent in the concept of attempted suicide based upon intent or lethality, as these aspects may be difficult to assess. The concept also avoids the broad connotations of the term self-harm and excludes habitual self-harming behaviors such as drug abuse. The concept of parasuicide focuses on the intent of achieving some kind of change through the act and excludes thoughts or wishes.

A definition of parasuicide used in the multicenter project of the WHO/EURO Multi-Centre Study on Parasuicide reads as follows:

> "an act with non-fatal outcome, in which an individual deliberately initiates a non-habitual behavior that, without intervention from others, will cause self-harm, or deliberately ingests a substance in excess of the prescribed or generally recognized therapeutic dosage, and which is aimed at realizing changes which the individual desired via the actual or expected physical consequences" (Platt, et al., 1992).

The term parasuicide has disadvantages. The connotations of the prefix "para" in certain languages are associated with "mimicking" and "pretending," implying that a parasuicidal patient has no intent to die. The term has also been the cause of some confusion in research and clinical practice as the term has come to have quite different connotations in Europe and overseas.

In the USA, the term parasuicide is often regarded as a subcategory of attempted suicide, characterized by low suicidal intent. In Europe, on the other hand, attempted suicide commonly is regarded as a subcategory of parasuicide, characterized by strong suicidal intent. Still others use the terms as mutually exclusive – parasuicide defines suicidal acts with low suicidal intent, while the term attempted suicide is reserved for situations where intent to die is evident.

These disadvantages have led the WHO/EURO group to suggest that both these terms, as well as the term deliberate self-harm be exchanged with the term "non-fatal suicidal behavior". The present definition of non-fatal suicidal behavior, used by the WHO/EURO group, reads as follows:

> "A non-habitual act with non-fatal outcome that the individual, expecting to, or taking the risk, to die or to inflict bodily harm, initiated and carried out with the purpose of bringing about wanted changes" (De Leo, et al., 2004).

Despite the confusion caused by these attempts at scientifically defining the terms used and the cohorts to be studied, in clinical practice the terms deliberate self-harm, parasuicide, attempted suicide and non-fatal suicidal behavior are commonly used interchangeably.

THE MAGNITUDE OF THE PROBLEM

The frequency of non-fatal suicidal behavior in a population is hard to reliably assess, as most acts probably do not come to medical attention and thus are not available for direct study. The behavior may also be underreported in self-report surveys. In a self-report survey of 6,020 adolescents in England (Hawton, et al., 2002), 6.9% reported an act of self-harm during the last year, with only 12.9% of these reporting that they had sought medial attention for the act.

Non-fatal suicidal acts that result in a visit to an emergency room are around ten times as common as suicides. Epidemiological studies have repeatedly shown a male dominance for suicide in Western society, while women dominate for attempted suicide (Söderberg, 2001). The acts often lead to admission to a somatic or psychiatric ward at the hospital and are the cause of much concern for consulting psychiatrists who are asked to assess the potential risk for completed suicide. Since such a risk may be hard to assess, prolonged periods of hospital-based psychiatric care are often suggested and sometimes enforced through involuntary admission to a psychiatric ward.

CAUSES AND PSYCHOPATHOLOGY

Deliberate self-harm has been shown to be associated with drug misuse, depression, anxiety, impulsivity and low self esteem, and is strongly associated with physical and sexual abuse (Hawton, et al., 2002; Söderberg, et al., 2004). Among those with repeated non-fatal suicidal behavior, there is a strong association with impulsivity, identity disturbance, affective instability and intense but unstable interpersonal relationships (Skodol and Bender, 2003). Within psychiatry, such characteristics are usually diagnosed as borderline personality disorder.

The validity of the borderline personality disorder concept has been strongly questioned. This is due in part to the lack of empirical support for a qualitative distinction between normal and abnormal personality functioning as well as an extensive overlap between and heterogeneity within the personality disorder categories (Skodol, et al., 2002). The categorical construct of borderline personality disorder may lead to an oversimplified reduction of the complex personality dimension, both in research and treatment. The diagnostic concept is at present the focus of substantial research efforts.

Among persons seeking medical attention due to recent non-fatal suicidal behavior, a borderline personality disorder has been identified in up to 55% (Söderberg, 2001). The repeated self-harm in this group has led to the notion among clinicians that their self-harming behavior is of a manipulative nature. However, repeated studies during the past 20 years have not been able to confirm this hypothesis, as differences in motives and precipitating factors between the borderline group and others has not been found (Söderberg, et al., 2004). These findings indicate that the notion of "manipulative" suicide attempts among persons diagnosed with borderline personality disorder is a reflection of frustration and resentment on the part of the helpers, rather than a characteristic of the patients.

Among persons diagnosed with borderline personality disorder the risk for completed suicide in the years following a suicide attempt is around 10%. This is in the same range as the suicide risk in major mood disorders and schizophrenia. Regardless of personality traits, the overall risk for completed suicide after a suicide attempt is highest in the year following the attempt and then diminishes. However, for persons diagnosed with borderline personality disorder, the risk for completed suicide remains elevated for more than a decade (Paris, 2002).

Since the median prevalence of borderline personality disorder in the community across studies is around 1% (Mattia and Zimmerman, 2001), the high prevalence of borderline personality disorder in repeated non-fatal suicidal behavior indicates a substantial need for a better understanding of the life experiences and sufferings of the individuals that exist behind the numbers.

The group is characterized by having experienced many adverse events during their lifetime, and many of the women in the group have suffered childhood sexual abuse (Söderberg, et al., 2004). Such abuse is regarded as a very serious adverse life event with long-term psychological consequences, including symptoms of depression, anxiety and low self-esteem as well as suicidal behavior.

An increasing number of studies have also linked the symptoms of borderline personality disorder to other forms of dysfunctional relationships, emotional neglect, abandonment and abuse during childhood. Attributing all the emotional pain these patients reveal to sexual abuse therefore trivializes other experiences of neglect, emotional torture and abandonment, both among those who have and those who have not been sexually abused (Zanarini, 2000; Goodman, et al., 2003). Sexual abuse may be seen as an indicator of severely dysfunctional relationships in childhood, and sexual abuse in itself may not be the most horrifying experience to the patients, although it may be to clinicians. In the words of Mary Zanarini, "Rather, it may be emblematic of the ongoing chaos and insensitivity that left them with long-term feelings of helplessness, worthlessness and inchoate rage" (Zanarini, 2000, p. 98).

Behind the repeated self-destructiveness, there are usually feelings of despair and a perceived unbearableness of the present situation or frame of mind, as well as a sense of lack of control over life circumstances (Paris, 2003; Söderberg, et al., 2004). The self-destructiveness may be seen as a way of gaining control - exerting the only power that remains, the power to end one's life (Gunderson and Ridolfi, 2001; Paris, 2003). In follow-up studies, many have described that their self-destructiveness has diminished parallel to the process of gaining control over life and having found possibilities for choosing other options (Paris, 2003; Söderberg, 2004).

Cultural Implications

The increasing frequency of non-fatal suicidal behavior seems to be related to the ever increasing pace of social change in modern society. This has implications for the future of both Western society and developing countries. The transition to urbanization and industrialization, the widespread mass media and the World Wide Web has unequivocally changed the identity process of the individual.

Previously, a person's identity was formed by her/his participation in the nearby community, where a person was regarded as an integrated part of the whole. Modern man, on the other hand, mainly lives in cities, often far from relatives and friends. Instead of meeting others as an integrated person well-defined by his place in society, she/he meets others in the context of temporal roles, to which she/he adapts in the context of work and other relationships. Several different roles may be held during a day, and encounters with others are related to the context of the temporal roles of those who interact. For anyone who lives separated from close private personal encounters, and/or does not carry an integrated sense of identity, this situation can lead to disintegration.

During the last decades, the pace of change has accellerated. Information is increasingly mediated through modern media instead of through narratives of the people we meet. Events far away permeate our homes and have an influence on everyday thoughts and life. Encounters with others no longer involve face-to-face roles, but the roles have instead become abstract, as the encounters often are through phone or other media. These abstract anonymous roles, for instance at a chatroom over the web, permit roles that disregard even such basics of identity as age and gender of the persons who interact.

In the present day, those who stand as models for our lives may not be people we have had close encounters with in daily life, but rather persons we have only met through the media. Media also influences the way we perceive ourselves, as imperatives of achievement, happiness and an attractive body are advertised daily. Even the confines of the characteristics of the individual body are challenged through the possibility of an "extreme makeover".

Modern life thus is characterized by the break-up of the close confines of human life, guided by proximity, face-to-face relations and traditional values transmitted through the generations, into a situation where each individual has to make his own choices from a wide variety of practical as well as moral possibilities. In sociological theory, this process is usually termed "modernity," and is regarded as having a profound influence on the formation of self and identity (Giddens, 1991). Instead of being defined by our position in a slowly developing community, the individual has to construct his own view of himself through a reflective process, a narrative of his identity. Giddens terms this process "the reflexive project of the self".

In this "reflexive project of the self", there are the ever changing possibilities of different roles. Seemingly contradictory to this, modern society also sets demands for uniqueness and authenticity. According to Taylor (1991), the modern process has resulted in a quest for authenticity, of being true to oneself, so much so that it is perceived as an imperative. Authenticity has come to be something we have to attain to be true and full human beings. Being authentic is to stay true to one's own originality – whatever that may be.

These tendencies of modern society have a profound influence on childhood experiences. In the context of constantly shifting styles, increasingly questioned norms and an increasing pace of social change, the room for development of a well-integrated personality diminishes while we constantly receive impulses that guide momentary but disintegrated actions. Among sensitive individuals, these characteristics of modern life promote the development of personality traits presently known as "borderline".

Implications for Treatment

The present trends in modern society poses radically new demands on the organization of psychiatric healthcare as well as on the development of working strategies and methods to meet the needs of persons formed by the modern society.

As an example, traditional hospitalization after a single non-fatal suicide attempt may be an adequate strategy – but for those with repeated non-fatal suicidal behavior, the value of prolonged periods of hospital-based psychiatric care is dubious. There is consensus that the focus should be on out-patient care and very short periods of hospitalization, since clinical experience indicates that prolonged hospitalization leads to accentuated self-destructiveness, as the treatment model reinforces such behavior (Gunderson and Ridolfi, 2001; Paris, 2003; Paris 2004; Stanley and Brodsky, 2005; Oldham, 2006; Fonagy and Bateman, 2006). The pros and cons of admission, therefore, should be carefully discussed with the person involved, with the focus on the person's own judgement of her/his ability to take control over anxiety and self-destructiveness, allowing her/him to exert responsibility for her/his own choices (Gunderson and Ridolfi, 2001). Basically, the need of the clinician for a "safe" handling of the situation should be disregarded.

Repeated non-fatal suicidal behavior also poses a challenge to the traditional therapeutic methods used. An increased need for long-term treatment characterized by close and frequent interaction can be expected since such methods seem necessary to broaden the basis for understanding the life circumstances and ways of thinking of the patients with severe trauma or severe symptoms. Such treatment methods have proved to be of crucial importance (Bateman and Fonagy, 2000; Söderberg, 2004), and can dramatically increase the rate of improvement (Fonagy and Bateman, 2006).

Changing expectations and demands on the therapeutic community as a whole can also be expected. In the present phase of modernity, therapists and therapeutic traditions are at the mercy of the trust and doubt that is characteristic of all institutions in the modern age (Giddens, 1991). In the flow of information, people are used to making their own revisions of the basis for their trust, and no longer accept the need to be "treated" according to the preferred methods of an individual expert. The responsibility for self-identity and self-development now lies on the shoulders of the individual, who will recognize the value of a therapeutic intervention with regard to whether this intervention is instrumental for her/his authenticity and individuality (Taylor, 1991).

In this context, a demand for mutuality and participation in the planning and process of therapy can also be expected. The process calls for a perspective of collaboration in therapeutic work, enabling the patients to take charge of their lives, helping them define their own needs, using a language that has common connotations for both the therapist and the patient (Ekman and Söderberg, 2009). The process of modernity thus seems to call for a redefinition of the positions of power in psychiatric health care (Wilson, 2000), enabling a process of empowerment for the individual seeking assistance.

Present Trends in Treatment Strategies

Persons with non-fatal suicidal behavior are a heterogeneous group. To find guidance for how to address their needs, the reliance is on clinical experience and the principles involved in those methods that have been shown to be fruitful – the Dialectical Behavior Therapy of Linehan (for a review, see Lieb, et al., 2004), and the mentalization-based partial-hospitalization programs of Bateman and Fonagy (2001, 2004). Both methods are orientated towards principles of accessibility to the therapist, well-defined and structured methodology, active participation of the patient in the development of the specific treatment strategies, and role predictability as a basis for reliable long-term relations with the staff.

The basic prerequisite in meeting persons who, due to their life experiences, have an emotional instability and difficulty in trusting others, is showing that one is worthy of their trust. (Livesley, 2005; Oldham, 2006). This is a continuous process which demands sincerity and predictability in the approach (Gunderson and Ridolfi, 2001). It includes a readiness to continue the relationship and to stay true to promises given, as well as knowing your methodology thoroughly. This familiarity with methods allows one to improvise in a structured way when the formalized strategies do not give guidance. Such treatment models have been shown to accelerate the rate of improvement, and merits optimism concerning the long-term outcome (Fonagy and Bateman, 2006).

Persons with repeated non-fatal suicidal behavior usually have an admirable honesty concerning their pain and its sources (Zanarini, 2000), and it takes courage to meet this pain. The need for support is usually vast and immediate, and often not possible to handle through traditional therapeutic models (Gunderson and Ridolfi, 2001; Paris, 2003; Söderberg, 2004; Fonagy and Bateman, 2006). It is important to acknowledge the limitations of such strategies to offer help, and to focus on the whole set of problems early in the process. An adequate support should be structured, instead of resorting to individual therapy contacts that in the end may only offer the patient another experience of the deceitfulness of man, enforcing feelings of abandonment, isolation and desperation (Gunderson and Ridolfi, 2001; Paris, 2003; Söderberg, 2004; Fonagy and Bateman, 2006).

For those with non-fatal suicidal behavior, a contribution from the field of social work known as "empowerment" may give guidance in treatment (Payne, 1997; Hamann, et al., 2003). Empowerment perspectives were developed during the 1970's in work with oppressed ethnic groups, and since then have been applied to a wide variety of settings, including psychiatry. The empowerment perspective places work with individuals and families in a collaborative context, aiming to remove the power basis inherent in the traditional medical model.

Empowerment perspectives argue for a participative approach and suppose that people want to be involved in decisions regarding their lives, and that they have the right to be involved in those decisions (Payne, 1997). Empowerment practices include making it possible for people to take charge of matters which affect them by defining their own needs, and to participate in subsequent planning and decision-making. Empowerment work aims at developing confidence, self-esteem, assertiveness, expectations, knowledge and skills, and is focused on encouraging people to become subjects rather than objects in their lives. This work also argues that the focus should be on the knowledge gained from the patients in a dialogical process based on their own descriptions, using their own language. The process should be focused on the person's own understanding of himself and his situation. The preconceived assumptions, policies and terminologies of the helper should be discarded, as such a language is an expression of a power relationship. Empowerment strategies regard each human being as the expert of his own life, and empowerment perspectives seriously challenge the medical model of expert-defined assessment, diagnostics and treatment, and redefines positions of power in healthcare settings (Hewitt-Taylor, 2004). Basically, the approach is built upon confidence in the person's own capacity to find her/his own solutions and strategies as well as a readiness to support her/him in this quest.

CONCLUSION

Deliberate self-harm, parasuicide, attempted suicide and non-fatal suicidal behavior define somewhat different groups of behavior, but the terms are often used interchangeably in clinical practice. Deliberate acts of self-harm is a growing problem especially among young persons in urbanized parts of the world, This may possibly reflect the increasing pace of social change that influences the formation of identity. This process encourages the development of personality traits characterized by impulsivity, affective instability, intense but unstable interpersonal relationships and a fragile sense of self among sensitive individuals.

The context of modernity seems to predispose those who have been subjected to severe adverse events in childhood to repeated deliberate acts of self-harm in early adult life. The frailty of such persons calls for long-term, stable, multidisciplinary treatment strategies based upon close and frequent interaction with predictability of the roles of the staff. Such treatment strategies have shown to be of crucial importance for the rate of improvement of severely traumatized persons with repeated non-fatal suicidal behavior, and are a cause of optimism regarding long-term outcome.

The continuous and ever increasing pace of change in society in both the Western world and developing countries indicates that deliberate acts of self harm can be expected to be even more common in the future, challenging present traditions in psychiatric healthcare. A demand for mutuality and participation in the planning and process of treatment can be expected, and therapeutic traditions have to change accordingly, possibly based around the principles of empowerment.

REFERENCES

Bateman, A. and Fonagy, P. (2004). *Psychotherapy for borderline personality disorder: mentalization-based treatment.* Oxford, England: Oxford University Press.

Bateman, A. and Fonagy, P. (2001). Treatment of borderline personality disorder with psychoanalytically oriented partial hospitalization: an 18-month follow-up. *American Journal of Psychiatry*, 158, 36-42.

Bateman, A. W. and Fonagy, P. (2000). Effectiveness of psychotherapeutic treatment of personality disorder. *British Journal of Psychiatry*, 177, 138-143.

De Leo, D., Burgis, S., Bertolote, J. et al. (2004). Definitions of suicidal behaviour. In D. De Leo, U. Bille-Brahe, A. Kerkhof and A. Schmidtke (Eds.) *Suicidal behavior: theories and research findings,* pp. 17-39. Göttingen: Hogrefe and Huber Publishers.

Ekman, I. and Söderberg, S. (2009). Across the street - not down the road. Staying alive through deliberate self-harm. In L. Sher and A. Vilens (Eds.) *Internet and suicide*, pp 221-232. New York: Nova Science Publishers.

Fonagy, P. and Bateman, A. (2006). Progress in the treatment of borderline personality disorder. *British Journal of Psychiatry*, 188, 1-3.

Giddens, A. (1991). *Modernity and self-identity: self and society in the late modern age.* London, England: Polity Press.

Goodman, M., Weiss, D. S., Koenigsberg, H. et al. (2003). The role of childhood trauma in differences in affective instability in those with personality disorders. *CNS Spectrum*, 8, 763-770.

Gunderson, J. G. and Ridolfi, M. E. (2001). Borderline personality disorder: suicidality and self-mutilation. *Annals of the New York Academy of Science,* 932, 61-73.

Hamann J., Leucht, S. and Kissling, W. (2003). Shared decision making in psychiatry. *Acta Psychiatrica Scandinavica*, 107, 403-409.

Hawton, K., Rodham, K., Evans, E. et al.. (2002). Deliberate self harm in adolescents: self report survey in schools in England. *British Medical Journal,* 325, 1207-1211.

Hewitt-Taylor, J. (2004). Challenging the balance of power: patient empowerment. *Nursing Standard*, 18, 33-37.

Lieb, K., Zanarini, M. C., Schmahl, C. et al. (2004). Borderline personality disorder. *Lancet*, 364, 453-461.

Livesley, W. J. (2005). Progress in the treatment of borderline personality disorder. *Canadian Journal of Psychiatry*, 50, 433-434.

Mattia, J. L. and Zimmerman, M. (2001). Epidemiology. In W. J. Livesley (Ed.) *Handbook of personality disorders*, pp. 107-123. New York: Guilford.

Oldham, J. M. (2006). Borderline personality disorder and suicidality. *American Journal of Psychiatry*, 163, 20-26.

Paris, J. (2004). Is hospitalization useful for suicidal patients with borderline personality disorder? *Journal of Personality Disorders*, 18, 240-247.

Paris, J. (2003). *Personality disorders over time: precursors, course, and outcome.* Washington DC: American Psychiatric Publishing.

Paris, J. (2002). Chronic suicidality among patients with borderline personality disorder. *Psychiatric Services*, 53, 738-742.

Payne, M. (1997). *Modern social work theory.* 2nd Ed. London, England: Macmillan.

Platt, S., Bille-Brahe, U., Kerkhof, A. et al. (1992). Parasuicide in Europe: the WHO/EURO multicentre study on parasuicide. I. Introduction and preliminary analysis for 1989. *Acta Psychiatrica Scandinavica*, 85, 97-104.

Skodol, A. E. and Bender, D. S. (2003). Why are women diagnosed borderline more than men? *Psychiatric Quarterly*, 74, 349-360.

Skodol, A. E., Gunderson, J. G., Pfohl, B. et al. (2002). The borderline diagnosis I: psychopathology, comorbidity, and personality structure. *Biological Psychiatry*, 51, 936-950.

Stanley, B. and Brodsky, B. S. (2005). Dialectical behaviour therapy. In J. M. Oldham, A. E. Skodol and D. S. Bender (Eds.) *American psychiatric publishing textbook of personality disorders*, pp. 307-320. Washington, DC: American Psychiatric Publishing.

Söderberg, S., Kullgren, G. and Salander Renberg, E. (2004). Life events, motives and precipitating factors in parasuicide among borderline patients. *Archives of Suicide Research*, 8, 153-162.

Söderberg, S. (2004). To leave it all behind. Factors behind parasuicide - Roads towards stability. Umeå University Medical Dissertations. Umeå: Umeå University. http://urn.kb.se/resolve?urn=urn:nbn:se:umu:diva-362

Söderberg, S. (2001). Personality disorders in parasuicide. *Nordic Journal of Psychiatry,* 55, 163-167.

Taylor, C. (1991). The malaise of modernity. Ontario, Canada: House of Anansi Press.

Wilson, H. J. (2000). The myth of objectivity: is medicine moving towards a social constructivist medical paradigm? *Family Practice*, 17, 203-209.

Zanarini, M. C. (2000). Childhood experiences associated with the development of borderline personality disorder. P*sychiatric Clinics of North America,* 23, 89-101.

PART 2: THE NEUROBIOLOGY OF SUICIDE

In: Suicide from a Global Perspective: Psychiatric Approaches ISBN: 978-1-61942-267-4
Editors: A. Shrivastava, M. Kimbrell, and D. Lester © 2012 Nova Science Publishers, Inc.

Chapter 6

THE PREFRONTAL CORTEX AND SUICIDE

Marco Innamorati, Maurizio Pompili, Gianluca Serafini, and David Lester

INTRODUCTION

Suicide is a major worldwide public health problem. Nearly one million lives are lost from suicide each year, and between 3%-5% of adults make at least one suicide attempt at some point in their life (Kessler, Borges and Walters, 1999; Szadoczky, Vitrai, Rihmer and Furedi, 2000; Weissman, et al., 1999). Despite intensive efforts, research has failed to find necessary and sufficient factors that indicate an increased likelihood for suicide, and effective prevention strategies have remained elusive, suggesting that our understanding of the interplay of factors that increase the risk of suicide remains incomplete. Furthermore, although a great deal of research has been published on sociopsychological factors affecting suicidal behavior, the results lack sufficient specificity.

In recent years, studies have indicated that up to 43% of the variability in suicidal behavior can be explained by genetics (Brent and Mann, 2005; McGuffin, Marusic and Farmer, 2001). Thus, combining independent clinical and biological predictors may provide improved predictive models (Mann, et al., 2006). The aim of the present chapter is to review research on the neurobiological basis of suicide behavior.

THE NEUROBIOLOGY OF SUICIDE

A great deal of research analyzing the neurobiological basis of suicide has been published in the last few decades. A search of two of the major scientific databases for the neurocognitive sciences (MedLine and PsychInfo) identified more than 4,000 records containing the keywords suicide and neurobiology (or serotonin, prefrontal cortex or brain). Research has identified two main brain areas implicated in suicidal behavior, the prefrontal cortex and the dorsal and medial raphe nuclei in the mid-brain.

Prefrontal Cortex Dysfunction and Suicidal Behavior

Many studies have identified abnormalities of the serotonergic system in suicidal individuals, particularly in the ventral prefrontal cortex (Arango, Underwood, Gubbi and Mann, 1995; Mann and Arango, 2001; Stanley and Mann, 1983; Stanley, Virgilio and Gershon, 1982) , as well as several other possible abnormalities, such as reduction in messenger RNA and protein levels of cyclic adenosine monophosphate response element binding, CRE-DNA binding activity, and basal and cyclic adenosine monophosphate–stimulated protein kinase A activity (Dwivedi, et al., 2003), noradrenergic overactivity (Arango, Ernsberger, Sved and Mann, 1993), alterations in the levels of endocannabinoid and in the density of the CB1 receptors (Vinod and Hungund, 2006), lower grey-matter cholesterol content (Lalovic, et al., 2007), elevated cholecystokinin mRNA levels (Bachus, Hyde, Herman, Egan and Kleinman, 1997), expression of proteins involved in glial function, neurodegeneration and oxidative stress neuronal injury (Schlicht, et al., 2007), and higher β-adrenergic receptor binding (Mann, Stanley, McBride, and McEwen, 1986).

The prefrontal cortex has extensive connections to limbic structures and other cortical areas and, therefore, has an important role in many emotional and cognitive functions. The prefrontal cortex is the seat of executive functions and is also involved in behavioral and cognitive inhibition (Shallice and Burgess, 1996). Stuss and Benson (1986) suggested that the frontal lobe is involved in four basic functions: sequencing, drive, control and self-analysis.

Sequencing is the ability to maintain meaningful information units. Drive allows for the modulation and inhibition of cerebral activity. For example, Davidson, et al. (2000) argued that anger involves the activation of the orbital prefrontal and anterior cingulate cortical regions as part of an effort to suppress emotions, including an inhibitory projection to the amygdala. Lesions of the prefrontal cortex interfere with the inhibition of the conditioned response (Gewirtz, Falls and Davis, 1997; Morgan, Romanski and LeDoux, 1993). Control includes the planning, monitoring and anticipation of cognitive and noncognitive activities. Neuroimaging studies indicate that the prefrontal cortex becomes activated during imagined actions as part of the process of carrying out willful acts and provides insight into consequences of future actions (Frith, Friston, Liddle and Frackowiak, 1991; Ingvar, 1994). This self-analysis facilitates evaluating the meaningfulness of the cognitive process for the individual.

Wheeler, et al. (1997) proposed a functional division of the prefrontal cortex into two domains, the first related to cognitive functions, mostly dependent on the dorsolateral cortical areas, and the latter related to affective functions, dependent on medial and orbitofrontal cortical areas. Following brain injury to the orbitofrontal and ventromedial prefrontal cortex, patients display gross alterations in social and emotional behavior with largely preserved cognitive functions (Bechara, Tranel and Damasio, 2000; Damasio, 1994; Malloy, Bihrle, Duffy and Cimino, 1993; Rolls, 1999).

Van Heeringen and Marusic (2003) hypothesized that two major neural networks in the frontal regions of the brain are implicated in suicidal behavior (Deakin, 1996). (1) A social cognitive component is thought to be modulated by the frontal and temporal cortex in conjunction with the hippocampus, and mediated by serotonin $(5\text{-HT})_{1A}$ and noradrenalin neurotransmission systems. (2) Executive functions and problem-solving are modulated by the prefrontal cortex in conjunction with the amygdala and mediated by $(5\text{-HT})_{2A}$ and dopamine neurotansmission systems. Dysfunctions in the networks are associated with problems in attention, memory and fluency and a cognitive style found in suicidal individuals (sensitivity to particular life events accompanied by feelings of defeat, the sense of being trapped and the absence of hopes for rescue).

Early investigators hypothesized that cognitively rigid individuals were more prone to suicidal behavior (Duberstein, Conwell and Caine, 1994; Neuringer, 1964) as were those with poor interpersonal problem-solving skills (Pollock and Williams, 2004; Schotte and Clum, 1987). More recently, neuropsychological studies have identified several dysfunctions related to executive functions in suicidal individuals. In their review of the research, of suicidal individuals, LeGris and van Reekum (2006) found a lack of convergence between the results on completed suicides and attempted suicides. One problem in this research may lie in studying attempted suicides with varying lethality. Only those with high-lethality are similar biologically to individuals who complete suicide (Mann and Malone, 1997).

Keilp, et al. (2001) studied the neuropsychological performance of unmedicated subjects who had a major depressive episode with or without a suicidal history. Subjects with a history of high-lethality suicide attempts exhibited deficits in executive functioning that were independent of deficits associated with depression alone and independent of differences in prior education, occupational attainment, apparent intellectual capacity or the severity of the depression. These deficits were not consistent with global dysfunction but rather with selective dysfunctions of the prefrontal area. Patients who had made severe attempts were not impaired on a number of measures commonly used to evaluate superior prefrontal region activity, such as the number of categories or perseverative errors on the Wisconsin Card Sorting Test and Trail Making Test performance (Taylor, 1996). The deficits were in language fluency, verbally-mediated logical reasoning, and verbal learning, consistent with dysfunction in inferior prefrontal subregions (Paulesu, Frith and Frackowiak, 1993; Peterson, et al., 1999; Posner and Raichle, 1994).

Jollant, et al. (2005) evaluated decision making strategies in violent and nonviolent suicide attempters without a current DSM Axis I disorder by administering the computerized version of the Iowa Gambling Task (Bechara, Damasio, Damasio and Lee, 1999). The research identified impaired performance on the task in the suicide attempters when compared to healthy control subjects and when the violent suicide attempters were compared to the controls. However, no significant differences were found between the two groups of suicide attempters. Marzuk, et al. (2005) found that depressed patients with suicidal ideation performed significantly worse than non-suicidal depressed patients on several measures of executive functioning after controlling for age, IQ, severity of depression and prior suicide attempts.

Raust, et al. (2007) investigated prefrontal cortex functions in patients with suicidal behavior, separating dorsolateral and orbitofrontal cortex functions. Multivariate analysis indicated significant deficits in the executive functions of the patients with suicidal behavior, with impairment in visuospatial conceptualization, spatial working memory, inhibition, and visual attention (or reading fluency). Differentiation between dorsolateral functions and orbitofrontal functions showed no specific dysfunction of the orbitofrontal region in patients with suicidal behavior. However, the authors did not separate violent from non-violent attempters, nor take into account DSM pathologies.

CONCLUSION

Neuropsychological dysfunction may contribute to suicidal risk by impairing decision making during acute psychiatric crises or may reflect neurobiological abnormalities associated with suicidal risk. At least one study of cognitive performance in patients with a history of attempted suicide suggested that the deficits may diminish with treatment. However, even though patients with damage to the prefrontal cortex can sometimes perform appropriately in laboratory settings, they often fail to apply this knowledge in their daily social interactions (Bach, Happe, Fleminger and Powell, 2000; Damasio, 1994).

Although research has indicated causal relationships between dysfunction in cortical areas and suicidal behavior, identification of the specific pathways requires further study. In the absence of imaging data, it cannot be asserted that a given deficit is due to dysfunction in a particular area of the brain or to neural networks mediated by multiple areas (Keefe, 1995).

REFERENCES

Arango, V., Ernsberger, P., Sved, A. F., and Mann, J. J. (1993). Quantitative autoradiography of alpha 1- and alpha 2-adrenergic receptors in the cerebral cortex of controls and suicide victims. *Brain Research,* 630, 271-282.

Arango, V., Underwood, M. D., Gubbi, A. V., and Mann, J. J. (1995). Localized alterations in pre- and postsynaptic serotonin binding sites in the ventrolateral prefrontal cortex of suicide victims. *Brain Research,* 688, 121-133.

Bach, L. J., Happe, F., Fleminger, S., and Powell, J. (2000). Theory of mind: independence of executive function and the role of frontal cortex in acquired brain injury. *Cognitive Neuropsychiatry,* 5, 175–192.

Bachus, S. E., Hyde, T. M., Herman, M. M., Egan, M. F., and Kleinman, J. E. (1997). Abnormal cholecystokinin mRNA levels in entorhinal cortex of schizophrenics. *Journal of Psychiatric Research,* 31, 233-256.

Bechara, A., Damasio, H., Damasio, A. R., and Lee, G. P. (1999). Different contributions of the human amygdala and ventromedial prefrontal cortex to decision-making. *Journal of Neuroscience,* 19, 5473-5481.

Bechara, A., Tranel, D. and Damasio, H. (2000). Characterization of the decision-making deficit of patients with ventromedial prefrontal cortex lesions. *Brain,* 123, 2189-2202.

Brent, D. A. and Mann, J. J. (2005). Family genetic studies, suicide, and suicidal behavior. *American Journal of Medical Genetics C: Seminar in Medical Genetics,* 133(1), 13-24.

Damasio, A. (1994). *Descartes error: Emotion, reason and the human brain.* New York: G. P. Putnam.

Davidson, R. J., Putnam, K. M. and Larson, C. L. (2000). Dysfunction in the neural circuitry of emotion regulation: a possible prelude to violence. *Science,* 289, 591-594.

Deakin, J. F. W. (1996). 5-HT, antidepressant drugs and the psychosocial origins of depression. *Journal of Psychopharmacology,* 10, 31-38.

Duberstein, P. R., Conwell, Y. and Caine, E. D. (1994). Age differences in the personality characteristics of suicide completers: preliminary findings from a psychological autopsy study. *Psychiatry,* 57, 213-224.

Dwivedi, Y., Rao, J. S., Rizavi, H. S., Kotowski, J., Conley, R. R., Roberts, R. C. et al. (2003). Abnormal expression and functional characteristics of cyclic adenosine monophosphate response element binding protein in postmortem brain of suicide subjects. *Archives of General Psychiatry,* 60, 273-282.

Frith, C. D., Friston, K., Liddle, P. F., and Frackowiak, R. S. (1991). Willed action and the prefrontal cortex in man: a study with PET. *Proceedings in Biological Science,* 244, 241-246.

Gewirtz, J. C., Falls, W. A. and Davis, M. (1997). Normal conditioned inhibition and extinction of freezing and fear-potentiated startle following electrolytic lesions of medical prefrontal cortex in rats. *Behavioral Neuroscience,* 111, 712-726.

Ingvar, D. H. (1994). The will of the brain: cerebral correlates of wilful acts. *Journal of Theoretical Biology,* 171, 7-12.

Jollant, F., Bellivier, F., Leboyer, M., Astruc, B., Torres, S., Verdier, R. et al. (2005). Impaired decision making in suicide attempters. *American Journal of Psychiatry,* 162, 304-310.

Keefe, R. S. (1995). The contribution of neuropsychology to psychiatry. *American Journal of Psychiatry,* 152, 6-15.

Keilp, J. G., Sackeim, H. A., Brodsky, B. S., Oquendo, M. A., Malone, K. M., and Mann, J. J. (2001). Neuropsychological dysfunction in depressed suicide attempters. *American Journal of Psychiatry,* 158, 735-741.

Kessler, R. C., Borges, G. and Walters, E. E. (1999). Prevalence of and risk factors for lifetime suicide attempts in the National Comorbidity Survey. *Archives of General Psychiatry,* 56, 617-626.

Lalovic, A., Levy, E., Luheshi, G., Canetti, L., Grenier, E., Sequeira, A. et al. (2007). Cholesterol content in brains of suicide completers. *International Journal of Neuropsychopharmacology,* 10(2), 159-166.

LeGris, J. and Van Reekum, R. (2006). The neuropsychological correlates of borderline personality disorder and suicidal behaviour. *Canadian Journal of Psychiatry,* 51, 131-142.

Malloy, P., Bihrle, A., Duffy, J., and Cimino, C. (1993). The orbitomedial frontal syndrome. *Archives of Clinical Neuropsychology,* 8, 185-201.

Mann, J. J. and Arango, V. (2001). Neurobiology of suicidal behavior. In D. Wasserman (Ed.), *Suicide: An unnecessary death,* pp. 29–34. London: Martin Dunitz.

Mann, J. J., Currier, D., Stanley, B., Oquendo, M. A., Amsel, L. V., and Ellis, S. P. (2006). Can biological tests assist prediction of suicide in mood disorders? *International Journal of Neuropsychopharmacology,* 9, 465-474.

Mann, J. J. and Malone, K. M. (1997). Cerebrospinal fluid amines and higher-lethality suicide attempts in depressed inpatients. *Biological Psychiatry,* 41, 162-171.

Mann, J. J., Stanley, M., McBride, P. A., and McEwen, B. S. (1986). Increased serotonin2 and beta-adrenergic receptor binding in the frontal cortices of suicide victims. *Archives of General Psychiatry,* 43, 954-959.

Marzuk, P. M., Hartwell, N., Leon, A. C., and Portera, L. (2005). Executive functioning in depressed patients with suicidal ideation. *Acta Psychiatrica Scandinavica,* 112, 294-301.

McGuffin, P., Marusic, A. and Farmer, A. (2001). What can psychiatric genetics offer suicidology? *Crisis,* 22, 61-65.

Morgan, M. A., Romanski, L. M. and LeDoux, J. E. (1993). Extinction of emotional learning: contribution of medial prefrontal cortex. *Neuroscience Letters,* 163, 109-113.

Neuringer, C. (1964). Rigid thinking in suicidal individuals. *Journal of Consulting Psychology,* 28, 54-58.

Paulesu, E., Frith, C. D. and Frackowiak, R. S. (1993). The neural correlates of the verbal component of working memory. *Nature,* 362, 342-345.

Peterson, B. S., Skudlarski, P., Gatenby, J. C., Zhang, H., Anderson, A. W., and Gore, J. C. (1999). An fMRI study of Stroop word-color interference: evidence for cingulate subregions subserving multiple distributed attentional systems. *Biological Psychiatry,* 45, 1237-1258.

Pollock, L. R. and Williams, J. M. (2004). Problem-solving in suicide attempters. *Psychological Medicine,* 34, 163-167.

Posner, M. I. and Raichle, M. E. (1994). *Images of mind.* New York: Freeman.

Raust, A., Slama, F., Mathieu, F., Roy, I., Chenu, A., Koncke, D. et al. (2007). Prefrontal cortex dysfunction in patients with suicidal behavior. *Psychological Medicine,* 37, 411-419.

Rolls, E. T. (1999). *The brain and emotion.* Oxford: Oxford University Press.

Schlicht, K., Buttner, A., Siedler, F., Scheffer, B., Zill, P., Eisenmenger, W. et al. (2007). Comparative proteomic analysis with postmortem prefrontal cortex tissues of suicide victims versus controls. *Journal of Psychiatric Research,* 41, 493-501.

Schotte, D. E. and Clum, G. A. (1987). Problem-solving skills in suicidal psychiatric patients. *Journal of Consulting and Clinical Psychology,* 55, 49-54.

Shallice, T. and Burgess, P. (1996). The domain of supervisory processes and temporal organization of behaviour. *Philoophicals Transactions of the Royal Societyof London B: Biological Science,* 351, 1405-1411.

Stanley, M. and Mann, J. J. (1983). Increased serotonin-2 binding sites in frontal cortex of suicide victims. *Lancet,* 1, 214-216.

Stanley, M., Virgilio, J. and Gershon, S. (1982). Tritiated imipramine binding sites are decreased in the frontal cortex of suicides. *Science,* 216, 1337-1339.

Stuss, D. T. and Benson, F. D. (1986). *The frontal lobes.* New York: Raven Press.

Szadoczky, E., Vitrai, J., Rihmer, Z., and Furedi, J. (2000). Suicide attempts in the Hungarian adult population: their relation with DIS/DSM-III-R affective and anxiety disorders. *European Psychiatry,* 15, 343-347.

Taylor, S. F. (1996). Cerebral blood flow activation and functional lesions in schizophrenia. *Schizophrenia Research,* 19, 129-140.

Van Heeringen, C. and Marusic, A. (2003). Understanding the suicidal brain. *British Journal of Psychiatry,* 183, 282-284.

Vinod, K. Y. and Hungund, B. L. (2006). Role of the endocannabinoid system in depression and suicide. *Trends in Pharmacological Science,* 27, 539-545.

Weissman, M. M., Bland, R. C., Canino, G. J., Greenwald, S., Hwu, H. G., Joyce, P. R. et al. (1999). Prevalence of suicide ideation and suicide attempts in nine countries. *Psychological Medicine,* 29, 9-17.

Wheeler, M. A., Stuss, D. T. and Tulving, E. (1997). Toward a theory of episodic memory: the frontal lobes and autonoetic consciousness. *Psychological Bulletin,* 121, 331-354.

In: Suicide from a Global Perspective: Psychiatric Approaches ISBN: 978-1-61942-267-4
Editors: A. Shrivastava, M. Kimbrell, and D. Lester © 2012 Nova Science Publishers, Inc.

Chapter 7

Serotonin and Suicide

J. K. Trivedi, Rajul Tandon, Sachin Sharma, and Mohan Dhyani

Introduction

Serotonin (5-hydoxytryptamine or 5-HT) was first recognized as a powerful vasoconstrictor in blood serum. The greatest concentration of 5-HT (90%) is found in the enterochromaffin cells of the gastrointestinal tract. Most of the remainder of the body's 5-HT is found in platelets and the CNS. The neurons of the Raphe nuclei are the principal source of 5-HT release in the brain.

The studies on the firing rate of serotonergic soma in Raphe nuclei indicate that serotonin has a general effect on behavior by modulating the tone of nervous system activity. The functions of serotonin are numerous and appear to involve control of appetite, sleep, memory and learning, temperature regulation, mood, behavior (including sexual and hallucinogenic behavior), cardiovascular function, muscle contraction and endocrine regulation. Understanding of the functions and disorders related to serotonin is still progressing. Seven types of serotonin receptors are now recognized: 5-HT_1 through 5-HT_7, with numerous subtypes. The physiological functions of these receptors are a subject of intense research in conjunction with subtype-specific drugs targeting these receptors.

Biological Factors in Suicide

Suicide is the leading course of fatality in psychiatric disorders. There has been research on the biological basis of suicidal behavior for the last two decades. The search for biological markers and etiology of suicidal behavior was spurred partly by the inability of psychologically-oriented studies to adequately explain and predict suicidal behavior.

The idea that suicide and suicidal behavior might involve specific biological processes arose from early attempts to investigate the functioning of serotonin in patients with depression. Before the era of genetic polymorphisms, gene expression studies in the brain or neuroimaging, biochemical measures in the blood and the cerebrospinal fluid (CSF) were the only available approaches. In a classic series of papers, Asberg and colleagues (reviewed in Asberg, 1997) showed that the CSF concentration of 5-hydroxyindoleacetic acid (5-HIAA) was reduced in patients with depression. They observed that a high proportion of individuals with low CSF 5-HIAA subsequently went on to attempt or complete suicide. Later studies reported that measures of low 5-HT function were associated with suicidal behavior, not only in depression, but also in schizophrenia and other psychiatric disorders (Arango, et al., 1997). These studies have given rise to the idea that suicide has a biological basis that is independent of depression. Variation in this dimension would explain the variation in the risk of suicide in depression as well as in schizophrenia and other psychiatric illnesses (Deakin, et al., 2003).

Biological changes associated with suicidal behavior could include neuroendocrinal changes and structural changes. Various neuroendocrine pathways involved in behavior modification are studied indirectly through pharmacochallenge because direct access to neurotransmitters and its receptors in the CNS is difficult to achieve. Pharmacochallenge studies in suicide (see Mann, et al., 1989) are divided into two types: transmitter-nonspecific and transmitter-specific.

Transmitter-Nonspecific Neuroendocrine Studies

Hypothalamus-Pituitary-Adrenal Axis (HPA-Axis)

Early studies (Bunney and Fawcett, 1965; Krerger, 1974) conclusively linked suicidality with HPA-axis hyperactivity, showing increased plasma concentration of cortisol and urinary 17-hydroxycorticosteroids. However, later studies (Kocsis, et al., 1986), using the abovementioned markers, failed to replicate the findings. Preliminary studies using central corticotropin releasing factor binding (Nemeroff, et al., 1988) and preopiomelanacortin mRNA (Lopez, et al., 1990) as markers of HPA-axis activity have shown more definitive results regarding the correlation between HPA-axis hyperactivity and suicide.

Hypothalamus-Pituitary-Thyroid Axis (HPT-Axis)

Studies seeking a correlation with suicidality have yielded inconclusive results. One group, Baki, et al. (1983), studying a population with various diagnoses, has even reported enhanced TSH response in patients with suicidal behavior.

Transmitter-Specific Neuroedocrine Studies

Catecholamines

Studies of pharmacochallenge involving the noradrenergic system in suicidal patients are both scarce and inconclusive, with contradictory findings.

Dopaminergic System

Low levels of homovanillic acid (HVA), a dopamine metabolite, in the CSF has been reported in many studies of suicidal patients (Baki, et al., 1984; Ibor-Lopez, et al., 1985). Some studies (Roy, et al., 1986) have shown the coexistence of low HVA and disordered HPA axis function.

THE SEROTONIN-SUICIDE LINK

The search for neurobiological markers of suicide has inevitably focused on studies of postmortem brains for the obvious reason that planned prospective studies would be impractical and unethical. Studies of the biology of recurrent self-harm, in contrast, have involved the full armamentarium of biological psychiatry. Nevertheless, almost the entire effort has been devoted to investigating a single neurotransmitter, 5-HT, for the following reasons.

(1) Most effective antidepressants drugs directly or indirectly enhance 5-HT function, and an enormous amount of effort has gone into investigating abnormal 5-HT function in patients with depression.

(2) Serotonin has been associated with disorders of impulse control, such as antisocial behavior, aggression, and drug and alcohol abuse (Dolan, et al., 2001). Indeed, impulsivity and inwardly-directed aggression have been thought by many to be the trait associated with suicidal behavior independently of whether the driver is a depressive illness, schizophrenia or a temporary life disturbance (Deakin, et al., 2003).

SEROTONIN NEUROTRANSMISSION

Serotonin synthesizing cells are located in the midline (raphe) nucleus of the brain stem. A few hundred thousand 5-HT-containing neurons innervate the entire forebrain, principally from two raphe nuclei (the dorsal and medial raphe nucleus). 5-HT neurotransmission can be divided into (a) presynaptic and (b) postsynaptic components.

Presynaptic Mechanisms

5-HT is synthesized in raphe neurons from tryptophan by tryptophan hydoxylase. Intravenous administration of large amounts of tryptophan can cause 5-HT-mediated effects, notably in increasing prolactin and growth hormone (GH) secretion. 5-HT is stored in synaptic vesicles and released by the arrival of action potentials at the nerve terminal. Its action in the synaptic cleft is terminated by 5-HT reuptake channels, known as 5-HT transporters. The primary mechanism of SSRIs is to occlude the 5-HT transporter. 5-HT is metabolized intracellularly by monoamine oxidase to the stable 5-HIAA.

Presynaptic 5-HT Measures

5-HIAA and Tryptophan

Many studies report decreased levels of 5HIAA in the CSF and the brain in, not only depressed patients, but also in those who harm themselves in association with personality disorders (Mann, et al., 2001). Low 5-HIAA implies decreased synthesis of the neuro-transmitter, and this depends on tryptophan availability and on the activity of tryptophan hydroxylase. Some studies report a lowered ratio of tryptophan to large neutral amino acids (which compete for transport into the brain) in depressed patients and in recent attempted suicides. Tryptophan hydoxylase has a functional genetic polymorphism in the population, and some studies reveal that the less active forms occur more commonly among people who attempt suicide recurrently and impulsively. An increased incidence of suicide attempts has been found to be associated with low CSF 5-HIAA. (Roy, 1986, Lopez, et al., 1985).

The 5-HT Transporter (5-HTT)

A number of studies report a reduction in antidepressant drug binding to the 5-HTT in postmortem studies. In the largest study, Mann, et al. (2000) concluded that depression was associated with a widespread reduction in 5-HTT binding in the frontal cortex, whereas suicide was associated with reductions in the ventrolateral parts, a frontal region concerned with the inhibition of behavior. Thus, low 5-HT innervation of the ventrolateral prefrontal cortex may contribute to impulsivity and, thereby, influence whether patients with depressive symptoms engage in suicidal acts. While 5-HTT binding in the cortex is not yet resolvable by positron emission tomography (PET), decreases in subcortical sites in depression have been described (D'haenen, 2001). Amongst the different allelic forms of the 5-HTT gene, the allele for the less active form is more common in depressed patients (Furlong, et al., 1998). Neumeister, et al. (2002) reported that healthy volunteers with no family history of depression developed depressed mood for a few hours after tryptophan depletion, and this methodology might be a way to explore the role of 5-HT and its polymorphisms in suicidal ideation and intent.

Post-Synaptic Mechanisms

5-HT Receptors

The effects of 5-HT are mediated by seven families of 5-HT receptors. 5-HT_{1A} and 5-HT_{2A} are the most prevalent subtypes in the human brain. In vivo PET imaging studies report a significant reduction in cortical 5-HT_{1A} receptor binding sites in depression (Sargent, et al., 2000). However, sample sizes are small because of the expense of the technique, and there is no reported link with suicidal behavior or thoughts. Reduced 5-HT_{1A} receptor binding in the brains from depressed suicides has been reported in two studies (reviewed in Deakin, et al., 2003). A number of studies have found increases in radioligand binding to the 5-HT_{2A} receptors in the postmortem brains of suicides (Kamali, et al., 2001). In contrast, reduced in vivo radioligand binding to the 5-HT_{2A} receptors using SPECT has been reported in patients with depression who were not suicidal (D'haenen, 2001).

An increase in postsynaptic 5-HT_{2A} receptors has been reported by most studies of suicides. Arango, et al. (1995) reported that higher 5-HT_{1A} and lower serotonin transporter binding are greatest in the orbital and lateral prefrontal cortex (PFC - the area involved in mediating inhibition). Abnormalities in this area of the brain, or reduced serotonergic input into this area of the PFC, may result in a failure to adequately inhibit suicidal feelings and thoughts.

Serotonin Receptor Binding Studies

Postmortem studies have reported that suicides have greater serotonin receptor 2A (5-HTR_{2A}) binding in the prefrontal cortex than normal subjects (Stanley, et al., 1983; Mann, et al., 1986; Arango, et al., 1995). Gustavo, et al. (1999) strengthened this finding, along with suggestion that the HTR2A variation significantly affects 5-HTR_{2A} binding.

Distal to the receptor, Pacheco, et al. (1996) reported that, in the prefrontal cortex of suicides, there were alterations in the functioning of second messenger signal transduction. The phosphoinositide signaling mechanism and G-protein levels are significantly reduced.

Recent development in brain imaging with selective labelled ligands has allowed assessment of certain brain 5-HTT receptor subtypes in vivo.

Common Markers of Serotonergic Neurotransmission

There are several markers of serotonergic activity (its precursor, the parent compound, its binding sites, the enzyme degrading it, and its metabolite) which are related to the brain itself or to the platelet as a model for brain serotonergic activity.

[1] In the brain
1. Serotonin.
2. 5-HIAA.
3. [3H] (i.e., titrated imipramine binding).
4. [3H] titrated spiroperidol binding.
5. MAO activity.

[2] In blood
1. Platelet MAO activity
2. Ratio of plasma tryptophan to other neutral amino acids (important determinants of tryptophan transport into CNS).
3. Platelet [3H] imipramine binding
4. Platelet serotonin intake
5. Free tryptophan (the rate limiting factor in the synthesis of serotonin).

[3H] Imipramine Binding

This is probably related to and the best marker for the presynaptic serotonin uptake sites. Contradictory results (higher, normal or lower binding) have been reported in suicides since the initial report of fewer binding sites by Stanley, et al. (1982). The receptor is thought to be located on 5-HT nerve terminals and is associated with the 5-HT transporter. Hence, imipramine binding sites are an index of the number and/or functional status of the 5-HT nerve terminals. Gross-Isseroff, et al. (1989) reported that [3H] impiramine binding was elevated in some brain regions, such as the pyramidal and molecular layers of the hippocampus, and decreased in others, such as the post-central gyrus and insula.

[3H] Spiroperidol Binding

This is a marker of post-synaptic serotonin-2 binding sites. Studies have reported increased binding, consistent with decreased serotonergic neurotransmission suggested by the CSF studies. The majority of the studies have found an increased number of 5-HT2 receptors in the prefrontal cortex of suicides which is consistent with decreased serotonergic activity (Mann, et al., 1989)

MAO Activity

Though initial studies found lower MAO activity in alcoholic suicides than in controls, later studies have found it to be similar to the controls.

Blood Platelet Activity

Buchsbaum, et al. (1976) reported an increased incidence of suicide attempts in subjects with very low platelet MAO activity and in their relatives. Buchsbaum, et al. (1977) also found a correlation between low MAO activity and suicidal behavior, but only in those who were also augmenters on evoked response tests. Gottfries, et al. (1980) found that MAO activity was lower in depressed individuals who made violent suicide attempts than in those making nonviolent or no attempts.

Plasma Tryptophan/Neutral Amino Acid Ratio

Branchay, et al. (1984) found this ratio to be lower in alcoholics, especially those with a history of suicidal and aggressive/impulsive behavior.

More about Serotonin-Related Markers

Platelet Function in Suicide Attempters

Platelets contain a 5-HT_{2A} receptor that is genetically, pharmacologically and mechanistically the same as the 5-HT_{2A} receptor in the central nervous system. McBride, et al. (1986) found a positive correlation between receptor density and the lethality of recent suicidal behavior. Pandey, et al. (1997) found that receptor density was increased in suicidal subjects independent of their psychiatric diagnosis, and that increased 5-HT_{2A} density was significantly higher in subjects with a recent suicide attempt compared with those with past suicide attempts.

Cholesterol Studies

Kaplan, et al. (1997) proposed a cholesterol-serotonin hypothesis - that low cholesterol results in reduced serotonergic function and, thereby, predisposes individuals to impulsive behaviors associated with the risk of accident or suicide.

Functional 5-HT Neurotransmission and Suicidal Behavior

Most neurochemical studies involve static measures of specific aspects of 5-HT function. It is very difficult to know what the functional consequences are. Drug challenge studies were developed to provide functional measures of 5-HT neurotransmission, net of the presynaptic and postsynaptic change.

The Neuroendocrine Axis, Serotonin and Suicide

Neuroendocrine assessments of central 5-HT functions are based on the fact that an increase in central 5-HT function leads to increased secretion of GH, ACTH and prolactin and secondary secretion of cortisol in response to increased ACTH. There are various probes used to study neuroendocrine axis related to 5-HT.

5-HT Precursors (I.E., 5-Hydroxytryptophan and L-Tryptophan)

Meltzer, et al. (1984) reported enhanced cortisol response in patients with suicidal behavior when given oral 5-HTP representing post-synaptic 5-HT_2 receptor upregulation due to decreased presynaptic 5-HT function. A study using L-TRP i.v. administration by Cowen (1990) was inconclusive due to the confounding factor of weight loss.

Indirect Agonist: Fenfluranine

Fenfluramine acts on the 5-HT transporter to cause 5-HT release. Coccaro, et al. (1994) showed a direct correlation between a history of attempted suicide and diminished prolactin response to fenfluramine in patients with various diagnoses (mood disorder and personality disorders). The correlation was stronger with suicidal behavior than with depression. 5-HT dysregulation in individuals with personality disorders was associated more with traits of aggression and impulsivity. There was no correlation between the timing of the suicide attempt, sampling or the response to fenfluramine. Considering all of the above, it was concluded that this biological characteristic is associated with the traits of irritability and impulsive aggression whether directed inwardly or outwardly. Strickland, et al. (2002) and Malone, et al. (1996) also showed a correlation between lowered prolactin response to fenfluramine and particularly lethal suicidal attempts.

Direct Agonist

Studies with meta-chlorophenylpiperazine (MCPP - a non selective post-synaptic 5-HT agonist) yielded negative findings since these failed to show any correlation between the MCPP challenge and hormonal responses in suicidal patients (Korn, et al., 1992; Brown, et al., 1992). A study using the selective 5-HT_{1A} receptor agonist flesinoxan demonstrated blunting of cortisol response in suicidal patients.

Uptake Inhibitors

Intravenous clomipramine (CMI) has been used successfully as a challenge agent. Anderson, et al. (1992) reported lower PRL responses in patients who had a history of suicide attempts as compared with nonsuicidal patients. Golden, et al. (1991) found no correlation between PRL or cortical responses to CMI and suicidality in a relatively large group of patients across a variety of nosological categories.

Depression, Aggression and Suicide Risk

Aggression and depression have a particularly strong relationship to both suicide and 5-HT. Depression is so commonly paired with suicide that it is difficult to dissociate it in research from suicide. In fact, most of the studies focus on the biology of depressives rather than that of suicides (Van Praag, et al., 1986). However, not all suicides are depressed or suffering from personality disorders, and suicide attempters often have high levels of aggression (Van Praag, et al., 1986). Suicide risk peaks when high levels of depression and aggression coincide. Brown and Goodwin (1986) suggested that aggression and depression stem from the same biological syndrome, and that aggression is simply a more primitive or evolutionary early response to low 5-HT. The aggression response could reflect the activity of the brain stem under low 5-HT, whereas depression is the result of low 5-HT in the frontal cerebral hemispheres.

Relationship with Violent Methods

Low levels of CSF 5-HIAA have been found in patients who have made a violent suicide attempt (Banki, et al., 1983; Traskman, et al., 1981). An increased number of violent attempts associated with the aggression-depression combination would certainly lead to higher suicide risk, since violent suicide attempts are more likely to be successful (Davison and Neale, 1994).

Biological Changes in the Brain Stem

Low levels of 5-HT in the prefrontal cortex of suicidal patients has been shown to be due to fewer 5-HT synthesizing neurons in the dorsal raphe nucleus of the brain stem which project in the prefrontal cortex (Arango and Under wood, 1997).

Genetic Polymorphism and Suicidal Risk

Nielson, et al. (1994) reported that tryptophan hydoxylase (TPH) is deficient in suicide attempters. The TPH gene shows polymorphism with two alleles, U and L. The genotype of UL and LL is associated with the risk of attempted suicide. The LL genotype is associated with impulsive-aggressive behavior. The L allele is associated with repetitive suicidal behavior (see the review by Tandon, et al., 2001). A recent study by Zill. et al. (2004) suggested associations between TPH_2 gene polymorphisms and completed suicide.

Treatment Implications

Antidepressants produce effects that are the opposite of the alteration found in the same monoaminergic receptors in suicides, namely the $5\text{-}HT_{2A}$ and the beta-adrenergic receptors (Stanley and Mann, 1984). It is, therefore, reasonable to hypothesize that the effect of antidepressants may account for the anti-suicidal action of those compounds. Since suicidal behavior is found in syndromes unrelated to depression, antidepressants may be effective for the suicidal component of such psychiatric syndromes.

It has been suggested that drugs like carbamazepine, lithium and propranolol, which are effective in some cases of aggression, have important interactions with serotonergic systems and should be evaluated in impulsive suicidal behavior.

Clinical Prediction of Suicidal Risk

Some studies have suggested that the combination of a clinical and a biological variable, or of two biological variables, may allow better prediction of increased suicide risk. Traskmann, et al. (1981) found that, within a year of leaving the hospital, 21% of the patients with the combination of a suicide attempt and a CSF 5-HIAA level below 90 nmoles/L had committed suicide. However, routine determinations of CSF monoamine metabolite levels are impracticable in most settings. Some studies advocate platelet measures of the serotonin system (Roy, et al., 1987). There is clearly a need for further studies of possible peripheral biological markers of suicidality.

Conclusion

By searching for biological markers for suicide, one can presumably identify subjects that are at risk for suicidal behavior. The studies so far have raised more questions than answers, and predicting suicidal behavior from biological markers is unfeasible as of now.

References

Andersson, A., Eriksson, A. and Marcusson, J. (1992). Unaltered number of brain serotonin uptake sites in suicide victims. *Journal of Psychopharmacology*, 6, 509-513.

Arango, V. and Underwood, M. D. (1997). Serotonin chemistry in the brain of suicide victims, In R. W. Maris, M. M. Silverman and S. S. Canetto (Eds.) *Review of suicidology*, pp. 237-250. New York: Guilford.

Arango, V., Underwood, M. D., Perper, J. L., and Mann, J. J. (1995). Localized alteration in pre and postsynaptic serotonin binding sites in the lateral prefrontal cortex of suicide victims. *Journal of Neurochemistry*, 41, 256-265

Asberg, M. (1997). Neurotransmitters and suicidal behavior: the evidence from cerebrospinal fluid studies. *Annals of the New York Academy of Sciences*, 836, 158-181.

Banki, C. M. and Arato, M. (1983). Amine metabolite and neuroendocrine response related to depression and suicide. *Journal of Affective Disorders*, 5, 223-232.

Banki, C. M., Arato, M., Papp, Z. et al. (1984). Biochemical markers in suicidal patients. *Journal of Affective Disorders*, 6, 341-350.

Branchey, L. and Branchey, M. (1984). Depression, suicide and aggression in alcoholics and relation to plasma amino acids. *Psychiatry Research*, 12, 219-226.

Brown, S. L., Botsis, A. J. and Van Praag, H. M. (1992). Suicide: CSF and neuroendocrine challenge studies. *International Review of Psychiatry*, 4, 141-148.

Brown, G., L., Goodwin, F. K. and Bunney, W. E. Jr. (1982). Human aggression and suicide: their relationship to neuropsychiatric diagnoses and serotonin metabolism. In B. T. Ho, J. C. Schoolar and E. Usdin (Eds.) *Serotonin in biological psychiatry*. New York: Raven.

Bunney, W. and Fawcett, J. (1965). Possibility of a biochemical test for suicide potential. *Archives of General Psychiatry*, 13, 232-239.

Buschbaum, M. S., Coursey, R. D. and Murphy, D. L. (1976). The biochemical high risk paradigm: behavioral and familial correlates of low platelet monoamine oxidase activity. *Science*, 194, 339-341.

Buschbaum, M. S., Haier, R. J. and Murphy, D. L. (1977). Suicide attempts, platelet monoamine oxidase and the average evoked response. *Acta Psychiatrica Scandinavica*, 56, 69-79.

Coccaro, E. F. and Kavoussi, R. J. (1994). Neuropsychopharmacologic challenge in biological psychiatry. *Clinical Chemistry,* 40, 319-327.

Coccaro, E. F., Siever, L. J., Klar, H. et al. (1989). Serotonergic studies in patients with affective and personality disorders: correlates with suicidal and impulsive aggressive behavior. *Archives of General Psychiatry*, 46, 587-599.

Cowen, P. J., McCance, S. L., Gelder, M. G., and Grahame-Smith, D. G. (1990). Effect of amitriptyline on endocrine responses to intravenous L-tryptophan. *Psychiatry Research*, 31, 201-208.

Deakin, B. and Del Ben, C. (2003). Biological aspects of suicide and suicidal behavior. *Psychiatry (UK)*, 2(7), 5-7.

D'Haenan, H. (2001). Imaging the serotonergic system in depression. *European Archives of Psychiatry and Clinical Neuroscience*, 251(supplement 2), 76-80.

Dolan, M., Anderson, I. M. and Deakin, J. F. W. (2001). Relationship between 5-HT function and impulsivity and aggression in male offenders with personality disorders. *British Journal of Psychiatry*, 178, 352-359.

Furlong, R. A., Hol, L., Walsh, C. et al. (1998). Analysis and meta-analysis of two serotonin transporter gene polymorphism in bipolar and unipolar affective disorders. *American Journal of Medical Genetics,* 81, 58-63.

Gottfries, C. G. Von Knorring, L. (1980). Platelet monoamine oxidase activity in mental disorders. *Progress in Neuropsychopharmacology*, 4, 185-92.

Gross-Isseroff, R., Israeli, M. and Biegon, A. (1988). Autoradiographic analysis of serotonergic markers in brains of suicide victims. Presented at the symposium, *Neurochemical Correlates of Affective disorders and their Treatment,* Copenhagen.

Gross-Isseroff, R., Israeli, M. and Biegon, A. (1989). Autoradiographic analysis of tritated imipramine binding in the human brain postmortem: effects of suicide. *Archives of General Psychiatry*, 46, 237-241.

Gustavo, T., Richard, B., Karen, D., Tonino, A., Alain, D. L., Monique, S., Chawky, N., and Vanier, C. (1999). Prediction of level of serotonin-2A receptor binding by serotonin receptor-2A genetic variation in postmortem brain sample from subjects who did or did not commit suicide. *American Journal of Psychiatry*, 156, 1456-1458.

Jacobs, B. L. and Fornal, C. A. (1993). 5-HT and motor control: a hypothesis *Trends in Neuroscience*, 16, 346-352.

Kamali, M., Oquendo, M. A. and Mann, J. J. (2001). Understanding the neurobiology of suicidal behavior. *Depression and Anxiety*, 14, 164-176.

Kaplan, J. R., Muldoon, M. F., Manuck, S. B., and Mann, J. J. (1997). Assessing the observed relationship between low cholesterol and violence related mortality. *Annals of the New York Academy of Sciences*, 836, 57-80.

Kocsis, J. H., Kennedy, S., Brown, R. P. et al. (1986). Suicide and adrenocortical function. *Psychopharmacology Bulletin*, 22, 650-655.

.Korn, M. L., Asnis, G., Brown, S. L. et al. (1992). Serotonin receptor sensitivity and suicide. *Biological Psychiatry*, 32, 209-210.

Krieger, G. (1974). The plasma level of cortisol as a predictor of suicide. *Diseases of the Nervous System*, 35, 237-240.

Lopez, J. F., Palkovitz, M., Arato, M. et al. (1990). Localization and quantification of pro-opiomelanocortin mRNA and glucocorticoid receptor mRNA in pituitary of suicide victims. *Neuroendocrinology*, 56, 491-501.

Lopez-Ibor, J. J., Saiz-Ruiz, J. and De Los Cobos, J. C. P. (1985). Biologic correlations of suicide and aggressivity in major depression (with melancholia): 5-hydroxyindoleacetic acid and cortisol in cerebrospinal fluid, dexamethasone suppression test and therapeutic response to 5-hydroxytroptophan, *Neuropsychobiology*, 14, 67-74.

Malone, K. M., Corbitt, E. M., Szanto, K. et al. (1996). Antidepressant pharmacotherapy and suicidal behavior during major depression. Paper presented at the National Clinical Drug Evaluation Unit, 34th Annual Meeting, Florida.

Malone, K. M., Haas, G. L., Sweeney, J. A., and Mann, J .J. (1997). Major depression and the risk of attempted suicide. *Journal of Affective Disorders*, 34, 173-185.

Mann, J. J. (1989). Neurobiological models. In J. J. Mann (Ed.) *Models of depressive disorders: Psychological, biological and genetic perspectives*. New York: Plenum.

Mann, J. J., Brent, D. A. and Arango, V. (2001). The neurobiology and genetics of suicide and attempted suicide: a focus on the serotonergic system. *Neuropsychopharmacology*, 24, 467-477.

Mann, J. J. and Cohen, L. S. (1986). Serotonin and serotonergic receptors in suicide. *Annals of the New York Academy of Sciences*, 487, 122-127.

Mann, J. J., Huang, Y. Y., Underwood, M. D. et al. (2000). A serotonin transporter gene promoter polymorphism and prefrontal cortical binding in major depression and suicide. *Archives of General Psychiatry*, 57, 729-738.

Mann, J. J. and Stanley, M. (1984). Postmortem monoamine oxidase enzyme kinetics in the frontal cortex of suicide victims and controls. *Acta Psychiatrica Scandinavica*, 69, 135-139.

Mann, J. J., Stanley, M., McBride, P. A., and McEwen, B. S. (1986). Increased serotonin-2 and beta-adrenergic receptor binding in the frontal cortices of suicide victim. *Archives of General Psychiatry,* 43, 954-959.

Meltzer, H. Y., Perline, R., Tricou, B. J. et al. (1984). Effect of 5-hydroxy-tryptophan on serum cortisol levels in major affective disorders: II. Relation to suicide, psychosis and depressive symptoms. *Archives of General Psychiatry*, 41, 379-387.

Nemeroff, C. B., Owens, M. J., Bissette, G. et al. (1988). Reduced corticotropin releasing factor binding sites in the frontal cortex of suicide victim. *Archives General Psychiatry*, 45, 577-579.

Neumeister, A. and Konstantinidis, A. J. et al. (2002). Association between 5-HTTLPR and behavioral responses to tryptophan depletion in healthy women with and without family history of depression. *Archives of General Psychiatry*, 59, 613-620.

Pacheco, M. A. and Stockmeier, C. A. (1996). Alterations in phosphoinositide signaling and G- protein levels in depressed suicide brain. *Brain Research*, 723, 37-45.

Pandey, G. N. (1997). Altered serotonin function in suicide: evidence from platelet and neuroendocrine studies. *Annals of the New York Academy of Sciences*, 836, 182-183.

Roy, A. (1986). Genetics of suicide. *Annals of the New York Academy of Sciences*, 487, 97-105.

Roy, A., Everett, D., Pickar, D., and Paul, S. (1987). Platelet titrated imipramine binding and serotonin uptake in depressed patients and controls. *Archives of General Psychiatry*, 44, 320-327.

Sargent, P. A., Kjaer, K. H., Bench, C. J. et al. (2000). Brain serotonin-1A receptor binding measured by PET with [11C]WAY-100635: effects of depression and antidepressant treatment. *Archives of General Psychiatry*, 57, 174-180.

Stanley, M. and Mann J. J. (1983). Increased serotonin-2 binding sites in frontal cortex of suicide victims. *Lancet*, 1, 214-216.

Stanley, M., McBride, P. A. et al. (1986). Increased serotonin2 and beta-adrenergic receptor binding in the frontal cortex of suicide victims. *Archives of General Psychiatry*, 43, 954-959.

Stanley, M., Virgilio, J. and Gershon, S. (1982). Titrated imipramine binding sites are decreased in the frontal cortex of suicides. *Science*, 216, 1337-1339.

Strickland, P. L., Deakin, J. F. W., Percival, C., Dixon, J., Gator, R. A., and Goldberg, D. P. (2002). Biosocial origins of depression in the community: interaction between social adversity, cortisol and serotonin neurotransmission. *British Journal of Psychiatry*, 180, 168-173.

Tandon, R., Trivedi, J. K. et al. (2001). Recent advances in the understanding of suicide. *Indian Journal of Behavoural Science*, 11(2), 43-51.

Traskman, L., Asberg, M., Bertilsson, L. et al. (1981). Monoamine metabolites in CSF and suicidal behavior. *Archives of General Psychiatry*, 38, 631-636.

Van Praag, H. M., Putchik, R. and Conte, H. (1986). The serotonin hypothesis of aggression: critical appraisal of the evidence. *Annals of the New York Academy of Sciences*, 487, 150-167.

In: Suicide from a Global Perspective: Psychiatric Approaches ISBN: 978-1-61942-267-4
Editors: A. Shrivastava, M. Kimbrell, and D. Lester © 2012 Nova Science Publishers, Inc.

Chapter 8

TOWARD IDENTIFYING A GENE FOR SUICIDE

Brigitta Bondy and Peter Zill

INTRODUCTION

It is well known that attempted and completed suicide run in families which means that relatives of suicidal individuals are a high-risk population. Although biological, psychological, sociological and economic factors contribute to the complex etiology of suicidal behavior, evidence for a genetic liability is convincing. Twin studies have shown that, overall, about 18% of monozygotic (MZ) twin pairs were concordant for death by suicide as compared to 0.7% of dizygotic (DZ) twin pairs (Roy, 2006). Furthermore, in adoption studies, the rate of suicide was elevated about six times in the biological relatives of suicides compared to the biological relatives of non-suicidal adopted persons, thereby underlining the genetic contribution to suicide. From these data, it is estimated that 43% of the variability in suicidal behavior may be explained by genetics, while the remaining 57% is explained by environmental factors (Brent and Mann, 2005), and so both genetic and nongenetic factors may be targets for preventive therapeutic tactics.

THE LINK BETWEEN MENTAL MORBIDITY AND SUICIDE

Several arguments suggest that suicidal behavior is a disorder in its own right, although psychiatric disorders are a major contributing factor in about 90% of attempted suicides. The majority of all suicides occur in relation to mood disorders, but other risk factors, such as life stress, schizophrenia, alcoholism and drug abuse, may be related to suicidality. Furthermore, there are some clinical features, including personality traits, hopelessness, life stress, a history of physical or sexual abuse during childhood, and a history of head injury or neurological disorders, that increase the probability of suicidal behavior (Mann, 2003). Personality traits, especially impulsive-aggression, neuroticism and anxiety, as well as anger-related traits, have been proposed as intermediary risk factors (Baud, 2005). Since personality traits themselves are partly under genetic control, they may contribute to the familial loading of suicidal behavior.

Although the presence of psychopathology is a strong predictor for suicide, only a minority of people with these diagnoses commit suicide. This implies that psychiatric disorder might be a necessary, but insufficient, risk factor for suicide, indicating that a vulnerability for suicidal behavior might be independent from the main psychiatric disorders (Baud, 2005). Thus, the genetically influenced susceptibility of suicidal behavior seems to be determined through at least two components: the inherited psychiatric disorders and the inherited impulsive-aggression and other personality traits (Brent and Mann, 2005).

THE CURRENT STATUS OF GENETIC STUDIES

Suicidal behavior is a complex phenomenon involving psychological and biological characteristics. Genetic association studies have been carried out for about two decades on the basis of neurobiological findings, which are now converging on several key areas. The most important is a dysfunction within the serotonergic system, which is involved in regulation of mood, anxiety, cognition, impulsivity and aggression and may, therefore, be correlated with suicidal risk, depression, susceptibility to aggressive behavior and high-lethality suicidal behavior (Popova, 2006). Research suggests that the hypothalamic-pituitary-adrenal axis and an excess activity of the noradrenergic system are both involved in the response to stressful life events and in the pathophysiology of depression and might, therefore, have impact on suicide risk (Mann, 2003). However, multiple systems play a role in regulating the risk of suicide and, given this, the identification of new candidate genes seems mandatory.

GENES OF THE SEROTONERGIC SYSTEM

The first serotonergic gene investigated was tryptophan hydroxylase (TPH), the rate-limiting enzyme in the biosynthesis of serotonin (5-HT). Today two different TPH isoforms are known, TPH1 and TPH2, the genes for these being located on chromosomes 11 and 12, respectively (Walther, et al., 2003). It is further known that TPH2 is expressed in brain but not in peripheral tissues in mice (Walther, et al., 2003) and men (Zill, et al., 2004), and TPH2 has been proposed as the brain specific enzyme.

The early association studies were carried out with intronic polymorphisms of the TPH1 gene, an A to C substitution at nucleotides 779 (A779C) and at 218 (A218C), which are in tight, but incomplete, linkage disequilibrium. After the first report by Nielsen, et al. (1994) of an association between the 779AA genotype and higher CSF 5-HIAA concentrations in violent alcoholic offenders, many studies followed, relating the variants to suicidal behavior in different psychiatric disorders. Despite some positive reports, the list of negative findings is long. A meta-analysis has combined the data of all investigated polymorphisms and finally confirmed an association between suicidal behavior and the A779C/A218C polymorphisms (Li and He, 2006). Furthermore, there is now no doubt concerning a relationship between aggression, irritability and anger-related traits and the TPH1 779A allele.

Concerning the brain specific TPH2 gene, there is recent supportive evidence for various polymorphisms and haplotypes contributing to the risk for suicidality and several suicide-related personality traits (Gutknecht, et al., 2007; Zhou, et al., 2005; Ke, et al., 2006; Lopez, et al., 2007; Zill, et al., 2004), although negative findings also exist, suggesting that the observed association might be based on an association with affective disorders (Harvey, et al., 2007). Although the functional consequences of the TPH2 polymorphisms are unknown, and although the data are still limited, the TPH2 gene deserves further evaluation as the candidate gene for suicidal behavior.

The majority of association studies were carried out with the serotonin transporter (5-HTT) gene, as 5-HTT terminates serotonin action via its uptake from the synaptic cleft. A common polymorphism in the 5'-regulatory region, with a 44 base pair deletion, resulting in either the S (short) or L (long) allele (5-HTTLPR) with altered transcriptional activity, has been related to anxiety-related personality traits and to several clinical features in depression (Serretti, et al., 2006). Research has been conducted to document the association of the 5-HTTLPR with suicidal behavior, but the results are not consistent. Recent meta-analyses could not verify an association between the alleles and suicidality *per se*, but clearly produced evidence for an association between the S allele (with lower transcriptional activity) and violent suicidal behavior, independent of clinical diagnosis, demographic or sociocultural parameters (Li and He, 2007; Bondy, et al., 2006).

Other serotonergic candidate genes are those coding for different types of 5-HT receptors. The most intensively investigated are the 5-HT2A (T102C and A-1438G variants) and the 5-HT1B receptor genes, but most of the studies do not find an association between any of these polymorphisms and suicide in Caucasian, Jewish or Brazilian populations (Bondy, et al., 2006). A recent systematic review and meta-analysis for attempted and completed suicide found no association with the 5-HT2A T102C variants.

Genes Involved in Transmitter Synthesis and Degradation

As not only 5-HT, but also noradrenaline (NA) and dopamine (DA), are important modulators of mood and behavior, neurotransmitter synthesizing and degrading enzymes might contribute to suicidality. Monoamine-oxydase-A (MAO-A) plays a key role in the metabolism of 5-HT and most studies have been carried out with a 30 bp repeated sequence upstream of coding sequences, being present in 3, 3.5, 4 or 5 copies. Alleles with 3.5 or 4 copies are transcribed more efficiently, and these high activity alleles are associated with more impulsive aggression in men who had attempted violent suicide (Courtet, et al., 2005). Although at present there seems to be no relation between the MAO-A gene and the vulnerability for suicidality, an excess of high activity MAO-A gene promoter alleles may influence the methods used in suicide attempts.

Some variants in tyrosine hydroxylase (TH), the rate-limiting enzyme in the synthesis of noradrenalin and dopamine, are associated with some personality traits common among suicidal individuals, such as adjustment disorder, anger and hostility, but overall there is not much interest in and success with this gene (Wasserman, et al., 2007).

Catechol-O-methyltransferase (COMT), the major catecholamine-degrading enzyme has a functional polymorphism at position 158 (Val/Met) which is responsible for substantial variability in COMT enzymatic activity. The Val allele is associated with high activity (H allele) and the Met allele with low activity (L allele). For several ethnic groups, it has been shown that the Met allele is associated with a higher propensity for violence and, despite some negative findings, a recent meta-analysis gave evidence of a weak association between the 158Met allele and suicidal behavior in men which could be related to increased lethality of the suicidal behavior (Kia-Keating, et al., 2007).

The Search for New Candidate Genes

Several recent studies have expanded the search to identify new mechanisms and candidate genes. Thus, under the assumption that anxiety and stress response are involved in suicidal behavior (Mann, 2003), several mechanisms modulating these effects are of interest. In particular, acute or chronic stressful life events may contribute to a person's constitutional predisposition and, thereby, to suicidality. As the hypothalamic-pituitary-adrenal axis plays a critical role in the reaction to stress, and alterations in this system may be linked to aggression and impulsivity, polymorphisms in regulating genes, such as the corticotrophin-releasing-hormone (CRH), are of interest (De, et al., 2007). Other approaches include the study of the effects of cannabinoids on anxiety-related responses, γ-aminobutyric acid (GABA) as a main inhibitory transmitter, and neuropeptide or growth factors. However these studies are only just beginning (Bondy, et al., 2006).

Gene-Environment Interaction in Suicide

Gene-environment interactions are highly relevant since suicidal behavior is complex, with contributing genetic and environmental factors. This approach assumes that environmental pathogens cause the disorder and that genes, or an interaction of different genes, influence the susceptibility to pathogens. These environmental causes are considered only as contributors because exposure to them does not always generate the disorder (Caspi and Moffitt, 2006). These studies are new, but some of the initial findings are intriguing. Thus, the L-allele of the 5-HTTLPR polymorphism has been shown to moderate the influence of stressful life events on the later development of depression and to reduce suicidality (Caspi, et al., 2003). This study has been replicated in an investigation of the recently identified triallelic 5-HTTLPR in substance-dependent patients with and without childhood trauma and suicidal behavior (Roy, et al., 2007). Although extensive studies have to follow in order to confirm these results, this is a promising step forward in identifying vulnerability genes.

CONCLUSION

As there is abundant evidence that serotonergic transmission plays a pivotal role in mood, impulsiveness and aggression, and that intent to die and lethality are correlated positively with abnormalities in the serotonergic system, it is no surprise that molecular genetic studies in suicide research focus on serotonergic genes. Despite tremendous effort and many investigations, only two genes, one coding for the tryptophan hydroxylase 1 (TPH1 A218C) and the other for the serotonin transporter (5-HTTLPR), have been reliably found to be involved in the vulnerability for suicidal behavior.

It may be suggested both of these variants lead to more pronounced serotonergic dysfunction, with higher levels of anger and more violent and repeated suicidal acts (Courtet, et al., 2005). In contrast to this, the data with the MAO-A gene, which has been consistently associated with impulsive aggressive personality traits, do not indicate a direct relationship with suicidal behavior, but it might orient the suicidal act towards violence in people with other suicide risk factors (Courtet, et al., 2005). The findings for the serotonin receptors have been predominantly negative, as have been the studies of catecholamine synthesizing, metabolizing enzymes and dopaminergic receptors.

Despite the well-established heritability of suicidal behavior, the results of the molecular studies are not convincing. Among the possible reasons are the several pitfalls of association studies, such as the small sample sizes in many studies, as well as the different phenotypes ranging from suicidal ideation, with low intent to die, up through violent suicidal behavior. Moreover, suicidal behavior is a complex disorder and, therefore, the predisposition consists of numerous genetic factors. In the majority of the studies, only one single polymorphism in one gene is investigated, and so gene-gene interactions cannot be unravelled. Furthermore, the field of gene-environment interaction, which is rather important in the development of vulnerability (Balazic and Marusic, 2005), has been neglected until recently.

Despite these criticisms, there is no doubt that variants in genes remain an important risk factor in the phenomenon of suicide, in particular when an individual is confronted with stress, such as negative life events, and somatic disorders. Further studies are needed to identify more robustly the susceptibility genes using well-characterized suicide phenotypes. Some genetic factors may be related to aggressiveness and impulsivity, which have their effects independently of, or additively to, a mental disorder (Balazic and Marusic, 2005), and the link to impulsive-aggressive behavior should be clarified.

REFERENCES

Balazic, J. and Marusic, A. (2005). The completed suicide as interplay of genes and environment. *Forensic Science International*, 147(Supplement), S1-S3.

Baud, P. (2005). Personality traits as intermediary phenotypes in suicidal behavior: genetic issues. *American Journal of Medical Genetics C: Seminar in Medical Genetics*, 133(1), 34-42.

Bondy, B., Buettner, A. and Zill, P. (2006). Genetics of suicide. *Molecular Psychiatry*, 11, 336-351.

Brent, D. A. and Mann, J. J. (2005). Family genetic studies, suicide, and suicidal behavior. *American Journal of Medical Genetics C: Seminar in Medical Genetics*, 133(1), 13-24.

Caspi, A. and Moffitt, T. E. (2006). Gene-environment interactions in psychiatry: joining forces with neuroscience. *Nature Reviews: Neuroscience*, 7, 583-590.

Caspi, A., Sugden, K., Moffitt, T. E., Taylor, A., Craig, I. W., Harrington, H. et al. (2003). Influence of life stress on depression: moderation by a polymorphism in the 5-HTT gene. *Science*, 301, 386-389.

Courtet, P., Jollant, F., Buresi, C., Castelnau, D., Mouthon, D., and Malafosse, A. (2005). The monoamine oxidase A gene may influence the means used in suicide attempts. *Psychiatric Genetics*, 15, 189-193.

Courtet, P., Jollant, F., Castelnau, D., Buresi, C., and Malafosse, A. (2005). Suicidal behavior: relationship between phenotype and serotonergic genotype. *American Journal of Medical Genetics C: Seminar in Medical Genetics*, 133(1), 25-33.

De Luca, V., Tharmalingam, S. and Kennedy, J. L. (2007). Association study between the corticotropin-releasing hormone receptor 2 gene and suicidality in bipolar disorder. *European Psychiatry*, 22, 282-287.

Gutknecht, L., Jacob, C., Strobel, A., Kriegebaum, C., Muller, J., Zeng, Y. et al. (2007). Tryptophan hydroxylase-2 gene variation influences personality traits and disorders related to emotional dysregulation. *International Journal of Neuropsychopharmacology*, 10, 309-320.

Harvey, M., Gagne, B., Labbe, M., and Barden, N. (2007). Polymorphisms in the neuronal isoform of tryptophan hydroxylase 2 are associated with bipolar disorder in French Canadian pedigrees. *Psychiatric Genetics*, 17, 17-22.

Ke, L., Qi, Z. Y., Ping, Y., and Ren, C. Y. (2006). Effect of SNP at position 40237 in exon 7 of the TPH2 gene on susceptibility to suicide. *Brain Research*, 1122, 24-26.

Kia-Keating, B. M., Glatt, S. J. and Tsuang, M. T. (2007). Meta-analyses suggest association between COMT, but not HTR1B, alleles, and suicidal behavior. *American Journal of Medical Genetics B: Neuropsychiatric Genetics*, 144, 1048-1053.

Li, D. and He, L. (2006). Further clarification of the contribution of the tryptophan hydroxylase (TPH) gene to suicidal behavior using systematic allelic and genotypic meta-analyses. *Human Genetics*, 119, 233-240.

Li, D. and He, L. (2007). Meta-analysis supports association between serotonin transporter (5-HTT) and suicidal behavior. *Molecular Psychiatry*, 12, 47-54.

Lopez, V. A., Detera-Wadleigh, S., Cardona, I., Kassem, L., and McMahon, F. J. (2007). Nested association between genetic variation in tryptophan hydroxylase II, bipolar affective disorder, and suicide attempts. *Biological Psychiatry*, 61, 181-186.

Mann, J. J. (2003). Neurobiology of suicidal behaviour. *Nature Reviews: Neuroscience*, 4, 819-828.

Nielsen, D. A., Goldman, D., Virkkunen, M., Tokola, R., Rawlings, R., and Linnoila, M. (1994). Suicidality and 5-hydroxyindoleacetic acid concentration associated with a tryptophan hydroxylase polymorphism. *Archives of General Psychiatry*, 51, 34-38.

Popova, N. K. (2006). From genes to aggressive behavior: the role of serotonergic system. *Bioessays*, 28, 495-503.

Roy, A., Hu, X. Z., Janal, M. N., and Goldman, D. (2007). Interaction between childhood trauma and serotonin transporter gene variation in suicide. *Neuropsychopharmacology*, 32, 2046-2052.

Roy, A. (2006). Family history of suicide and impulsivity. *Archives of Suicide Research*, 10, 347-352.

Serretti, A., Calati, R., Mandelli, L., and De Ronchi, D. (2006). Serotonin transporter gene variants and behavior: a comprehensive review. *Current Drug Targets*, 7, 1659-1669.

Walther, D. J., Peter, J. U., Bashammakh, S., Hortnagl, H., Voits, M., Fink, H., et al. (2003). Synthesis of serotonin by a second tryptophan hydroxylase isoform. *Science*, 299, 76.

Wasserman, D., Geijer, T., Sokolowski, M., Rozanov, V., and Wasserman, J. (2007). Nature and nurture in suicidal behavior, the role of genetics: some novel findings concerning personality traits and neural conduction. *Physiology and Behavior*, 92, 245-249.

Zhou, Z., Roy, A., Lipsky, R., Kuchipudi, K., Zhu, G., Taubman, J. et al. (2005). Haplotype-based linkage of tryptophan hydroxylase 2 to suicide attempt, major depression, and cerebrospinal fluid 5-hydroxyindoleacetic acid in 4 populations. *Archives of General Psychiatry,* 62, 1109-1118.

Zill, P., Buttner, A., Eisenmenger, W., Moller, H. J., Bondy, B., and Ackenheil, M. (2004). Single nucleotide polymorphism and haplotype analysis of a novel tryptophan hydroxylase isoform (TPH2) gene in suicide victims. *Biological Psychiatry*, 56, 581-586.

Zill, P., Buttner, A., Eisenmenger, W., Bondy, B., and Ackenheil, M. (2004). Regional mRNA expression of a second tryptophan hydroxylase isoform in postmortem tissue samples of two human brains. *European Neuropsychopharmacology*, 14, 282-284.

In: Suicide from a Global Perspective: Psychiatric Approaches ISBN: 978-1-61942-267-4
Editors: A. Shrivastava, M. Kimbrell, and D. Lester © 2012 Nova Science Publishers, Inc.

Chapter 9

THE NEUROBIOLOGY OF SUICIDAL BEHAVIOUR IN CHILDREN AND ADOLESCENTS

Tsvi Fischel, Amir Krivo, and Gil Zalsman

INTRODUCTION

Suicidal behavior in adolescents has been found to have biochemical, genetic and psychological correlates (Apter, et al., 1990; Brent, et al., 2003; Mann, 2003). Suicidal behavior refers to the occurrence of suicide attempts and ranges from fatal acts (completed suicide), high-lethality and failed suicide attempts (where serious intention and careful planning are evident, and survival is fortuitous), to low-lethality attempts.

Usually impulsive attempts that are triggered by interpersonal crises seem to be ambivalent and contain a strong element of appeal for help (Beck, 1973; Stengel, 1976). Intent and lethality are positively correlated and related to biological abnormalities that mostly involve the serotonergic system. The clinical and neurobiological study of attempted suicide can provide information about completed suicide because the two populations are clinically and demographically similar (Mann, 2003).

Among adolescents, the annual rate of suicide attempts that require medical attention is 2.6%, while suicide is much less prevalent. Among 15 to 19 year olds, the completed suicide rates in 1998 in the USA were 14.6 per 100,000 in boys and 2.9 in girls (Brent, 2002). There is a strong relationship between attempted suicide in adolescent psychiatric patients and eventual death from suicide (Garrison, et al., 1991). Predisposition to suicidal behavior might be genetically transmitted as a trait independent of Axis I or II diagnoses (Brent, et al., 1996). Suicide and suicidal behavior in adolescents are linked to a wide variety of psychiatric disorders, including affective disorder, alcohol and substance abuse, conduct disorder, and schizophrenia (Shaffer, 1988). Over 90% of adolescent and adult suicides appear to have at least one Axis I disorder (Brent, 1995).

Several neurobiological systems are linked to suicide and suicidal behavior, mainly the hypothalamic axes and the serotonergic system (5-HT). Data have been collected utilizing several methodologies including hormonal suppression tests, sleep studies, post-mortem studies and genetic factor analysis. Currently, it is believed that the most plausible biological system related to suicidality, impulsive violence and anxiety is the serotonergic system (Apter, et al., 1990, 1993b; Mann, 2003, Zalsman, 2006a).

The Involvement of the Neuroendocrine System

Hypothalamic-Pituitary-Adrenal (HPA) Axis

Administration of dexamethasone in healthy adults suppresses the release of cortisol (dexamethason suppression test – DST). Non-suppression or early escape from dexamethsone suppression is considered to be partly the result of corticosteroid receptor down-regulation at the level of the hippocampus, hypothalamus or pituitary and contributes to HPA-axis hyperactivity in depressed adults. Some evidence in adults indicates that DST non-suppression is a predictor of suicide, but not non-fatal suicidal behavior (Coryell, 2001). Dahl and colleagues (1992) found no difference between suicidal and non-suicidal depressed children on the DST. In another study (Pfeffer, 1991), it was found that, although there was no association between suicidal behavior and DST non-suppression in prepubertal children, the patients with persistent suicidal behavior had significantly higher pre-dexamethasone 4 PM cortisol levels. In a comparison of depressed adolescents and healthy controls, it was found that both had similar cortisol secretion patterns with the exception of sleep onset, when the cortisol secretion in the depressed group was higher. Most of this difference was attributable to suicidal or inpatient depressed adolescents (Dahl 1991). Interestingly, sexually abused girls had significantly lower basal, net and total, corticotropin-releasing-hormone stimulated ACTH responses in comparison to non-abused subjects, but higher rates of suicidal ideation, suicide attempts and dysthymia (De Vellis, 1994). Because the results from adult studies have shown that, in general, HPA function is altered more frequently in older patients, and that dexamthasone resistance becomes more common with age, age-related differences may explain some of the discrepancies found in studies of children and adolescents (Zalsman, 2006).

Growth Hormone (GH)

GH secretion, from the anterior pituitary, is stimulated by GH-releasing hormones (GHRH) and inhibited by somatostatin. Other stimulants of GH release are the alpha-2-adrenoreceptors, muscarinic cholinergic receptors and activation of dopamine receptors. In depressed children and adolescents, increased nocturnal secretion of GH has been reported (Kutcher, 1991; Puig-Antich, 1984). It may be that muscarinic hypersensitivity at sleep onset leads to excessive somatostatin inhibition and increased release of GH. Muscarinic hypersensitivity could be the consequence of a serotonin deficit since, under normal conditions, serotonin modulates the cholinergic surge that accompanies sleep onset (Zalsman, 2006).

Ryan, et al. (1988) suggested that lower GH secretion in the response to desmethylimipramine in depressed adolescents may be related to the presence of a suicide plan or attempt during the depressive episode. Dahl, et al. (1992b) found no difference between adolescents with major depression and controls on GH measures. However, the group with depression and with suicidal behavior (a definite plan or attempt) showed a blunting of sleep GH secretion compared with the non-suicidal group. In a follow up of the subjects, ten years after the original study, 38% of the control group adolescents developed some form of depressive disorder, whereas 62% remained depression free. Twenty-three percent from the depressive group made suicide attempts during the follow-up period. The original data from the sleep studies and GH examination were compared again, reclassifying subjects based on the updated data. During the follow-up period, suicide attempters secreted more GH during the first 4 hours of sleep and during the whole 24-hour period compared to the other three groups. The depressive nonsuicidal group had demonstrated an earlier, steeper GH release curve when compared with depression-free controls, whereas the depressed, suicide attempters did not differ from controls. The role of GH on adolescents' suicidality remains unclear and needs further investigation.

The Serotonergic System

There is accumulating evidence of serotonergic system disruption in suicidality in adults as well as in children and adolescents. There appears to be a high correlation between the medical damage resulting from a suicide attempt and the number of 5HT receptors in a given individual (Mann, et al., 1992). Tyano and colleagues (2006) compared the relationship of measured plasma serotonin and psychometric measures in depressed suicidal adolescents and controls. A significant negative correlation was found between plasma serotonin levels and the severity of suicidal behavior among the suicidal inpatients. However, there was no difference in serotonin levels between psychiatric patients with different psychiatric disorders. The biology of adolescent suicide attempters is under-studied and seems to be somewhat different in terms of their response to serotonin-related medication (Brent and Birmaher, 2002). Higher levels of B_{max} were found in the 5HT2A receptors in suicidal patients, independent of diagnosis (Pandey, et al., 1995). Postmortem studies have demonstrated higher 5HT2A receptor binding in the postmortem brains of adolescent suicides (Pandey, et al., 2002), replicating the abnormalities observed in adults.

In adults, low cerebrospinal fluid (CSF) levels of 5-hydroxyindolacetic acid (5-HIAA) have been found to be related to suicidal behavior, especially more lethal suicide attempts, regardless of psychiatric diagnosis (Mann, et al., 1992). Moreover, low CSF 5-HIAA has been shown to be predictive of violent suicide attempts and completed suicide, suggesting that those measures represent trait rather than state measures (Traskman and Asberg, 1986). A two-year follow-up of a group of children and adolescents with disruptive behavior disorders showed that the CSF 5-HIAA level predicted the severity of physical aggression during the follow-up but did not predict suicide attempts (Kruesi, 1992). It may be that these results were negative at the time of the study since this group remains at risk for suicidality later in life.

Neuroendocrine Challenge Studies

The prolactin response to fenfluramine is an important index of serotonergic function (Malone, et al., 1996; Sher, et al., 2003). Fenfluramine causes the release of serotonin and inhibits serotonin reuptake. In adults, a history of highly lethal suicide attempts is associated with a blunted prolactin response to fenfluramine (Malone, et al., 1996). Patients with a history of very lethal suicide attempts have a blunted prolactin response compared with individuals with major depression but no history of very lethal suicide attempts, and a blunted prolactin response to fenfluramine may be a biochemical trait for suicidality, as is low CSF 5-HIAA.

Kaufman (1998) gave groups of depressed abused children, depressed non-abused children, and non-depressed, non-abused children a $_{L}$-5-hydroxytriptophan challenge in order to examine the measure of prolactin release and found that children with a positive family history for suicide attempts from all three groups had a more robust prolactin release after the challenge in comparison to children without a family history of suicide attempts. These results suggested that suicidal behavior in youth is associated with a different pattern of serotonergic abnormality compared with adults, a pattern that may include greater 5-HT_{1A} or 5-HT_{2A} receptor responsiveness (with serotonin affecting prolactin release) (Zalsman. 2006).

Platelet Studies

Platelets have been used as a less invasive approach for modeling brain serotonin neurons, since they share many properties (both are derived from the embryonic neural crest and contain serotonin, 5-HT_{2A} receptors, MAO-B and serotonin transporters), an approach that is more suitable for the pediatric age-group. This method has questions regarding its validity since platelets are not part of the neural circuit that can be modulated by other neurotransmitter systems. One study (Ambrosini, 1992) examined platelet serotonin transporter binding (B_{max}) using 3H-imipramine in depressed children and found an inverse relationship between 3H-imipramine binding and the presence of suicidal behavior. In contrast, Pine, et al. (1995) compared 3H-imipramine binding in the platelets of adolescents with conduct disorder who had attempted suicide with those of nonsuicidal controls with conduct disorder and found no difference between the two groups. However, the suicidal group showed significant seasonal variations of 3G-imipramine binding with the lowest amount in late winter and early spring.

Serotonin uptake by platelets may represent a number of serotonin transporter binding sites on the membranes of platelets. Suicidality was not found as a factor affecting the lower V_{max} values of depressed adolescents (Modai, 1989). The serotonin amplified the aggregation in children with mood disorders, although lower tryptophan levels are found in the blood of children who had recently attempted suicide as compared to the levels found in the blood of normal controls (Pffefer, 1998). Various measures of serotonin receptor contents of precursors in platelets have not yielded a consistent picture (Zalsman, 2006). A significant positive correlation between platelet serotonin transporter density and anger scores, and a negative correlation between platelet count and trait anxiety, was observed in a suicidal versus a non-suicidal group of adolescent inpatients. The serotonin transporter promoter (5-

HTTLPR) polymorphism was not associated with transporter binding and suicidality (Zalsman, 2005).

Postmortem Studies

Pandey, et al. (2002) examined the right prefrontal cortex (Broadman's area 8/9) in 15 teenage suicide victims compared with 15 matched normal subjects. They found that 5-HT_{2A} receptor protein and mRNA levels were higher in the prefrontal cortex and hippocampus but not in the nucleus accumbens of the adolescent suicides. These higher levels were restricted to the pyramidal cells of layer V. In adults, most autopsy studies of suicides reveal various abnormalities in serotonin function in the brainstem and prefrontal cortex, where more 5-HT_{1A} and 5-HT_{2a} binding and lower serotonin transporter bindings are reported, mostly in the ventral prefrontal cortex (Arango, 1995). Serotonergic function may be a mechanism whereby genetic factors influence the suicide threshold. Its stability, as shown by genetic studies of CSF 5-HIAA over time, suggests that serotonergic function is a trait which may contribute to its potential use as a predictor of suicide and suicide attempts (Traskman-Bendz, 1992).

Sleep Studies

In addition to disturbances in the quality of sleep reported by adult suicidal patients, some studies have also shown sleep polysomnography abnormalities when compared to nonsuicidal patients, including increased REM time and REM activity (Sabo, 1991). In children and adolescents, the findings have not been consistent. Some studies have shown no differences between suicidal and nonsuicidal depressed adolescents (Rau, 1996), while others show higher sleep latency in suicidal adolescents (Khan, 1990) and possibly shorter REM latency compared with other depressed adolescents (Armitage, 2001) as well as significantly higher REM density among suicidal depressed adolescents (Goetz, 1991). Further studies are needed to clarify the relationship between sleep abnormalities and suicidal behavior.

Genetic Factors Linked to Suicidality

Suicidal behavior runs in families, probably as a factor independent of major depression. Adults who complete suicide or attempt suicide have a higher rate of familial suicidal acts (Roy, 1983). Rates for suicide (Roy, 1991) and suicide attempts (Roy, 1995) are higher in monozygotic versus dizygotic twins. Adoption studies (Schulsinger, 1979) have shown a higher reported rate of suicide in the biological parents of adoptees who complete suicide compared with the biological relatives of control adoptees, even after controlling for rates of psychosis and mood disorders. The heritability of suicide and suicide attempts is comparable to the heritability of other psychiatric disorders, such as bipolar disorder and schizophrenia (Statham, 1998). Several studies have shown a higher rate of suicidal behavior in families of children and adolescents who have attempted or completed suicide, compared with controls, independent of the diagnosis of depression (Shafii, 1985; Pfeffer, 1994).

These results could be caused by the genetic transmission of underlying psychiatric illnesses or non-genetic family influences, such as imitation or exposure to violence in the family. Brent, et al. (1996) conducted a family study of adolescent suicides and demographically similar controls. The rate of suicide attempts in first-degree relatives of the suicides was higher than the controls, even after adjusting for differences in the rates of Axis I and II diagnoses in the families, including depression, which suggested that suicidal behavior may be transmitted as an independent factor from Axis I and II disorders. Several studies have attempted to locate genetic markers for suicide, and interest has focused on genes for serotoninergic systems.

Candidate Genes

The promoter region of the serotonin transporter gene (5-HTTLPR) polymorphism is the center of investigation in relation to depression and suicidality. The short form of the allele (SL/SS) indicates a lower expression of the serotonin transporter, while the opposite is true for the long form (LL). It seems that the long form comes in two varieties: LA as the short form and LG as the long form (known as "tri-allelic-polymorphism" - see Zalsman [2006b]). No association was found between the different alleles and depression or suicidality in adolescents. A possible association with aggressive traits was reported (Zalsman, 2001a). In the pediatric age group, the candidate genes 5HT2A, COMT, TPH1 and DRD4III were also investigated for their association with depression and suicidality (Zalsman, 2001a, 2001b).

Gene-Environment Interaction

Stressful life events seem to have an etiologic influence on the vulnerability to depression and suicide. This vulnerability may be caused by genetic factors. The 5-HTTLPR polymorphism was found to moderate the influence of stressful life events on depression (Caspi, 2003). Young adults with one or two copies of the short allele exhibited more depressive symptoms and suicidality in response to stressful life events than individuals who are homozygous for the long allele. This finding was replicated in children, adolescents and young adults (Zalsman, 2006b).

Conclusion

It appears that suicidal behavior in children and adolescents correlates with several neurobiological evidences, independent of underlying psychiatric disorders. These include disturbances of the HPA-axis as well as GH secretion irregularities. However, the serotonergic system disturbances, as manifested by postmortem findings, serotonin receptor abnormalities on platelets and metabolite levels, as well as genetic studies, seem to be the clues for the mechanisms underlying suicidality that are most investigated and considered most critical.

In the future, it is hoped that utilizing a combination of neurobiological tools, such as genetic vulnerability, environmental factors and levels of 5-HIAA in the CSF, will help in recognizing populations at high risk for suicide.

REFERENCES

Ambrosini, P. J., Metz, C., Arora, R. C. et al. (1992). Platelet imipramine binding in depressed children and adolescents. *Journal of the American Academy of Child and Adolescent Psychiatry*, 32, 298-305.

Apter, A., Van Praag, H. M., Plutchik, R., Sevy, S., Korn, M., and Brown, S. L. (1990). Interrelationships among anxiety, aggression, impulsivity, and mood: a serotonergically linked cluster? *Psychiatry Research*, 32, 191-199.

Arango, V., Underwood, M. D., Gubbi, A. V. et al. (1995). Localized alterations in pre and postsynaptic serotonin binding sites in the ventrolateral prefrontal cortex of suicide victims. *Brain Research*, 688, 121-133.

Armitage, R., Emsile, G. J., Hoffmann, R. F. et al. (2001). Delta sleep EEG in depressed adolescent females and healthy controls. *Journal of Affective Disorders*, 63, 139-148.

Beck, A. T., Weissman, A., Lester, D., and Trexler, L. (1976). Classification of suicidal behaviors II: dimensions of suicidal intent. *Archives of General Psychiatry*, 33, 835-837.

Brent, D. A. (1995). Risk factors for adolescent suicide and suicidal behavior. *Suicide and Life-Threatening Behavior*, 19, 52-63.

Brent, D. A., Bridge, J., Johnson, B. A., and Connolly, J. (1996). Suicidal behavior runs in families: a controlled family study of adolescent suicide victims. *Archives of General Psychiatry*, 53, 1145–1152.

Brent, B. A. and Birmaher, B. (2002). Adolescent depression, *New England Journal of Medicine*, 347, 667-671.

Brent, D. A., Oquendo, M., Birmaher, B., Greenhill, L., Kolko, D., Stanley, B., Zelazny, J., Brodsky, B., Firinciogullari, S., Ellis, S. P., and Mann, J. J. (2003). Peripubertal suicide attempts in offspring of suicide attempters with siblings concordant for suicidal behavior. *American Journal of Psychiatry*, 160, 1486-1493.

Caspi, A., Sugden, K., Moffitt, T. E. et al. (2003). Influence of life stress on depression: moderation by a polymorphism in the 5-HTT gene. *Science*, 301, 386-389.

Coryell, W. and Schlesser, M. (2001). The dexamethasone suppression test and suicide prediction. *American Journal of Psychiatry*, 158, 748-753.

Dahl, R. E., Ryan, N. D., Puig-Antich, J. et al. (1991). 24-hour cortisol measures in adolescents with major depression: a controlled study. *Biological Psychiatry*, 30, 25-36.

Dahl, R. E., Kaufman, J., Ryan, N. D. et al. (1992). The dexamethasone suppression test in children and adolescents: a review and controlled study. *Biological Psychiatry*, 32, 109-126.

Dahl, R. E., Ryan, N. D., Williamson, D. E. et al. (1992b). Regulation of sleep and growth hormone in adolescent depression. *Journal of the American Academy of Child and Adolescent Psychiatry*, 31, 615-621.

De Bellis, M. D., Chrousos, G. P., Dorn, L. D. et al. (1994). Hypothalamic-pituitary-adrenal axis dysregulation in sexually abused girls. *Journal of Clinical Endocrinology and Metabolism*, 78, 249-255.

Garrison, C. Z., Jackson, K., Addy, C. L., McKeowan, R. E., Waller, J. (1991). Suicidal behaviors in young adolescents. *American Journal of Epidemiology*, 133, 1005-1014.

Goetz, R. R., Puig-Antich, J., Dahl, R. E. et al. (1991). EEG sleep of young adults with major depression: a controlled study. *Journal of Affective Disorders*, 22, 91-100.

Kahn, A. U. and Todd, S. (1990). Polysomnographic findings in adolescents with major depression. *Psychiatry Research*, 33, 313-320.

Kaufman, J., Birmaher, B., Perel, J. et al. (1998). Serotonergic functioning in depressed abused children: clinical and familial correlates. *Biological Psychiatry*, 44, 973-981.

Kruesi, M. J., Hibbs, E. D., Zahn, T. P. et al. (1992). A 2-year prospective follow-up study of children and adolescents with disruptive behavior disorders: prediction of cerebrospinal fluid 5-hydroxyindolacetic acid, homovanillic acid and autonomic measures. *Archives of General Psychiatry*, 49, 429-435.

Kutcher, S., Malkin, D., Silverberg, J. et al. (1991). Nocturnal cortisol, thyroid stimulating hormone and growth hormone secretory profiles in depressed adolescents. *Journal of the American Academy of Child and Adolescent Psychiatry*, 30, 407-414.

Mann, J. J., McBride, P. A., Brown, R. P., Linnoila, M., Leon, A. C., DeMeo, M., Mieczkowski, T., Myers, J., and Stanley, M. (1992). Relationship between central and peripheral serotonin indexes in depressed and suicidal patients. *Archives of General Psychiatry*, 49, 442-446.

Mann, J. J. (2003). Neurobiology of suicidal behaviour. *Nature Reviews: Neuroscience*, 4, 819-828.

Modai, I., Apter, A., Meltzer, M. et al. (1989). Serotonin uptake by platelets of suicidal and aggressive adolescent psychiatric inpatients. *Neuropsychobiology*, 21, 9-13.

Pandy, G. N., Dwivedi, Y., Rizavi, H. S. et al. (2002). Higher expression of serotonin 5-HT(2A) receptor in the postmortem brains of teenage suicide victims. *American Journal of Psychiatry*, 159, 419-429.

Pine, D. S., Trautman, P. D., Shaffer, D. et al. (1995). Seasonal rhythm of platelet [3H]imipramine binding in adolescents who attempted suicide. *American Journal of Psychiatry*, 152, 923-925.

Pfeffer, C. R., Strokes, P. and Shindledecker, R. (1991). Suicidal behavior and hypothalamic-pituitary-adrenocortical axis indices in child psychiatric inpatients. *Biological Psychiatry*, 29, 909-917.

Pfeffer, C. R., Normandin, L. and Kakuma, T. (1994). Suicidal children grow up: suicidal behavior and psychiatric disorders among relatives. *Journal of the American Academy of Child and Adolescent Psychiatry*, 33, 1087-1097.

Pfeffer, C. R., McBridge, A., Anderson, G. M. et al. (1998). Peripheral serotonin measures in prepubertal psychiatric inpatients and normal children: associations with suicidal behavior and its risk factors. *Biological Psychiatry*, 44, 568-577.

Puig-Antich, J., Goetz, R., Davies, M. et al. (1984). Growth hormone secretion in prepubertal children with major depression II: sleep-related plasma concentrations during a depressive episode. *Archives of General Psychiatry*, 41, 463-466.

Rao, U., Dahl, R. E., Ryan, N. D. et al. (1996). The relationship between longitudinal clinical course and sleep and cortisol changes in adolescent depression. *Biological Psychiatry*, 40, 474-484.

Roy, A. (1983). Family history of suicide. *Archives of General Psychiatry*, 40, 971-974

Roy, A., Segal, N. L., Centerwall, B. S., and Robinette, C. D. (1991). Suicide in twins. *Archives of General Psychiatry*, 48, 29-32.

Roy, A., Segal, N. L. and Sarchiapone, M. (1995). Attempted suicide among living co-twins of twin suicide victims. *American Journal of Psychiatry*, 152, 1075-1076.

Ryan, N. D., Puig-Antich, J., Rabinovich, H. et al. (1988). Growth hormone response to desmethylimipramine in depressed and suicidal adolescents. *Journal of Affective Disorders*, 15, 323-337.

Sabo, E., Renolds, C. F., Kupfer, D. J. et al. (1991). Sleep, depression and suicide. *Psychiatry Research*, 36, 265-277.

Shaffer, D. (1998). The epidemiology of teen suicide: an examination of risk factors. *Journal of Clinical Psychiatry*, 49, 36-41.

Shafii, M., Carrigan, S., Whittinghill, J. R. et al. (1985). Psychological autopsy of completed suicide in children and adolescents. *American Journal of Psychiatry*, 142, 1061-1064.

Schulsinger, F., Kety, S. S., Rosenthal, D., and Wender, P. H. (1979). A family study of suicide. In M. Schou and E. Strömgren (Eds.) *Origin, prevention and treatment of affective disorders*, pp. 277-287. New York: Academic.

Statham, D. J. et al. (1998). Suicidal behaviour: an epidemiological and genetic study. *Psychological Medicine*, 28, 839-855.

Stengel, E. (1973). *Suicide and attempted suicide*. Harmondsworth, UK: Penguin.

Traskman, L. and Asberg, M. (1986). Serotonergic function in personality disorder. In J. J. Mann and M. Stanley (Eds.) *Psychobiology of suicidal behavior,* pp. 168-174. New York: New York Academy of Sciences.

Traskman-Bendz, L., Alling, C., Oreland, L. et al. (1992). Prediction of suicidal behavior from biologic tests. *Journal of Clinical Psychopharmacology*, 61, 685-693.

Tyano, S., Zalsman, G., Ofek, H., Blum, I., Apter, A., Wolovik, L., Sher, L., Sommerfeld, E., Harell, D., Weizman, A. (2006). Plasma serotonin levels and suicidal behavior in adolescents. *European Neuropsychopharmacology*, 16, 49-57.

Zalsman, G., Frisch, A., Bromberg, M., Gelernter, J., Michaelovsky, E., Campino, A., Erlich, Z., Tyano, S., Apter, A., and Weizman, A. (2001a). Family-based association study of serotonin transporter promoter in suicidal adolescents: possible role in violence traits. *American Journal of Medical Genetics*, 105, 239-245.

Zalsman, G., Frisch, A., King, R. A., Pauls, D. L., Grice, D. E., Gelernter, J., Alsobrook, J., Michaelovsky, E., Apter, A., Tyano, S., Weizman, A., and Leckman, J. F. (2001b). Case-control and family based association studies of tryptophan hydroxylase A218C polymorphism and suicidality in adolescents. *American Journal of Medical Genetics*, 105, 451-457.

Zalsman, G, Anderson, G. M., Peskin, M., Frisch, A., King, R. A., Vekslerchik, M., Sommerfeld, E., Michaelovsky, E., Sher, L., Weizman, A., and Apter, A. (2005). Relationships between serotonin transporter promoter polymorphism, platelet serotonin transporter binding and clinical phenotype in suicidal and non-suicidal adolescent inpatients. *Journal Neural Transmission*, 112, 309-315.

Zalsman, G., Oquendo, M. A., Greenhill, L., Goldberg, P. H., Kamali, M., Martin, A., and Mann, J. J. (2006a). Neurobiology of depression in children and adolescents. *Child and Adolescent Psychiatric Clinics of North America*, 15, 843-868.

Zalsman, G., Huang, Y. Y., Oquendo, M. A., Burke, A. K., Hu, X. Z., Brent, D. A., Ellis, S. P., Goldman, D., and Mann, J. J. (2006b). Association of a triallelic serotonin transporter gene promoter region (5-HTTLPR) polymorphism with stressful life events and severity of depression. *American Journal of Psychiatry*, 163, 1588-1593.

In: Suicide from a Global Perspective: Psychiatric Approaches ISBN: 978-1-61942-267-4
Editors: A. Shrivastava, M. Kimbrell, and D. Lester © 2012 Nova Science Publishers, Inc.

Chapter 10

BIOLOGICAL MARKERS OF SUICIDAL BEHAVIOUR

Carl Ernst, Jelena Brezo, Tim Klempan, Aleksandra Lalovic, and Gustavo Turecki

INTRODUCTION

Pre-screening patients to determine who may be at risk for suicide is an important area of psychiatry. Currently, any preventive measures taken are based on risk factors such as presence of an Axis I disorder (e.g., a major depressive disorder) or an Axis II disorder (e.g., borderline personality disorder). Most of the literature investigating suicide has found that people with such disorders are more likely to commit suicide. In general, the presence of these traits can be a warning sign to the physician, yet many people are affected with these conditions and do not commit suicide.

Finding biological markers of suicidal behavior or, perhaps more appropriately, biological factors that are associated with a subgroup of patients who show suicidal behavior, could be an important preventive strategy to decrease the prevalence of suicide. While behavioral risk factors are based on self-rating questionnaires or interviews, screening for biological factors mediating suicide risk could be a more objective way of determining the extent to which someone may be at risk. Clearly, not all people at risk of suicide will have clear biological commonalities. Still, any effort that can be made to reduce the number of suicides warrants further investigation, particularly if used in conjunction with other risk moderators, such as the presence of a mood disorder.

This review hopes to serve as a brief overview of current research into biological markers of suicide. We will briefly discuss some well-studied potential biomarkers including those in the serotonergic system, those involved in the stress response, and cholesterol. Finally, we will examine some promising but less well studied molecules that may mediate suicide and related behaviors.

The Serotonergic System

The serotonergic system has received the most attention with regards to potential mediators of suicide risk. The activity of this system can be measured indirectly by measuring 5-HIAA (a product of serotonin catabolism) in the CSF. Alterations in the serotonergic system were first reported by Asberg and colleagues who associated low CSF 5-HIAA levels with depression and violent suicide attempts (Asberg, et al., 1976a, 1976b). Subsequently, a series of studies investigating peripheral and central markers of serotonergic activity were carried out. Platelets were extensively used in the past to investigate serotonergic function, with conflicting results (Elliott, 1984). Several serotonergic receptors have been investigated, but studies have focused primarily on the serotonin transporter, the serotonin 1A and the serotonin 2A receptors. A large number of postmortem brain studies have been carried out over the last few decades investigating serotonergic markers, but these studies have not always produced consistent results (Drevets, 2001). With the advance of brain imaging techniques, and the development of specific tracers for serotonergic receptors, more recent studies have investigated serotonergic function in the frontal cortex of suicide attempters with some promising findings (Arango, et al, 1997; Leyton, et al., 2006).

The search for genes whose variation may contribute to suicidal behaviors is now in its third decade. Spurred by evidence indicating that suicide risk may have a genetic component, association-based studies have investigated over thirty candidate genes. As has been the case with related psychiatric phenotypes, attention has centered on monoaminergic genes and, because of the biochemical data summarized above, most of the studies focused on genes regulating the availability of serotonin. The most studied are the serotonin transporter (SLC6A4) and tryptophan hydroxylase (TPH) genes.

In the case of SLC6A4, two variants have been investigated most often: the insertion/deletion promoter polymorphism (LPR) and the multiallelic intronic VNTR. In contrast to the weak association evidence for the VNTR variant, support for the role of LPR, in particular its low-activity S allele, is more substantial. The S allele and genotypes have been found to confer odds ratios between 1.7-4.8 and 2.3-6.5 respectively for a number of phenotypes, especially violent, impulsive and repeated suicide attempts (Bondy, et al., 2006). Two meta-analyses have confirmed its involvement in the predisposition to suicide attempts and violent suicides (Anguelova, et al., 2003; Lin and Tsai, 2004).

The two genes for TPH, TPH1 and TPH2, have been also extensively investigated. For the TPH1 gene, studies have focused primarily on non-coding, likely non-functional variants, located in intron 7, which are closely linked: A218C and A779C. The evidence implicating these polymorphisms is controversial. While an earlier meta-analysis found no association (Lalovic and Turecki, 2002), a more recent meta-analysis indicated that A218C confers a risk of 1.62 for suicidal behaviors (Bellivier, et al., 2004). TPH2, a more recent candidate, has so far been primarily studied in relation to completed suicides. One positive finding in a German sample (Zill, et al., 2004) suggests that polymorphisms between exons 5 and 7 may be associated with the development of suicidal behaviors, while a recent study in Canadian suicides indicates an association for the upstream region of this gene (de Lara, et al., 2007).

The exploration of candidate genes has also been extended to include serotonin receptors and catabolizing enzymes. HTR2A receptor's C102T variant, for example, has been found to be associated with both suicidal ideation and attempts, with CC genotypes increasing the risk

3.1 and 5.5 times respectively (Arias, et al., 2001; de Lara, et al., 2007). A meta-analysis, however, did not support the contribution of the HTR2A gene to suicidality (Anguelova, et al., 2003). The G allele of the C1019G polymorphism, which has been shown to be functional, is associated with the risk of suicide outcome and major depression (Lemonde, et al. 2003). No association was found with variants in the serotonin receptors HTR1D, HTR1E, HTR1F, HTR2C, HTR5A, HTR1A, or HTR6.

The HPA-Axis and Related Molecules

Interactions between the hypothalamic-pituitary-adrenocortical axis, noradrenergic system, and vulnerability to stress in relation to suicide has been proposed (Mann, 1998). It is possible to measure both the stress hormone cortisol (in blood or saliva) and the corticotrophin releasing hormone (in CSF), and there have been reports suggesting that these are down-regulated in patients with major depression (Roy, et al., 1987). One test that has been extensively used to investigate dysregulation of the stress response is the dexamethesone non-suppression test (Stokes, et al., 1984). There are interesting data suggesting that DST non-suppression may help predict suicidal behavior in patients with major depressive disorder (Coryell and Schlesser, 2001). However, it is possible that considering both stress hormone levels and indices of serotonergic function may provide a stronger prediction of the risk of a suicide attempt (Meltzer, et al., 1984).

Cholesterol and Lipid Metabolism

Low blood cholesterol level may be a biomarker of suicidal behavior. A multitude of studies have been conducted ranging from correlational studies that have found significantly lower levels of cholesterol in suicide attempters compared to controls, to experimental studies examining the behavioral effects of cholesterol-lowering through dietary modification or the use of medication. While most of the studies have focused on the relationship between peripheral levels of cholesterol and the risk of suicide and related behaviors, recent findings suggest that this association may also reflect brain cholesterol changes (Lalovic, et al., 2007). In a systematic review of the literature, Golomb (1998) examined cohort, case-control and cross-sectional studies that assessed serum cholesterol levels in relation to violent behavior and death (including attempted and completed suicide). The sum of the evidence reviewed pointed to a significant association between low or lowered serum cholesterol and suicide and violence. It remains unclear, though, what are the underlying molecular processes mediating this relationship.

Leptin is a substance in the blood that plays an important role in lipid metabolism and has been investigated as a possible biological marker of suicidal behavior. Leptin, classified as both a cytokine and a hormone, predominantly functions as a circulating satiety signal, and regulates energy balance by acting in the brain, but there is growing evidence to suggest that it may have other functions related to cognition and behavior (Durakoglugil, et al., 2005). Associations between low leptin levels and impulsivity, aggression and suicidal behavior, along with low serum cholesterol levels, have been demonstrated across different psychiatric diagnoses(Atmaca, et al., 2002; Westling, et al., 2004)

ADDITIONAL MARKERS THAT REQUIRE FURTHER STUDY

Catechol-0-methyl transferase (COMT) and monoamine oxidase A (MAOA) genes are two important enzymes involved in the catabolism of several neurotransmitter systems. MAOA's variable number tandem repeat (VNTR) and COMT's Val/Met polymorphisms show significant and in some cases gender-specific associations with violent behavior (Brunner, et al., 1993; Caspi, et al., 2002) and suicide attempts (Courtet, et al., 2005; Nolan, et al., 2000). Other systems, involving dopaminergic, noradrenergic, glutamatergic, GABAergic, and neurotrophic genes, have been studied to a lesser extent and with less encouraging results.

Monoamine oxidase B (MAOB) is an important protein in the brain, partially responsible for the homeostasis of serotonin in the synaptic cleft, and is also expressed in platelets. While no conclusive evidence exists for this potential marker, it may be a good candidate gene for future studies (Van Kempen, et al., 1992).

FUTURE DIRECTIONS: GENE EXPRESSION STUDIES

Microarray technology can measure the total gene expression in a biological sample and, as such, could be used to establish a gene expression signature for suicidal behavior. Implementation of microarray technology in psychiatric research remains in its infancy but shows promise in the discovery of, as yet unknown, aspects of depression and suicide neurobiology (Gwadry, et al., 2005; Konradi, 2005). To date only a small number of reports have emerged indicating a possible role of GABA/glutamate receptor misexpression (Choudary, et al., 2005), spermidine/spermine N^1-acetyltransferase (SSAT) (Lalovic, et al., 2007), and the neurogenesis-associated gene 14-3-3 epsilon (Yanagi, et al., 2005). The observation of notable oligodendroglial misexpression in the brains of individuals with major depression (Aston, et al., 2005) appears to be evident in the context of completed suicide (Klempan, et al., 2009). This suggests that fundamental processes related to a specific cell lineage are perturbed in the suicidal brain, similar to the accumulating evidence for myelination defects in schizophrenia.

Some studies have failed to demonstrate significant changes in gene expression associated with suicide following stringent correction for multiple testing (Sibille, et al., 2004), illustrating the potential variability in results imposed by different analytical approaches. Further factors, such as features of the clinical sample, medication use, method of death, sample quality, microarray platform and data normalization, are likely to act as additional confounding factors. The outlook on the biological underpinnings of suicidal behavior will evolve as this form of study becomes more commonplace, directing more focused investigations of particular pathways and genes.

CONCLUSION

To date, there is no conclusive marker that can predict suicidal behavior, although some promising leads exist. It is clear, though, that prediction of suicidal behavior is a complex and difficult task that will not be accomplished by considering one single marker or risk factor. To be effective, biological predictors will need to be considered in the context of several other clinical, psychological and social risk factors. Further studies into the investigation of biological markers of suicidal behavior will need to take this complexity into account.

REFERENCES

Anguelova, M., Benkelfat, C. and Turecki, G. (2003). A systematic review of association studies investigating genes coding for serotonin receptors and the serotonin transporter II: suicidal behavior. *Molecular Psychiatry*, 8, 646-653.

Arango, V., Underwood, M. D. and Mann, J. J. (1997). Postmortem findings in suicide victims: implications for in vivo imaging studies. *Annals of the New York Academy of Sciences*, 836, 269-287.

Arias, B., Gasto, C., Catalan, R. et al. (2001). The 5-HT(2A) receptor gene 102T/C polymorphism is associated with suicidal behavior in depressed patients. *American Journal of Medical Genetics*, 105, 801-804.

Asberg, M., Thoren, P., Traskman, L. et al. (1976a). "Serotonin depression": a biochemical subgroup within the affective disorders? *Science*, 191, 478-480.

Asberg, M., Traskman, L. and Thoren, P. (1976b). 5-HIAA in the cerebrospinal fluid: a biochemical suicide predictor? *Archives of General Psychiatry*, 33, 1193-1197.

Aston, C., Jiang, L. and Sokolov, B. P. (2005). Transcriptional profiling reveals evidence for signaling and oligodendroglial abnormalities in the temporal cortex from patients with major depressive disorder. *Molecular Psychiatry*, 10, 309-322.

Atmaca, M., Kuloglu, M., Tezcan, E. et al. (2002). Serum cholesterol and leptin levels in patients with borderline personality disorder. *Neuropsychobiology*, 45, 167-171.

Bellivier, F., Chaste, P. and Malafosse, A. (2004). Association between the TPH gene A218C polymorphism and suicidal behavior: a meta-analysis. *American Journal of Medical Genetics B: Neuropsychiatric Genetics*, 124, 87-91.

Bondy, B., Buettner, A. and Zill, P. (2006). Genetics of suicide. *Molecular Psychiatry*, 11, 336-351.

Brunner, H. G., Nelen, M., Breakefield, X. O. et al. (1993). Abnormal behavior associated with a point mutation in the structural gene for monoamine oxidase A. *Science*, 262, 578-580.

Caspi, A., McClay, J., Moffitt, T. E. et al. (2002). Role of genotype in the cycle of violence in maltreated children. *Science*, 297, 851-854.

Choudary, P. V., Molnar, M., Evans, S. J. et al. (2005). Altered cortical glutamatergic and GABAergic signal transmission with glial involvement in depression. *Proceedings of the National Academy of Sciences*, 102, 15653-15658.

Coryell, W. and Schlesser, M. (2001). The dexamethasone suppression test and suicide prediction. *American Journal of Psychiatry*, 158, 748-753.

Courtet, P., Jollant, F., Buresi, C. et al. (2005). The monoamine oxidase A gene may influence the means used in suicide attempts. *Psychiatric Genetics*, 15, 189-193.

De Lara, C. L., Brezo, J., Rouleau, G. et al. (2007). Effect of tryptophan hydroxylase-2 gene variants on suicide risk in major depression. *Biological Psychiatry*, 62, 72-80.

Drevets, W. C. (2001). Neuroimaging and neuropathological studies of depression: implications for the cognitive-emotional features of mood disorders. *Current Opinion in Neurobiology*, 11, 240-249.

Durakoglugil, M., Irving, A. J. and Harvey, J. (2005). Leptin induces a novel form of NMDA receptor-dependent long-term depression. *Journal of Neurochemistry*, 95, 396-405.

Elliott, J. M. (1984). Platelet receptor binding studies in affective disorders. *Journal of Affective Disorders*, 6, 219-239.

Golomb, B. A. (1998). Cholesterol and violence: is there a connection? *Annals of Internal Medicine*, 128, 478-487.

Gwadry, F. G., Sequeira, A., Hoke, G. et al. (2005). Molecular characterization of suicide by microarray analysis. *American Journal of Medical Genetetics C: Seminars in Medical Genetics*, 133, 48-56.

Klempan, T. A., Sequeira, A., Canetti, L. et al. (2009). Altered expression of genes involved in ATP biosynthesis and GABAergic neurotransmission in the ventral prefrontal cortex of suicides with and without major depression. *Molecular Psychiatry*, 14, 175-189.

Konradi, C. (2005). Gene expression microarray studies in polygenic psychiatric disorders: applications and data analysis. *Brain Research: Brain Research Reviews*, 50, 142-155.

Lalovic, A., Levy, E., Luheshi, G. et al. (2007). Cholesterol content in brains of suicide completers. *International Journal of Neuropsychopharmacology*, 10, 159-166.

Lalovic, A. and Turecki, G. (2002). Meta-analysis of the association between tryptophan hydroxylase and suicidal behavior. *American Journal of Medical Genetics*, 114, 533-540.

Lemonde, S., Turecki, G., Bakish, D. et al. (2003). Impaired repression at a 5-hydroxytryptamine 1A receptor gene polymorphism associated with major depression and suicide. *Journal of Neuroscience*, 23, 8788-8799.

Leyton, M., Paquette, V., Gravel, P. et al. (2006). Alpha-[11C]Methyl-L-tryptophan trapping in the orbital and ventral medial prefrontal cortex of suicide attempters. *European Neuropsychopharmacology*, 16, 220-223.

Lin, P. Y. and Tsai, G. (2004). Association between serotonin transporter gene promoter polymorphism and suicide: results of a meta-analysis. *Biological Psychiatry*, 55, 1023-1030.

Mann, J. J. (1998). The neurobiology of suicide. *Nature Medicine*, 4, 25-30.

Meltzer, H. Y., Perline, R., Tricou, B. J. et al. (1984). Effect of 5-hydroxytryptophan on serum cortisol levels in major affective disorders II: relation to suicide, psychosis, and depressive symptoms. *Archives of General Psychiatry*, 41, 379-387.

Nolan, K. A., Volavka, J., Czobor, P. et al. (2000). Suicidal behavior in patients with schizophrenia is related to COMT polymorphism. *Psychiatric Genetics*, 10, 117-124.

Roy, A., Pickar, D., Paul, S. et al. (1987). CSF corticotropin-releasing hormone in depressed patients and normal control subjects. *American Journal of Psychiatry*, 144, 641-645.

Sibille, E., Arango, V., Galfalvy, H. C. et al. (2004). Gene expression profiling of depression and suicide in human prefrontal cortex. *Neuropsychopharmacology*, 29, 351-361.

Stokes, P. E., Stoll, P. M., Koslow, S. H. et al. (1984). Pretreatment DST and hypothalamic-pituitary-adrenocortical function in depressed patients and comparison groups: a multicenter study. *Archives of General Psychiatry*, 41, 257-267.

Van Kempen, G. M., Notten, P. and Hengeveld, M. W. (1992). Repeated measures of platelet MAO activity and 5-HT in a group of suicidal women. *Biological Psychiatry*, 31, 529-530.

Westling, S., Ahren, B., Traskman-Bendz, L. et al. (2004). Low CSF leptin in female suicide attempters with major depression. *Journal of Affective Disorders*, 81, 41-48.

Yanagi, M., Shirakawa, O., Kitamura, N. et al. (2005). Association of 14-3-3 epsilon gene haplotype with completed suicide in Japanese. *Journal of Human Genetics*, 50, 210-216.

Zill, P., Buttner, A., Eisenmenger, W. et al. (2004). Single nucleotide polymorphism and haplotype analysis of a novel tryptophan hydroxylase isoform (TPH2) gene in suicide victims. *Biological Psychiatry*, 56, 581-586

In: Suicide from a Global Perspective: Psychiatric Approaches ISBN: 978-1-61942-267-4
Editors: A. Shrivastava, M. Kimbrell, and D. Lester © 2012 Nova Science Publishers, Inc.

Chapter 11

SUICIDE, PERSONALITY AND NEURODEVELOPMENT

Jayanti Chotai

INTRODUCTION

Suicidal behavior spans a spectrum of behavior that ranges from completed suicide, suicide attempts to, at the mildest end, suicidal ideation. In a recent European cross-sectional household survey, the lifetime prevalence of suicidal ideation was 7.8%, and that of suicide attempts was 1.8%. These prevalences were higher among women and varied considerably across countries and geographical areas. In persons with depression, anxiety disorder, or alcohol dependence, the lifetime prevalence was increased up to 30% for suicidal ideation and up to 10% for suicide attempts (Bernal, et al., 2006).

Up to 90% of those who commit suicide have a diagnosable psychiatric disorder at the time of death (Hawton, et al., 1998). The distribution among the different diagnoses varies in different studies and is also gender-specific. These diagnoses include depressive and related disorders (20%-30% in men, 40%-60% in women), alcohol dependence (30%-40% in men, 10%-18% in women), personality disorders, schizophrenia, as well as anxiety and adjustment disorders (Arsenault-Lapierre, et al., 2004). There are also gender differences and personality differences in healthcare seeking behavior and in the suicidal process. About half (33%-70%) of suicides have been reported to have had a history of contacts with psychiatric healthcare services (Chotai and Salander Renberg, 2002). Although there is generally an over-representation of men in completed suicides (2 to 3 times), the male/female ratios for the suicides is larger for those without previous psychiatric contacts.

The relationships between various aspects of suicide and suicidal behavior are further confounded by an interplay between the availability, acceptability and lethality of different suicide methods. These circumstances vary with time, and suicide methods are distributed differently in different sociodemographic strata (Chotai, et al., 2002).

Although most persons who commit suicide have a psychiatric disorder, the majority of individuals who have a psychiatric disorder do not commit suicide. For example, the lifetime risk of suicide mortality among patients with affective disorders is about 2%-8% (Bostwick and Pankratz, 2000) and among those with schizophrenia is about 5% (Palmer, et al., 2005). Psychiatric illness often leads to negative psychosocial complications, such as broken relationships, job loss or some other crisis. The severity of these complications and how the subject reacts to these complications depend, to a large extent, on characteristics of the subject, including personality traits, other than the psychiatric illness. Therefore, a vulnerability to suicidal behavior, independently of psychiatric morbidity, is believed to be present in those who commit suicide (Mann, et al., 1999; Chotai and Salander Renberg, 2002). These traits may have a familial component that may be transmitted independently of psychopathology, such as an impulsive-aggression personality trait (Kim, et al., 2005; Roy, 2006).

As a result of this, a stress-diathesis model (also known as a stress-vulnerability model or a trigger-threshold model) has received increasing attention in the literature (Mann, et al., 1999; Mann, 2003). The stressor can be an acute worsening of a psychiatric disorder, some substance abuse, adverse events, or a psychosocial crisis. The diathesis (or predisposition) is influenced by genetic factors, childhood experiences, personality traits and personality-related traits such as hopelessness, impulsivity and aggression (Mann, 2003). Research suggests also that the diathesis may be influenced by circumstances around the gestational and perinatal period of the subject. These circumstances may be modulating several neurodevelopmental aspects probably involving the development of the monoamine neurotransmitter systems, with long-term effects extending into adulthood.

PERSONALITY IN SUICIDAL BEHAVIOR

Several different instruments have been employed to study personality. Among the three most widely used instruments are the following. The *Eysenck Personality Questionnaire* (EPQ; Eysenck and Eysenck, 1964) measures three dimensions of personality: neuroticism, extraversion, and psychoticism. The *NEO Five Factor Inventory* (NEO-FFI; Costa and McCrae, 1992) measures five personality dimensions: neuroticism, extraversion, openness to experience, conscientiousness, and agreeableness. The *Temperament and Character Inventory* (TCI; Cloninger, et al., 1994) measures seven dimensions of personality. Four of these are called temperaments: novelty seeking, harm avoidance, reward dependence, and persistence. The remaining three are character dimensions: self-directedness, cooperativeness, and self-transcendence. Besides these, several other personality traits have been studied in research on suicide, including hopelessness, impulsiveness, aggression, impulsive-aggression, hostility, trait anger, and trait anxiety.

The development of personality from early childhood is probably influenced by complex interactions among many environmental and genetical factors, but empirical research shows that a majority of personality traits attain stability around age 30 years, and change very little after that (Terracciano, et al., 2006).

Suicidal behavior is associated with several personality traits, in particular with personality trait scores that deviate substanstially from the average in some direction (Brezo, et al., 2006), and these associations are, in certain cases, gender-specific. High scores on hopelessness, neuroticism, psychoticism, harm avoidance and impulsivity-aggression are correlated with suicidal ideation. High extraversion, on the other hand, is correlated negatively with suicidal ideation. Although similar personality correlates are found also among suicide attempters, the relationship between personality traits and different types of suicidal behavior may be complex. For example, among older depressed patients, Heisel, et al. (2006) found that elevated openness to experience increased the likelihood of reporting suicide ideation, although other research has shown that it may decrease the risk of death by suicide. Heisel, et al. concluded that the personality-mediated expression of suicide ideation may be adaptive in certain contexts. Personality traits may also be mediators in a broader context. One study found that some sociodemographic factors predicted an elevated lifetime risk of suicide attempts, but that these risks were mediated through the personality traits of harm avoidance and self-directedness (Grucza, et al., 2005).

NEUROBIOLOGY IN SUICIDAL BEHAVIOR

On the one hand, genetic factors have been found to modulate various personality traits (Reif and Lesch, 2003), with heritability estimates of between 40% and 60% . On the other hand, genetic factors have been found to contribute significantly to the complex phenomenon of suicidal behavior (Bondy, et al., 2006). This suggests that both personality and suicidal behavior likely share several common genetic factors, and this has led several researchers to suggest that personality is an intermediate endophenotype between genetical factors and suicidal behavior (Baud, 2005; Savitz, et al., 2006).

The effect of genetic factors on suicidal behavior is mediated, to a large extent, by the neurotransmitter systems, notably by the serotonin, noradrenaline and dopamine systems (Mann, 2003). Therefore, the search for genes underlying personality, or a vulnerability to suicidal behavior, has focused on genes that regulate neurotransmitter functions and the turnover of neurotransmitters in the brain. There are a large number of studies that have investigated the degradation products (metabolites) of these neurotransmitters in the cerebrospinal fluid of humans. The levels of these metabolites are considered to be indicators of the corresponding neurotransmitter turnover in the brain.

Converging research suggests that the serotonergic system is a major biochemical trait involved in the regulation of the threshold in suicide, impulsivity and aggression, so that lower serotonergic activity is correlated with higher risk for suicidal behavior (Mann, 2003; Bondy, et al., 2006). The roles of noradrenaline and dopamine in suicidal behavior are not yet well-understood.

Genes influence the neurodevelopment of the brain and, thereby, influence neuro-transmitter functions. However, neurodevelopment is also known to be influenced by the environment, and each period of neurodevelopment may be particularly sensitive to specific environmental factors. This is true not only regarding neurodevelopment during childhood, but also regarding the fetal period before birth and during the perinatal period around birth. Neonatal infections are known to influence the postnatal development of brain neurotransmitter systems, and studies have shown that perinatal maternal circumstances, such as poor nutrition, stress, smoking and drugs, affect subsequent neurodevelopment (Chotai, et al., 2006).

Season of Birth, Suicide and Neurodevelopment

Some of the maternal influences on the fetus vary in concert with the different seasons of the year (winter, spring, summer or autumn), particularly in high latitudes. Such seasonally varying circumstances include ambient temperature, infections, social rhythms, eating habits, physical activity and the availability of sunshine. Therefore, circumstances surrounding a developing fetus and circumstances just after birth are dependent on the season during which the gestation and the perinatal period take place. Season of birth (or month of birth) is a proxy for such seasonally varying circumstances. A person born in say, March, experiences the second trimester of the pregnancy around November-December, experiences the perinatal period around March, and conception takes place around June,. Depending on which period of neurodevelopment is considered to be particularly sensitive for the trait being investigated, specific months of birth will constitute a proxy for the specific type of season that was prevalent during this sensitive period.

It has been known for many years that schizophrenia is associated with the season of birth. Schizophrenics show a 5%-8% excess of births during winter-spring months and a deficit of births during autumn months (Davies, et al., 2003). Schizophrenia is considered to be a neurodevelopmental disorder, and the consequences of negative effects during the fetal life or during childhood may appear first during adulthood. Today, there is a large body of research demonstrating an association between the season of birth and various types of neurological and psychiatric morbidity in adulthood. This association is likely to be mediated, at least in part, through the neurotransmitter systems.

In recent years, season of birth has been found to be associated with adult neurotransmitter turnover and with some aspects of suicidal behavior. In a register study of all completed suicides during 1952-1993, it was found that, among men, the suicides who were born during the spring months (March-April) used hanging significantly more often, whereas those born during the autumn months (September-October) used poisoning or car exhaust significantly more often (Chotai, et al., 1999; Chotai and Adolfsson, 2002). In a sample of adult patients with mood, anxiety and adjustment disorders, it was found that the cerebrospinal fluid (CSF) level of the serotonin metabolite 5-HIAA was lowest for men born around March-April and highest for those born around September-October (Chotai and Åsberg, 1999; Chotai and Adolfsson, 2002). Therefore, the association between season of birth and suicide methods has been thought to be a result of a suicidality trait independent of major psychiatric disorders, probably modulated by the serotonergic system (Chotai and Adolfsson, 2002; Chotai and Salander Renberg, 2002). The season of birth variation of CSF levels of 5-HIAA has been demonstrated also in a recent study of newborn infants, but the minimum levels here were obtained for a birth month around January (Chotai, et al., 2006).

Other studies have shown a significant season of birth variation in some personality traits. In two studies, novelty seeking was lowest in adults born during the winter months around December (Chotai, et al., 2001; Chotai, et al., 2003) and, in another study, the trait of being a "morning type" was highest for those born during the winter months (Natale, et al., 2002). This may be mediated by a season of birth variation in the dopaminergic system as indicated by the level of the dopamine metabolite HVA found in the above CSF studies, in which the winter-borns had higher levels of HVA.

In conclusion, it is worth noting that, although statistical significant associations between season of birth and personality traits or suicidal behavior have been obtained, the magnitude of the season of birth effect is relatively small, and so season of birth cannot be used to predict suicide in individual cases. The attributable fraction (or etiological fraction) is around 5% for the season of birth effects (Chotai, et al., 2001). However, this is comparable to attributable fractions obtained for the effect of specific gene alleles on personality traits, which is frequently less than 5%. Suicidal behavior (and personality) is probably modulated by a large number of genetical and environmental components, each contributing a small effect on its own.

REFERENCES

Arsenault-Lapierre, G., Kim, C. and Turecki, G. (2004). Psychiatric diagnoses in 3275 suicides: a meta analysis. *BMC Psychiatry*, 4, 37.

Baud, P. (2005). Personality traits as intermediary phenotypes in suicidal behavior: genetic issues. *American Journal of Medical Genetics Part C (Seminars in Medical Genetics),* 133(1), 34-42.

Bernal, M., Haro, J. M., Bernert, S. et al. (2006). Risk factors for suicidality in Europe: results from the ESEMED study. *Journal of Affective Disorders*, doi:10.1016/j.jad.2006.09.018.

Bondy, B., Buettner, A. and Zill, P. (2006). Genetics of suicide. *Molecular Psychiatry*, 11, 336-351.

Bostwick, J. M. and Pankratz, S. S. (2000). Affective disorders and suicide risk: a reexamination. *American Journal of Psychiatry*, 157, 1925-1932.

Brezo, J., Paris, J. and Turecki, G. (2006). Personality traits as correlates of suicidal ideation, suicide attempts, and suicide completions: a systematic review. *Acta Psychiatrica Scandinavica,* 113, 180-206.

Chotai, J. and Adolfsson (2002). Converging evidence suggests that monoamine neurotransmitter turnover in human adults is associated with their season of birth. *European Archives of Psychiatry and Clinical Neuroscience,* 252, 130-134.

Chotai, J. and Åsberg, M. (1999). Variations in CSF monoamine metabolites according to the season of birth. *Neuropsychobiology*, 39, 57-62.

Chotai, J., Salander Renberg, E. and Jacobsson, L. (1999). Season of birth associated with the age and method of suicide. *Archives of Suicide Research*, 5, 245-254.

Chotai, J., Forsgren, T., Nilsson, L. G. et al. (2001). Season of birth variations in the temperament and character inventory of personality in a general population. *Neuropsychobiology*, 44, 19-26.

Chotai, J. and Salander Renberg, E. (2002). Season of birth variations in suicide methods in relation to any history of psychiatric contacts support and independent suicidality trait. *Journal of Affective Disorders*, 69, 69-81.

Chotai, J., Salander Renberg, E. and Jacobsson, L. (2002). Method of suicide in relation to some sociodemographic variables in northern Sweden. *Archives of Suicide Research*, 6, 111-122.

Chotai, J., Lundberg, M.. and Adolfsson, R. (2003). Variations in personality traits among adolescents and adults according to their season of birth in the general population: further evidence. *Personality and Individual Differences*, 35, 897-908.

Chotai, J., Murphy, D. L. and Constantino, J. N. (2006). Cerebrospinal fluid monoamine metabolite levels in human newborn infants born in winter differ from those born in summer. *Psychiatry Research*, 145, 189-197.

Cloninger, C. R., Pryzbeck, T. R., Svrakic, D. M. et al. (1994). *The Temperament and Character Inventory (TCI): A guide to its development and use*. St Louis: Washington University Center for Psychobiology of Personality.

Costa, P. T. and McCrae, R. R. (1992). *Revised NEO Personality Inventory (NEOPI-R) and NEO Five Factor Inventory (NEO-FFI*). Odessa, FL: Psychological Assessment Resources.

Davies, G., Welham, J., Chant, D. et al. (2003). A systematic review and meta-analysis of Northern Hemisphere season of birth studies in schizophrenia. *Schizophrenia Bulletin*, 29, 587-593.

Eysenck, H. J. and Eysenck, S. B. G. (1964). *Manual of the Eysenck Personality Inventory*. London, UK: London University Press.

Grucza, R. A., Przybeck, T. R. and Cloninger, C. R. (2005). Personality as a mediator of demographic risk factors for suicide attempts in a community sample. *Comprehensive Psychiatry,* 46, 214-222.

Hawton, K., Appleby, L., Platt,S. et al. (1998). The psychological autopsy approach to studying suicide: a review of methodological issues. *Journal of Affective Disorders*, 50, 269-276.

Heisel, M. J., Duberstein, P. R., Conner, K. R. et al. (2006). Personality and reports of suicide ideation among depressed adults 50 years of age or older. *Journal of Affective Disorders*, 90, 175-180.

Kim, C. D., Seguin, M., Therrien, N. et al. (2005). Familial aggregation of suicidal behavior: a family study of male suicide completers from the general population. *American Journal of Psychiatry,* 162, 1017-1019.

Mann, J. J. (2003). Neurobiology of suicidal behavior. *Nature Reviews: Neuroscience*, 4, 819-828.

Mann, J. J., Waternaux, C., Haas, G. L. et al. (1999). Toward a clinical model of suicidal behavior in psychiatric patients. *American Journal of Psychiatry*, 156, 181-189.

Natale, V., Adan, A. and Chotai, J. (2002). Further results on the association between morningness-eveningness preference and the season of birth in human adults. *Neuropsychobiology*, 46, 209-214.

Palmer, B. A., Pankratz, S. and Hostwick, J. M. (2005). The lifetime risk of suicide in schizophrenia: a reexamination. *Archives of General Psychiatry*, 62, 247-253.

Reif, A. and Lesch, K. P. (2003). Toward a molecular architecture of personality. *Behavioural Brain Research*, 139, 1-20.

Roy, A. (2006). Family history of suicide and impulsivity. *Archives of Suicide Research*, 10, 347-352.

Savitz, J. B., Cupido, C. L., Ramesar, R. S. (2006). Trends in suicidology: personality as an endophenotype for molecular genetic investigations. *PLoS Medicine* 3(5), e107.

Terracciano, A., Costa, P. T. and McCrae, R. R. (2006). Personality plasticity after age 30. *Personality and Social Psychology Bulletin*, 32, 999-1009.

PART 3: SUICIDE AND PSYCHIATRIC DISORDER

In: Suicide from a Global Perspective: Psychiatric Approaches ISBN: 978-1-61942-267-4
Editors: A. Shrivastava, M. Kimbrell, and D. Lester © 2012 Nova Science Publishers, Inc.

Chapter 12

Suicide and Mental Morbidity

Jess G. Fiedorowicz, Donald W. Black, and William H. Coryell

Introduction

Diagnosable psychiatric disorder appears to be one of the most robust risk factors for suicide. In fact, psychological autopsy studies suggest that more than 90% of completed suicides have a mental illness at the time of the act, with depressive disorders and alcohol-related disorders being the most frequent (Arsenault-Lapierre, et al., 2004). It has been suggested that many of the remaining cases are likely suffering from a mental disorder that the psychological autopsy failed to detect (Ernst, et al., 2004). In many cases, two or more psychiatric disorders are present, further elevating risk. Co-occurring alcohol and drug-related disorders are common (Henriksson, et al., 1993). Notably, only a minority of suicide completers receive adequate, if any, treatment, prior to death (Suominen, et al., 1998). Thus, mental illness serves as a natural target for understanding suicide and directing suicide prevention efforts. For practical purposes, the presence of a mental disorder should be considered necessary, but not sufficient for suicide to occur (Black and Winokur, 1990).

Review

Suicide refers to the deliberate act of killing oneself with the expectation or knowledge of its outcome. There is a growing tendency for research to widen the discussion to include suicidal ideation, acts of deliberate self-harm, and suicide attempts. Yet, while many of these components of suicidality are related to suicide completion, they remain surrogate endpoints. Risk factors for these surrogate outcomes, with gender as a notable example, are not directly correlated with completed suicides (Black and Winokur, 1990). For clarity and salience, this chapter will focus on completed suicide unless otherwise specified.

The psychological autopsy method is a validated means of integrating information from survivors, other informants, and medical records to assess the suicide's mental condition at or around the time of the act (Kelly and Mann, 1996).

Because this method relies on informants and medical records to generate diagnostic data, little information may be available in some cases, likely resulting in an underestimate of the mental morbidity associated with suicide (e.g., if social isolation due to depression is present).

This method, however, avoids the selection bias associated with the study of clinical populations and provides a reliable estimate of mental morbidity among the general population of suicide completers. Studies from clinical samples are biased toward more suicides in women and younger persons when compared with general population studies (Black, 1998).

Common diagnoses uncovered by psychological autopies include major depressive disorder, bipolar disorder, schizophrenia, anorexia nervosa, alcohol and drug-related disorders, and borderline personality disorder.

Psychiatric disorders have been identified as a risk factor for suicide in both industrialized and developing nations. Co-occurring diagnoses are common and appear to confer additional risk.

Perhaps the lowest rates of psychiatric disorder from psychological autopsy studies have been found in China. There, a large, geographically representative study ascertained psychiatric diagnoses in 63% of suicide completers (Phillips, et al., 2002). It is not clear whether this lower rate reflects cultural differences in reporting, surveillance bias, a greater influence of other risk factors, or a true difference in risk. The prevalence of major mental morbidity may be underestimated because of a cultural propensity to under-report depressive symptoms and a lack of available medical records. Only 7% of those who had completed suicide in this study had ever seen a mental health professional.

A meta-analysis of 27 English language psychological autopsy studies of suicide completers through 2002 attempted to synthesize these estimates (Arsenault-Lapierre et al., 2004). The meta-analysis suggested that 87.3% of suicide completers had a diagnosable mental disorder at the time of the act, with 15 of the 27 studies reporting estimates of at least 90%. Only 14 of the 27 studies assessed Axis II psychopathology. A summary of their results by geographic region is presented in Table 12-1. Many psychological autopsy studies are limited to identifying only the principal diagnosis or restricting the sources of information for assessment.

Table 12-2 shows the results of three studies that were selected based on the following criteria: published after 1985, allowed multiple diagnoses to be recorded, obtained information from both a review of records and interviews, assessed at least 100 suicides, and included a formal assessment for personality disorders (Rich, et al., 1986; Henriksson, et al., 1993; Foster, et al., 1997). These three studies identified mental disorders in 90% to 98% of suicide completers.

The psychiatric diagnoses most associated with suicide will be discussed below in greater detail. While general population risk factors for suicide are generally similar across diagnostic categories, risk factors specifically or uniquely associated with the specific diagnostic categories are highlighted.

Table 12-1. Percent of suicides associated with psychiatric diagnosis by region

	Mood Disorder	Personality Disorder	Substance Use Disorder	Schizophrenia	Any Psychiatric Disorder
Asia	51.3	17.7	26.7	8.4	83.0
Europe	48.5	16.8	18.6	7.5	88.8
North America	36.6	13.4	40.1	4.2	89.7
Oceania	32.7	17.7	24.1	24.3	78.9
All Studies	43.2	16.2	25.7	9.2	87.3

Adapted from Arsenault-Lapierre et al. (2004). Statistically significant regional differences were noted for affective disorders, substance-related disorders, and schizophrenia or other psychotic disorders. 15/27 studies uncovered psychiatric diagnoses in at least 90% of suicides.

Table 12-2. Psychiatric diagnoses in three general population studies of suicide

Author	Rich et al.	Henriksson et al.	Foster et al.
Year Published	1986	1993	1997
Country	United States	Finland	N. Ireland
#Suicides	283	229	118
Criteria	DSM-III	DSM-III-R	DSM-III-R
Any psychiatric diagnosis	91%	98%	90%
Mood disorder	44%	59%	37%
Alcohol disorder	54%	43%	40%
Drug use disorder	45%	5%	8%
Schozophrenia	3%	7%	8%
Other psychotic disorder	11%	7%	5%
Personality disorder	7%	31%	44%
Anxiety disorder	-	11%	10%
Organic mental disorders	4%	2%	3%

Studies were selected from a review of the literature and, for inclusion in this table, had to have been published after 1985, allowed multiple diagnoses, utilized review of records and interviews, sampled at least 100 suicides, and formally assessed for personality disorders. Studies of special population (i.e., geriatric populations) were not included.

#A later reassessment of data from the Rich, et al. San Diego suicide study found that this initial prevalence of personality disorders was underestimated.

MOOD DISORDERS

Mood disorders are the most frequently identified diagnoses after a review of cases of completed suicide (Barraclough, et al., 1974; Henriksson, et al., 1993; Conwell, et al., 1996), and across age groups (Marttunen, et al., 1991; Henriksson, et al., 1995). An inferred lifetime suicide risk of 15% for mood disorders from proportional mortality statistics has been widely-cited but is likely inaccurate. Compared to a non-affectively ill population risk of less than 0.5%, the lifetime risk of suicide for patients with a mood disorder has been estimated at 2.2%, although this figure increases to as high as 8.6% for those with a history of hospitalization for suicidality (Bostwick and Pankratz, 2000). Patients with mood disorders typically commit suicide during depressive phases, although an elevation in risk has also been reported during mixed episodes for those with bipolar disorder. A meta-analysis conducted by Harris and Barraclough (1997) suggests that the lifetime risk of suicide is increased 12-fold by a diagnosis of dysthymia, 15-fold by a diagnosis of bipolar disorder, and 20-fold by a diagnosis of major depression. These figures are shown in Table 12-3, along with the differential risk associated with other psychiatric diagnoses.

Table 12-3. Standardized mortality ratios (SMR) for suicide by psychiatric diagnosis from clinical cohorts

	SMR	Suicides Observed	Geographic Regions Represented
Psychiatric Disorders			
Anorexia Nervosa	22.5	25	Europe, North America
Major Depression	20.4	351	Europe, North America, Oceania
Bipolar Disorder	15.1	93	Europe, North America
Dysthymia	12.1	1436	Europe, North America
Schizophrenia	8.5	1176	Asia, Europe, N. America
Anxiety Disorders	6.5	163	Europe, North America, Oceania
	Substance Abuse Disorders		
Mixed Drug	21.0	158	Europe, North America
Sedative/Hypnotic	17.8	69	Europe
Opioid	14.0	64	Europe, North America
Alcohol	5.9	641	Africa, Asia, Europe, N. America, Oceania
	Axis II		
Any Personality Disorder	7.1	30	Europe, North America

Adapted from the meta-analysis by Harris, et al. (1997). The use of almost exclusively clinical samples, limited durations of follow-up, and publication bias may overestimate the magnitude of reported effects. Broad categories of geographical regions listed do not imply balanced or equal representation among merged studies.

Risk factors for suicide in depressed patients include a history suicide attempts or plans, male gender, being single or living alone, inpatient care, and hopelessness (Coryell, 2006). Hopelessness and measures of suicidality are among the most robust predictors of suicide in clinical populations with major depression (Coryell and Young, 2005). Other risk factors identified in mood disorder patients include a family history of suicide, life events, loss of pleasure or interest, and younger age. In bipolar disorder, mixed states and rapid cycling have also been associated with suicide. Studies contrasting suicide rates by mood disorder subtype have been inconsistent, with some suggestion of increased suicide completions with unipolar depression and increased suicide attempts with bipolar disorder (Lester, 1993). While type II bipolar disorder has been demonstrated to be overrepresented in several European studies (Rihmer, et al., 1990; Rihmer, et al., 1995), two recent prospective studies have failed to show any added risk from bipolar II disorder (Angst, et al., 2005; Coryell and Young, 2005). Time spent in depressive states, however, does appear to be correlated with functional impairment (Judd, et al., 2005) and suicide attempts (Oquendo, et al., 2000; Valtonen, et al., 2005). Overall, it does not appear that subtypes of affective disorder have different risk of suicide. Psychosis does not appear to increase the risk of suicide in patients with affective disorders (Coryell and Tsuang, 1982; Black et al., 1988), although studies of hospital suicides may suggest otherwise (Krupinski, et al., 1998).

Alcohol and Other Drug Use Disorders

Alcohol and other drug use disorders may result in up to a 6 to 20-fold increase in the lifetime risk of suicide (Table 12-3). Alcohol dependence is thought to contribute to at least one- quarter of completed suicides and often occurs in the context of a comorbid mood or anxiety disorder. Even higher rates of alcoholism have been found among suicide completers in Eastern Europe (Kolves, et al., 2006). Alcohol intoxication is common in the setting of suicide even outside a diagnosis of alcohol abuse or dependence. Suicides in alcoholism are often complicated by the occupational, interpersonal and physical sequelae of alcohol misuse. Unlike mood or psychotic disorders, where the risk of suicide occurs early in the course of illness and often shortly after hospitalization, the duration from the onset of alcoholism to suicide is often much longer (Black and Winokur, 1990).

The mean duration from onset of excessive drinking to suicide spans approximately two decades. Compared with controls, suicides in those with alcoholism tend to be older, are more likely to be divorced or widowed, and have made previous suicide attempts (Murphy, et al., 1992). Compared with depressed completed suicides, suicides in alcoholism were more likely to have communicated their suicide intent, have poor social support, to be unemployed, live alone, and have a comorbid medical disorder (Murphy, et al., 1992). Other identified risk factors for suicide in persons with alcoholism include male gender, continued drinking, recent binges, a major depressive episode, previous treatment for alcoholism, unemployment and living alone. Antisocial behaviors, depressive symptoms, and use of other substances is also associated with suicide attempts in men with alcoholism (Black, et al., 1986).

A disturbing trend is that drug use has been more frequently identified in suicide completers over the past few decades. This appears to be particularly true among younger patients and is thought to have contributed to the rise in youth suicides in some countries.

Drug use commonly occurs in conjunction with alcohol misuse and is commonly associated with other psychiatric syndromes. Risk factors specific to suicide completion in drug users have not clearly been identified.

Cocaine use, depressive symptoms, antisocial traits, and concomitant alcohol use have been associated with increased risk of suicidal thoughts (Cottler, et al., 2005). Withdrawal from drugs, including cocaine and heroin, may be associated with significant physical and emotional distress, which has been associated with suicidality and may acutely increase suicide risk (Ward and Schuckit, 1980). Accidental overdose may also result in death and has been associated with concomitant alcoholism, social maladjustment, and legal issues (Puschel, et al., 1993).

SCHIZOPHRENIA

Kraepelin (1919) underestimated the risk for suicide in *Dementia Praecox and Paraphrenia* when, commenting on mortality, he stated "life is threatened only very slightly by dementia praecox" (p. 211). Schizophrenia may increase the risk of suicide up to 8-fold as shown in Table 12-3.

In recent reviews, schizophrenia is commonly credited with a 10% or greater lifetime risk of suicide, although this figure has been questioned. A more recent estimate of lifetime risk suggests that 4.9% of persons with schizophrenia will commit suicide, and the greatest risk occurs following soon after illness onset (Palmer, et al., 2005). Because schizophrenia is less common than mood, personality and alcohol and drug use disorders, schizophrenia also tends to be less diagnosed in psychological autopsy studies, representing fewer than 10% of total suicides (Table 12-1).

Risk factors for suicide in schizophrenia include male gender, younger age, concomitant depression, recent hospitalization, a family history of depression or suicide, greater severity of illness and a high premorbid IQ (Black and Winokur, 1990; De Hert, et al., 2001). Recent loss has also been associated with suicide in schizophrenia.

The presence of depressive symptoms or a depressive syndrome represents the most consistently reported risk factor. Suicides are thought to be more likely during acute exacerbations of illness. One case-control psychological autopsy study noted a lower risk of suicide for those with Cluster A or C personality traits premorbidly (McGirr, et al., 2006) and suggested that these traits are associated with greater negative symptoms and diminished social networks, which may reduce the chance of interpersonal conflicts and negative life events. There appears to be no relationship between marital status and completed suicide (Hawton, et al., 2005). Likewise, unemployment appears to be unrelated to risk for suicide. Histories of violence and command hallucinations have been proposed as risk factors for suicide in schizophrenia (Montross, et al., 2005). While a history of both suicide attempts and suicidal ideation have been associated with completed suicide in schizophrenia, it has been suggested that patients with schizophrenia may be less likely to communicate suicidal intent than others at risk. Persons with schizophrenia are more likely to kill themselves by violent means, however (Hunt, et al., 2006).

Personality Disorders

Personality disorders have emerged as an important factor in many suicide completers. The risk for suicide, if associated with personality disorders and specific personality traits, is not entirely dependent upon co-occurring affective or psychotic disorders. Yet, many psychological autopsy studies omit a formal Axis II assessment. This may arise from the continued controversy and difficulty in conceptualizing personality disorders. A psychological autopsy study utilizing the five-factor model of dimensional personality assessment suggest that completed suicides may be associated with higher neuroticism, lower extraversion, and lower openness to experience (Duberstein, et al., 1994). Measures of impulsivity have been associated with a predilection to violent behaviors, suicide attempts and suicide completions (Apter, et al., 1993). Impulsivity has been further demonstrated to predict the long-term (> 1 year) risk of completed suicide in a large, prospective cohort study (Maser, et al., 2002). Borderline personality disorder has been consistently linked with an elevated risk of suicide (Pompili, et al., 2005). Suicide risk appears greatest in the early stages of follow-up and less with advancing age. Affective instability and impulsivity contribute to this risk. Co-existing mood and anxiety disorders further contribute to suicide risk. Despite a high frequency of suicide attempts, often of low perceived or actual lethality, previous suicide attempts remain an important predictor of suicide for persons with borderline personality disorder. Other risk factors identified for completed suicide include higher levels of education, younger age (adolescents and young adults), hopelessness and alcohol or substance misuse (Pompili, et al., 2005). Hopelessness may contribute to the lethality of suicidality in borderline personality disorder. The presence of any personality disorder may result in a 7-fold increase in the lifetime risk of suicide (Table 12-3). Further increases are seen among those who meet the criteria for more than one personality disorder, which may represent a marker of overall severity of pathological traits. A case-control study of 163 completed suicides suggested elevations in risk for all clusters of personality disorders, with a statistically significant odds ratio of 6.6 across genders for any personality disorder. Antisocial and schizoid personality disorders were the only personality disorders that did not show a significant association with suicide. Co-occurrence of personality disorders from more than one cluster resulted in a 16-fold elevation in risk for men and 20-fold elevation in risk for women after controlling for Axis I disorders (Schneider, et al., 2006). While the study of Schneider and colleagues did not demonstrate a statistically significant association between suicide and antisocial personality disorder, a follow-up study of 71 former inpatient males with antisocial personality disorder reported a SMR of 2.27 for suicide (Black, et al., 1996).

Anorexia Nervosa

The risk of suicide in anorexia varies significantly among studies, with more recently reported standardized mortality ratios between 1.4 and 17.8 (Nielsen, et al., 1998). In a recent meta-analysis of nine studies, 36 suicides were observed in 1,538 patients followed for 5 to 23 years, producing a standardized mortality ratio of 7.8 (Pompili, et al., 2004). This figure, shown in Table 12-3, is less than reported SMR of 22.5 in the meta-analysis of Harris and

Barraclough (1997), which may be an overestimate. Regardless of which figure is considered most accurate, suicide remains a major contributor to excess mortality in anorexia nervosa.

Previous studies suggest that patients with purging behaviors may be more likely to complete suicide. Patients with purging behaviors are thought to have greater impulsivity, higher rates of alcohol and drug use, and greater vulnerability to mood disorders (Vandereycken and Pierloot, 1983). Mood disorders are also common in anorexia and may correlate inversely with weight loss. Limited information is available regarding other specific risk factors for suicide in anorexia nervosa. However, suicide attempts have been associated in older patients with greater chronicity and treatment failures. It has also been suggested that uneasiness related to body image may be related to suicidality (Stein, et al., 2003). Many studies report data from cohorts of women, but data for men with anorexia is limited. While many of the risk factors for suicide in anorexia nervosa are also present in bulimia nervosa, the risk of suicide in bulimia remains under-studied, with a higher risk of suicide relative to the general population and a suggestion of a lower risk relative to anorexia (Pompili, et al., 2006).

Anxiety Disorders

Anxiety disorders are associated with elevated risk of suicide, as high as a 6-fold increase (Table 12-3). Follow-up studies of inpatients and outpatients with panic disorder have demonstrated an increased risk of death by suicide and unnatural causes (Coryell, et al., 1982; Coryell, et al., 1986). Risk factors for serious suicide attempts or suicide in panic disorder include younger age, not being married, personality disorders, major depression, and an early, insidious onset of illness (Noyes, et al., 1991). Individuals with obsessive-compulsive disorder may not be at increased risk for suicide (Coryell, 1981b). While not representative of general population or even clinical samples, an analysis of clinical trial data from the United States Food and Drug Administration databases found an increased risk in suicide across anxiety disorders in general, but was not powerful enough to assess difference in risk between groups (Khan, et al., 2002).

Somatoform Disorders

While recent studies have suggested some increased risk for suicide attempts in somatization disorder independent of mood or personality disorders (Khan, et al., 2002), this finding has not been extended to completed suicide (Coryell, 1981a), and this topic remains understudied.

Dementia and Other Neuropsychiatric Conditions

A number of other neuropsychiatric diseases have been associated with higher suicide rates including traumatic brain injury, epilepsy, Huntington's disease, Parkinson's disease and multiple sclerosis (Harris and Barraclough, 1997; Arciniegas and Anderson, 2002). The absolute number of suicides associated with these illness remains small, however, either because the suicide rate is only modestly increased or because the conditions are relatively uncommon. It remains unclear whether Alzheimer's dementia is associated with a greater risk of suicide.

CHILDHOOD AND ADOLESCENT SUICIDE

The presence of a mood disorder has been demonstrated as a risk factor for suicide in prepubertal children (Roche, et al., 2005), but there has been limited study of suicide in this lower risk age group. Risk factors for suicide among adolescents include the presence of a mood disorder, male gender, previous suicide attempts, a family history of suicide or suicide attempts, substance abuse in the immediate family, family discord and stressful life events (Beautrais, 2003; Roche, et al., 2005).

Alcohol and other drug abuse has also been commonly implicated in youth suicides (Renaud, et al., 2005). Compilation of long-term (> 10 year) follow-up studies of attention deficit disorders found a risk of suicide of 0.63% to 0.78% during follow-up (James, et al., 2004). There has been no systematic analysis of suicide risk with pervasive developmental disorders.

RECOMMENDATIONS

Knowledge about suicide and mental morbidity can help shape clinical recommendations at both the patient and the population level. At the patient level, access to clinicians who can provide comprehensive diagnostic assessments and treatment planning is critical. At the population level, suicide prevention efforts should emphasize access to care, destigmatization of mental illness, screening for mental illness, and ready availability of psychiatric services.

Patient Assessment

A comprehensive psychiatric examination that includes an accurate diagnostic assessment is essential to the successful management of psychiatric disorders. The evaluation will also lead to an understanding of important suicide risk factors. At that point, the appropriate treatment setting and level of care can be determined.

A comprehensive formulation can be developed wherein aspects of the patient's presentation are organized into those that are likely the result of brain disease, the provocation of psychological vulnerabilities, the product of maladaptive behaviors, or demoralization from a tragic illness or other life events (McHugh, 2005).

The psychiatric diagnosis and clinical data for suicide risk assessment can then be utilized for a summary of suicide risk, which may guide treatment.

Population Strategies for Prevention

Research related to suicide and mental morbidity can help direct policies and programs that aim to prevent suicide. A systematic review of suicide prevention strategies by Mann and colleagues (2005) emphasized improved recognition and treatment of depression and restricting access to lethal methods as essential elements. Improving access to care is also essential, but perhaps the most difficult recommendation to implement. Even in developed countries such as the USA, shortages of mental health providers in under-served areas limit access to care and the ability to provide close follow-up. The lack of mental health and crisis care for those with mental illness in developing countries is a major obstacle to global suicide prevention efforts.

A growing number of ecological studies suggest that the greater utilization of antidepressants is associated with lower suicide rates (Mann, et al., 2005). A cohort study of nearly 16,000 patients, followed for a mean of 3.4 years following hospitalization for a suicide attempt, showed a 32% decreased risk of suicide when individuals were treated with antidepressants. Similarly, educational programs for general practitioners on the treatment of depression have been demonstrated to increase antidepressant prescriptions and decrease suicide rates (Henriksson and Isacsson, 2006). Access to and provision of adequate treatment for depression represents a critical suicide prevention measure.

Lethal suicide methods vary regionally. Firearms remain the most common means in the USA, where firearms are readily accessible. Ingestion of chemicals such as pesticides or rat poison accounts for the majority of suicides in China (Phillips, et al., 2002). The World Health Organization has proposed a number of potential environmental modifications to prevent suicide (WHO, 1998). Restricting access to toxic substances, medications fatal in overdose, and firearms are important measures for policy making bodies to consider. Detoxification of domestic gas and automobile emissions (i.e., carbon monoxide) may also be addressed by similar regulations. Responsible reporting of suicide by the media and the use of barriers to deter jumping from high places are also suggested by the WHO.

Suicide prevention strategies that focus on a single risk factor are unlikely to be of substantial benefit. Failure to integrate prevention efforts further limits their utility. Nonetheless, with the strong relationship observed worldwide between psychiatric morbidity and suicide, access to psychiatric care and adequate treatment are paramount to any efforts to minimize the burden of suicide.

Conclusion

Suicide remains a major global public health issue. The WHO estimates that worldwide a suicide occurs every forty seconds. This figure is undoubtedly an underestimate. With estimates of underreporting ranging from 20% to 100%, rates of unrecorded suicides likely show considerable regional variation, complicating comparisons across geographic and political boundaries (Bertolote and Fleischmann, 2002). Studies which investigate the risk of suicide and accidental deaths may circumvent the impact of any such underestimation (Black, et al., 1985). Additional research on suicide is needed, particularly in the developing world. It has been estimated that nearly one-third of suicides worldwide occur in China and India, yet little is known about suicides in these countries. There is a similar lack of information about suicide in African countries. Despite these gaps, the association between psychiatric diagnosis and suicide is clear. While risk factors appear similar around the world, methods vary widely and may represent a pathoplastic feature of suicide as an illness behavior.

Complicating matters for clinicians is the fact that suicide is a rare event and cannot reliably be predicted on an individual basis (Goldstein, et al., 1991). At the population level, most completed suicides are associated with substantial mental morbidity. While suicide rates may vary with regional, demographic and other variables, psychiatric conditions remain a significant risk factor for suicide across countries and cultures. There is a burgeoning literature, which suggests that improved treatment of mental disorders may reduce suicide risk in certain populations. Thus, it is important for clinicians to rigorously pursue the assessment, diagnosis, and treatment of psychiatric illnesses as available resources permit. Suicide prevention programs may benefit from this knowledge by emphasizing the destigmatization, recognition, and treatment of psychiatric disorders.

REFERENCES

Angst, J., Angst, F., Gerber-Werder, R., and Gamma, A. (2005). Suicide in 406 mood-disorder patients with and without long-term medication: a 40 to 44 years' follow-up. *Archives of Suicide Research*, 9, 279-300.

Apter, A., Plutchik, R. and Van Praag, H. M. (1993). Anxiety, impulsivity and depressed mood in relation to suicidal and violent behavior. *Acta Psychiatrica Scandinavica*, 87, 1-5.

Arciniegas, D. B. and Anderson, C. A. (2002). Suicide in neurologic illness. *Current Treatment Options in Neurology*, 4, 457-468.

Arsenault-Lapierre, G., Kim, C. and Turecki, G. (2004). Psychiatric diagnoses in 3275 suicides: a meta-analysis. *BMC Psychiatry*, 4, 37.

Barraclough, B., Bunch, J., Nelson, B., and Sainsbury, P. (1974). A hundred cases of suicide: clinical aspects. *British Journal of Psychiatry*, 125, 355-373.

Beautrais, A. L. (2003). Suicide and serious suicide attempts in youth: a multiple-group comparison study. *American Journal of Psychiatry*, 160, 1093-1099.

Bertolote, J. M. and Fleischmann, A. (2002). Suicide and psychiatric diagnosis: a worldwide perspective. *World Psychiatry*, 1, 181-185.

Black, D. W. (1998). Iowa record-linkage study: death rates in psychiatric patients. *Journal of Affective Disorders*, 50, 277-282.

Black, D. W., Baumgard, C. H., Bell, S. E., and Kao, C. (1996). Death rates in 71 men with antisocial personality disorder: a comparison with general population mortality. *Psychosomatics*, 37, 131-136.

Black, D. W., Warrack, G. and Winokur, G. (1985). The Iowa record-linkage study: I Suicides and accidental deaths among psychiatric patients. *Archives of General Psychiatry*, 42, 71-75.

Black, D. W. and Winokur, G. (1990). Suicide and psychiatric diagnosis. In S. J. Blumenthal and D. J. Kupfer (Eds.) *Suicide over the life cycle: Risk factors, assessment, and treatment of suicidal patients*, pp. 135-153. Rockville, MD: American Psychiatric Publishing.

Black, D. W., Winokur, G. and Nasrallah, A. (1988). Effect of psychosis on suicide risk in 1,593 patients with unipolar and bipolar affective disorders. *American Journal of Psychiatry*, 145, 849-852.

Black, D. W., Yates, W., Petty, F., Noyes, R., Jr., and Brown, K. (1986). Suicidal behavior in alcoholic males. *Comprehensive Psychiatry*, 27, 227-233.

Bostwick, J. M. and Pankratz, V. S. (2000). Affective disorders and suicide risk: a reexamination. *American Journal of Psychiatry*, 157, 1925-1932.

Conwell, Y., Duberstein, P. R., Cox, C., Herrmann, J. H., Forbes, N. T., and Caine, E. D. (1996). Relationships of age and axis I diagnoses in victims of completed suicide: a psychological autopsy study. *American Journal of Psychiatry*, 153, 1001-1008.

Coryell, W. (1981a). Diagnosis-specific mortality: primary unipolar depression and Briquet's syndrome (somatization disorder). *Archives of General Psychiatry*, 38, 939-942.

Coryell, W. (1981b). Obsessive-compulsive disorder and primary unipolar depression: comparisons of background, family history, course, and mortality. *Journal of Nervous and Mental Disease*, 169, 220-224.

Coryell, W., Noyes, R. and Clancy, J. (1982). Excess mortality in panic disorder: a comparison with primary unipolar depression. *Archives of General Psychiatry*, 39, 701-703.

Coryell, W., Noyes, R., Jr. and House, J. D. (1986). Mortality among outpatients with anxiety disorders. *American Journal of Psychiatry*, 143, 508-510.

Coryell, W. and Tsuang, M. T. (1982). Primary unipolar depression and the prognostic importance of delusions. *Archives of General Psychiatry*, 39, 1181-1184.

Coryell, W. and Young, E. A. (2005). Clinical predictors of suicide in primary major depressive disorder. *Journal of Clinical Psychiatry*, 66, 412-417.

Coryell, W. H. (2006). Clinical assessment of suicide risk in depressive disorder. *CNS Spectrum*, 11, 455-461.

Cottler, L. B., Campbell, W., Krishna, V. A., Cunningham-Williams, R. M., and Abdallah, A. B. (2005). Predictors of high rates of suicidal ideation among drug users. *Journal of Nervous and Mental Diseases*, 193, 431-437.

De Hert, M., McKenzie, K. and Peuskens, J. (2001). Risk factors for suicide in young people suffering from schizophrenia: a long-term follow-up study. *Schizophrenia Research*, 47, 127-134.

Duberstein, P. R., Conwell, Y. and Caine, E. D. (1994). Age differences in the personality characteristics of suicide completers: preliminary findings from a psychological autopsy study. *Psychiatry*, 57, 213-224.

Ernst, C., Lalovic, A., Lesage, A., Seguin, M., Tousignant, M., and Turecki, G. (2004). Suicide and no axis I psychopathology. *BMC Psychiatry*, 4, 7.

Foster, T., Gillespie, K. and McClelland, R. (1997). Mental disorders and suicide in Northern Ireland. *British Journal of Psychiatry*, 170, 447-452.

Goldstein, R. B., Black, D. W., Nasrallah, A., and Winokur, G. (1991). The prediction of suicide: sensitivity, specificity, and predictive value of a multivariate model applied to suicide among 1906 patients with affective disorders. *Archives of General Psychiatry*, 48, 418-422.

Harris, E. C. and Barraclough, B. (1997). Suicide as an outcome for mental disorders: a meta-analysis. *British Journal of Psychiatry*, 170, 205-228.

Hawton, K., Sutton, L., Haw, C., Sinclair, J., Deeks, J. J. (2005). Schizophrenia and suicide: systematic review of risk factors. *British Journal of Psychiatry*, 187, 9-20.

Henriksson, M. M., Aro, H. M., Marttunen, M. J., Heikkinen, M. E., Isometsa, E. T., Kuoppasalmi, K. I., and Lonnqvist, J. K. (1993). Mental disorders and comorbidity in suicide. *American Journal of Psychiatry*, 150, 935-940.

Henriksson, M. M., Marttunen, M. J., Isometsa, E. T., Heikkinen, M. E., Aro, H. M., Kuoppasalmi, K. I., and Lonnqvist, J. K. (1995). Mental disorders in elderly suicide. *International Psychogeriatrics*, 7, 275-286.

Henriksson, S. and Isacsson, G. (2006). Increased antidepressant use and fewer suicides in Jamtland county, Sweden, after a primary care educational programme on the treatment of depression. *Acta Psychiatrica Scandinavica*, 114, 159-167.

Hunt, I. M., Kapur, N., Robinson, J., Shaw, J., Flynn, S., Bailey, H., Meehan, J., Bickley, H., Burns, J., Appleby, L., and Parsons, R. (2006). Suicide within 12 months of mental health service contact in different age and diagnostic groups: national clinical survey. *British Journal of Psychiatry*, 188, 135-142.

James, A., Lai, F. H. and Dahl, C. (2004). Attention deficit hyperactivity disorder and suicide: a review of possible associations. *Acta Psychiatrica Scandinavica*, 110, 408-415.

Judd, L. L., Akiskal, H. S., Schettler, P. J., Endicott, J., Leon, A. C., Solomon, D. A., Coryell, W., Maser, J. D., and Keller, M. B. (2005). Psychosocial disability in the course of bipolar I and II disorders: a prospective, comparative, longitudinal study. *Archives of General Psychiatry*, 62, 1322-1330.

Kelly, T. M. and Mann, J. J. (1996). Validity of DSM-III-R diagnosis by psychological autopsy: a comparison with clinician ante-mortem diagnosis. *Acta Psychiatrica Scandinavica*, 94, 337-343.

Khan, A., Leventhal, R. M., Khan, S., and Brown, W. A. (2002). Suicide risk in patients with anxiety disorders: a meta-analysis of the FDA database. *Journal of Affective Disorders*, 68, 183-190.

Kolves, K., Varnik, A., Tooding, L. M., and Wasserman, D. 92006). The role of alcohol in suicide: a case-control psychological autopsy study. *Psychological Medicine*, 36, 923-930.

Krupinski, M., Fischer, A., Grohmann, R., Engel, R., Hollweg, M., and Moller, H. J. (1998). Risk factors for suicides of inpatients with depressive psychoses. *European Archives of Psychiatry and Clinical Neuroscience*, 248, 141-147.

Lester, D. (1993). Suicidal behavior in bipolar and unipolar affective disorders: a meta-analysis. *Journal of Affective Disorders*, 27, 117-121.

Mann, J. J., Apter, A., Bertolote, J., Beautrais, A., Currier, D., Haas, A., Hegerl, U., Lonnqvist, J., Malone, K., Marusic, A., Mehlum, L., Patton, G., Phillips, M., Rutz, W., Rihmer, Z., Schmidtke, A., Shaffer, D., Silverman, M., Takahashi, Y., Varnik, A., Wasserman, D., Yip, P., and Hendin, H. (2005). Suicide prevention strategies: a systematic review. *Journal of the American Medical Association*, 294, 2064-2074.

Marttunen, M. J., Aro, H. M., Henriksson, M. M., and Lonnqvist, J. K. (1991). Mental disorders in adolescent suicide: DSM-III-R axes I and II diagnoses in suicides among 13- to 19-year-olds in Finland. *Archives of General Psychiatry*, 48, 834-839.

Maser, J. D., Akiskal, H. S., Schettler, P., Scheftner, W., Mueller, T., Endicott, J., Solomon, D., and Clayton, P. (2002). Can temperament identify affectively ill patients who engage in lethal or near-lethal suicidal behavior? A 14-year prospective study. *Suicide and Life-Threatening Behavior*, 32, 10-32.

McGirr, A., Tousignant, M., Routhier, D., Pouliot, L., Chawky, N., Margolese, H. C., and Turecki, G. (2006). Risk factors for completed suicide in schizophrenia and other chronic psychotic disorders: a case-control study. *Schizophrenia Research*, 84, 132-143.

McHugh, P. R. (2005). Striving for coherence: psychiatry's efforts over classification. *Journal of the American Medical Association*, 293, 2526-2528.

Montross, L. P., Zisook, S. and Kasckow, J. (2005). Suicide among patients with schizophrenia: a consideration of risk and protective factors. *Annals of Clinical Psychiatry*, 17, 173-182.

Murphy, G. E., Wetzel, R. D., Robins, E., and McEvoy, L. (1992). Multiple risk factors predict suicide in alcoholism. *Archives of General Psychiatry*, 49, 459-463.

Nielsen, S., Moller-Madsen, S., Isager, T., Jorgensen, J., Pagsberg, K., and Theander, S. (1998). Standardized mortality in eating disorders: a quantitative summary of previously published and new evidence. *Journal of Psychosomatic Research*, 44, 413-434.

Noyes, R., Jr., Christiansen, J., Clancy, J., Garvey, M. J., Suelzer, M., and Anderson, D. J. (1991). Predictors of serious suicide attempts among patients with panic disorder. *Comprehensive Psychiatry*, 32, 261-267.

Oquendo, M. A., Waternaux, C., Brodsky, B., Parsons, B., Haas, G. L., Malone, K. M., and Mann, J. J. (2000). Suicidal behavior in bipolar mood disorder: clinical characteristics of attempters and nonattempters. *Journal of Affective Disorders*, 59, 107-117.

Palmer, B. A., Pankratz, V. S. and Bostwick, J. M. (2005). The lifetime risk of suicide in schizophrenia: a reexamination. *Archives of General Psychiatry*, 62, 247-253.

Phillips, M. R., Yang, G., Zhang, Y., Wang, L., Ji, H., and Zhou, M. (2002). Risk factors for suicide in China: a national case-control psychological autopsy study. *Lancet*, 360, 1728-1736.

Pompili, M., Girardi, P., Ruberto, A., and Tatarelli, R. (2005). Suicide in borderline personality disorder: a meta-analysis. *Nordic Journal of Psychiatry*, 59, 319-324.

Pompili, M., Girardi, P., Tatarelli, G., Ruberto, A., and Tatarelli, R. (2006). Suicide and attempted suicide in eating disorders, obesity and weight-image concern. *Eating Behavior*, 7, 384-394.

Pompili, M., Mancinelli, I., Girardi, P., Ruberto, A., and Tatarelli, R. (2004) Suicide in anorexia nervosa: a meta-analysis. *International Journal of Eating Disorders*, 36, 99-103.

Puschel, K., Teschke, F. and Castrup, U. (1993). Etiology of accidental/unexpected overdose in drug-induced deaths. *Forensic Science International*, 62, 129-134.

Renaud, J., Chagnon, F., Turecki, G., and Marquette, C. (2005). Completed suicides in a youth centre population. *Canadian Journal of Psychiatry*, 50, 690-694.

Rich, C. L., Young, D. and Fowler, R. C. (1986). San Diego suicide study: I. Young vs old subjects. *Archives of General Psychiatry*, 43, 577-582.

Rihmer, Z., Barsi, J., Arato, M., and Demeter, E. (1990). Suicide in subtypes of primary major depression. *Journal of Affective Disorders*, 18, 221-225.

Rihmer, Z., Rutz, W. and Pihlgren, H. (1995). Depression and suicide on Gotland: an intensive study of all suicides before and after a depression-training programme for general practitioners. *Journal of Affective Disorders*, 35, 147-152.

Roche, A. M., Giner, L. and Zalsman, G. (2005). Suicide in early childhood: a brief review. *International Journal of Adolescent Medical Health*, 17, 221-224.

Schneider, B., Wetterling, T., Sargk, D., Schneider, F., Schnabel, A., Maurer, K., and Fritze, J. (2006). Axis I disorders and personality disorders as risk factors for suicide. *European Archives of Psychiatry and Clinical Neuroscience*, 256, 17-27.

Stein, D., Orbach, I., Shani-Sela, M., Har-Even, D., Yaruslasky, A., Roth, D., Meged, S. and Apter, A. (2003). Suicidal tendencies and body image and experience in anorexia nervosa and suicidal female adolescent inpatients. *Psychotherapy and Psychosomatics*, 72, 16-25.

Suominen, K. H., Isometsa, E. T., Henriksson, M. M., Ostamo, A. I., and Lonnqvist, J. K. 91998). Inadequate treatment for major depression both before and after attempted suicide. *American Journal of Psychiatry*, 155, 1778-1780.

Valtonen, H., Suominen, K., Mantere, O., Leppamaki, S., Arvilommi, P., and Isometsa, E. T. (2005). Suicidal ideation and attempts in bipolar I and II disorders. *Journal of Clinical Psychiatry*, 66, 1456-1462.

Vandereycken, W. and Pierloot, R. (1983). The significance of subclassification in anorexia nervosa: a comparative study of clinical features in 141 patients. *Psychological Medicine*, 13, 543-549.

Ward, N. G. and Schuckit, M. A. (1980). Factors associated with suicidal behavior in polydrug abusers. *Journal of Clinical Psychiatry*, 41, 379-385.

WHO. (1998). Suicide. In *Primary prevention of mental, neurological and psychosocial disorders*, pp. 75-87. Geneva, Switzerland: World Health Organization.

In: Suicide from a Global Perspective: Psychiatric Approaches ISBN: 978-1-61942-267-4
Editors: A. Shrivastava, M. Kimbrell, and D. Lester © 2012 Nova Science Publishers, Inc.

Chapter 13

SUICIDE IN MINOR MENTAL DISORDERS

Konstantinos N. Fountoulaki and Zoltan Rihmer

INTRODUCTION

Minor mental disorders (formerly called neurotic disorders) include a cluster of relatively mild, but frequently chronic, mental disorders that are often seen both in outpatient clinical practice and in the community. They include generalized anxiety disorder, dysthymia, panic and social anxiety disorders, and phobias. They are rarely seen alone. Usually they co-exist or they exist in combination with a major mental illness like unipolar depression or bipolar disorder (Merikangas, 2005).

Panic Disorder

Panic disorder is characterized by the presence of panic attacks which are a cluster of symptoms including, among others, the unexpected experience of dyspnea, palpitations, chest pain, choking, dizziness, feelings of depersonalization or derealization, paresthesias, hot and cold flashes, sweating, faintness and trembling or shaking. Sometimes panic disorder is accompanied by agoraphobia (Roy-Byrne, et al., 2006). The lifetime prevalence rate of DSM-III/DSM-IIIR and ICD-10 panic disorder (with or without agoraphobia) is between 0.4% and 3.6%. The highest lifetime prevalence rates have been reported from the USA and Western Europe and the lowest from Far East (Merikangas, 2005). Most recent studies from the USA showed that the lifetime rate is believed to be close to 5% (Bienvenu, 2006; Roy-Byrne, et al., 2006), and the age at onset is usually the early to middle 20s. Women may have higher rates than men (Merikangas, 2005). Panic disorder causes significant disability (Alonso, et al., 2004). The early neurobiological finding that sodium lactate infusion and hyperventillation can induce panic attacks in patients with panic disorder was followed by reports that many other substances like yohimbine, carbon dioxide, doxapram and cholecystokinin may have similar properties (Keck and Strohle, 2005), and it is believed that the biological substrate of panic disorder is likely to implicate serotonergic and noradrenergic systems, along with a genetic predisposition which seems to be crucial. As suggested by neuroimaging studies, the above may involve an amygdala-based fear network leading to an abnormal reactivity to stress (Sakai, et al., 2005; Strohle and Holsboer, 2003). Panic disorder is treated with antidepressants and anxiolytics (high-potency benzodiazepines) and with cognitive-behavioral psychotherapy.

Social Anxiety Disorder

Social anxiety disorder (formerly called social phobia) is a condition in which individuals suffer from an excessive fear concerning social situations. More specifically, in social situations, they feel embarrassed and fear that they will be humiliated. This leads them to actively and deliberately avoid these situations. Common social phobias involve fears of speaking or eating in public and urinating in public lavatories. The most severe forms of social anxiety disorder are highly disabling conditions although milder forms of the disorder widely exist in the general population (Alonso, et al., 2004). The lifetime prevalence of DSM-III/DSM-IIIR diagnosed social anxiety disorder is 0.5%-13.3% (Merikangas, 2005; Weissman, et al., 1996). However, as in the case of panic disorder, the lowest lifetime prevalence rates have been reported from Korea and Taiwan (Merikangas, 2005). Rates are highest among women, younger, single, less educated, and low socioeconomic class persons. Dysthimic disorder as well as major depression are the most common comorbid conditions (Merikangas, 2005). There are some data suggesting a dysfunction of the postsynaptic serotonin receptors and a hypersensitivity to challenge with caffeine, CO_2, and pentagastrin. Additionally, neuroimaging studies suggest a dysfunction of the striatal presynaptic dopamine transporter. It is likely that this condition can be treated with antidepressants and some form of psychotherapy, but hard data are lacking (Den Boer, 2000).

Generalized Anxiety Disorder

Generalized Anxiety Disorder (GAD) is characterized by the presence of unrealistic or excessive anxiety and worry, accompanied by motor tension, autonomic hyperactivity, vigilance and scanning, and apprehensive expectation. The lifetime prevalence of GAD is around 2.3%-7.9%, although rates as high as 13.1% have been also reported. Females are more frequently affected than males. Almost 90% of patients with GAD have at least one other psychiatric disorder during their lifespan, and mood disorders and panic disorder with or without agoraphobia are the most common. (Kessler, et al., 2002; Merikangas, 2005; Nelson, et al., 2000).

Dysthymic Disorder

Dysthymic disorder is a chronic subaffective disorder, lasting at least for two years, with insidious and typically early onset and a persistent or intermittent course (Klein, et al., 2006; Rihmer, 1999). Clinically, it is very close to a subthreshold chronic characterologic depression, and this is the way many psychiatrists perceive it. Its lifetime prevalence is between 3% and 6 % (Akiskal, 2001; Rihmer, 1999; Waraich, et al., 2004), and it causes a heavy burden on the individual (Alonso, et al., 2004).

Social Adjustment Dysthymic Disorder

In the form of Social Adjustment Dysthymic disorder, it leads many patients to invest whatever energy they have in work, leaving none for leisure and family or social activities. These persons are often high achievers in spite of the fact that they suffer from a form of existential depression, with feelings of being empty and lacking any joy in life outside work.

The profile of dysthymic disorder overlaps with that of recurrent major depressive disorder, but differs from it in the term of severity and duration and because symptoms tend to outnumber signs (i.e., more subjective than objective depression). Marked disturbances in appetite and libido or psychomotor agitation or retardation are not usually present, although subtle endogenous features (like diurnal variation of mood and activity) are not uncommon. Cognitive depressive symptoms and low self-esteem, as well as comorbid anxiety, are the rule (Regier, et al., 1993). The relationship between dysthymic disorder and major mood disorders was a common topic of debate till late 1980's. However, the recent concept of dysthymic disorder, also reflected in our official diagnostic systems, represents a major shift from the traditional view of chronic mild depressions as a neurotic or personality disorder to the current concept of dysthymia as a low-grade, chronic or fluctuating primary mood disorder, which is the mild form and often the antecedent of primary major mood disorders, sharing several familial-genetic, biological and treatment-response characteristics (Akiskal, 2001; Rihmer, 1999).

Treatment and Long-Term Outcome of Minor Mental Disorders

The World Health Organization reported that, beside schizophrenia and major mood disorders, minor mental disorders, especially panic disorder and GAD, are strongly associated with functional disability (Ormel, et al., 1994). This finding seems to be consistent across the major cultures around the world. The fact that most of these disorders have a mild clinical picture, which does not alarm the clinician as does major melancholic depression, does not mean that they are not incapacitating or that they do not possess a real threat towards the physical and mental capability of the individual. On the contrary, their chronic character, in addition to a relative refractoriness of some forms and the frustration they cause to the patient's environment, are often causes of great distress. If left untreated or if badly treated, the outcome is poor in a significant percentage of patients, and the most frequent long-term complication is the development of major depression (Akiskal, 2001; den Boer, 2000; Goodwin and Olfson, 2001; Klein, et al., 2006; Rihmer, 1999; Roy-Byrne, et al., 2006). It is fortunate that they seem to be self-restricting in the majority of cases in the general population and in the large number of patients treated in primary care. However this can raise problems. Suicidality today is a major problem, not only inside psychiatry, but also in the primary care setting and in medical patients who are poorly diagnosed, assessed and treated concerning their mental problems.

The treatment of these disorders is based on a combination of antidepressant pharmacotherapy, especially with newer agents like SSRIs and SNRIs, and some form of psychotherapy, usually cognitive-behavioral therapy. In some cases, anxiolytics are also needed, primarily at the early stage of the treatment (Baldwin and Polkinghorn, 2005; Blanco, et al., 2003; Davidson, 2003; Markowitz, et al., 2005; Mathew, et al., 2001; Schmitt, et al., 2005; Sheehan, 2002). What many physicians and psychiatrists seem to ignore today is that the above-mentioned pharmacological interventions have proven to be effective in the treatment of these disorders. The efficacy of psychological treatments has not been solidly shown yet, although some supportive research data do exist. In a randomized 16-week trial of 94 purely dysthymic patients showed that sertraline, with or without interpersonal psychotherapy, showed advantages relative to interpersonal psychotherapy or brief supportive psychotherapy (Markowitz, et al., 2005).

The existing literature indicates that panic disorder can treated with antidepressants, anxiolytics and cognitive-behavioral psychotherapy (Mathew, et al., 2001; Sheehan, 2002). It is likely social phobia can be treated with antidepressants and some form of psychotherapy, although hard data are lacking (Blanco, et al., 2003; Davidson, 2003; den Boer, 2000). Dysthymia can also be treated with antidepressants, with SSRIs preferred (Lima and Moncrieff, 2000). Antidepressant medication is increasingly seen as the medication treatment of choice for generalized anxiety disorder (Baldwin and Polkinghorn, 2005; Schmitt, et al., 2005).

THE RELATIONSHIP OF MINOR MENTAL DISORDERS AND SUICIDE

During recent decades, the understanding and prevention of suicide has become an important issue in medicine in general and, more specifically, in psychiatry. Psychological autopsy studies of suicides have shown that the majority were suffering from a mood disorder, usually major depression. However comorbidity was also a very frequent phenomenon (Henriksson, et al., 1993; Rihmer, 2007; Rihmer, et al., 2002).

Risk factors include male gender, previous suicide attempt(s), depression with comorbid mental disorders (especially personality disorders and substance abuse), permanent adverse life-situations and acute psycho-social stressors (Henriksson, et al., 1993; Rihmer, et al., 2002). However, predictive validity is poor. The major problem seems to be the fact that, although the risk factors include both primary (psychiatric-medical, such as depression), secondary (psychosocial, such as adverse life-situations) and tertiary (demographic, such as male gender), only the presence of primary risk factors seems to be the determining element (Rihmer, 2007; Rihmer, et al., 2002). From these primary factors, major depression and mixed episodes in bipolar disorder seem to be the strongest predictors.

The importance of minor mental disorders in suicidal behavior was demonstrated by two recent studies that showed that a pre-existing anxiety disorder, in combination with a major mood disorder, was associated with a higher risk of suicide attempts in comparison to major mood disorder alone (Sareen, et al, 2005a, 2005b; Szadoczky, , et al., 2000).

Psychopathological Understanding

From the viewpoint of the classic psychoanalytic theory, there is a strong relationship between depressive affect and suicidal behavior. Psychoanalytic and psychodynamic approaches consider suicide to be aggression turned inwards. The motivation to commit suicide may include hidden wishes to kill, to be killed and to die, as well as wish for a reunion with a lost figure.

Modern psychological approaches do not consider suicides as manifesting a similar psychological or personality structure. What seems to be the common element in suicides is the experience of hopelessness as a result of continuous frustration because of rigidly held unrealistic expectations. These may lead to suicide as the only way out for the individual (Gabbard, 2005). In accordance with this, it was found that suicide in dysthymia was significantly associated with hopelessness (Chioqueta and Stiles, 2003) and possibly with alexithymia in panic disorder (Iancu, et al., 2001).

Biological Correlates of Suicide in Minor Mental Disorders

Although suicide is not a nosological entity, but rather an end behavior, a series of studies of the cerebrospinal fluid (CSF) and neurochemical and receptor studies suggest that low brain serotonin activity might play a key role in suicidal behavior (Coccaro, 1989; Nordstrom, et al., 1994; Samuelsson, et al., 2006). The problem is that this is also true for depression in general, and research shows that major depression is a comorbid condition with minor mental disorders in most cases of suicide (Henriksson, et al., 1993; Rihmer, 2007; Rihmer, et al., 2002; Waraich, et al., 2004). The research does not entirely clarify this overlap. There are some data suggesting a predictive value for low concentrations of CSF 5-HIAA (Nordstrom, et al., 1994; Samuelsson, et al., 2006). Genetic studies suggest a role for the tryptophan hydroxylase 1 (TPH1) gene, which has been suggested as a risk factor for suicidal behavior, and for an insertion/deletion polymorphism of the serotonin transporter gene (5-HTTLPR) (Bondy, et al., 2006).

One of the rare studies dealing with dysthymia, and not with major depression, suggested that platelet monoamine oxidase (MAO) activity was significantly lower in female, but not in male, dysthymic patients who had attempted suicide (Tripodianakis, et al., 1998).

Another intriguing finding is that the level of emotional arousal might be of prime importance for the expression of aggression towards self or the others. Arousal, mostly in the form of anxiety, is increased in minor mental disorders, and the comorbidity of anxiety and depression seems to constitute a risk factor. It seems that serotonin activity cannot be linked with aggression unless an adequate level of emotional alertness is present (Coccaro, 1989). The problem may lay in the imbalance between the inhibition of behavior mediated through serotonin and the level of arousal mediated by catecholamines, particularly by acetylcholine (Brown and Goodwin, 1984; Depue and Spoont, 1986). Therefore, the patient may express aggression towards the environment or towards the self on the basis of a lower threshold. It is possible that the inhibition of behavior is mediated by serotonin and its release by norepinephrine and dopamine (Depue and Spoont, 1986).

Panic disorder patients with suicidal thoughts were reported to have lower serum total cholesterol and low-density lipoprotein levels than normal control subjects (Ozer, et al., 2004). The implications of such a finding are still unclear, but it is well documented that low serum cholesterol levels are associated with decreased central serotonin synthesis (Bernal, et al., 2007).

Psychological and Social Correlates of Suicide in Minor Mental Disorders

In spite of the fact that the primary factors influence the manifestation of suicidal behavior, the social and cultural environment may also play an important role. Thus, social support networks and religion may either promote or inhibit the manifestation of such behaviors, or modify their expression (Rihmer, et al., 2002). Several studies have suggested that low social and family support are significantly associated with suicide in men, but not in women. On the contrary, psychological factors such as depersonalization or anxiety may be more important for women. In younger patients, being female, younger, and divorced or widowed are reported to be associated with a higher prevalence of suicide ideation as well as attempts (Bernal, et al., 2007).

Suicide in Different Minor Mental Disorders

Significant controversy exists whether anxiety disorders are independently associated, with suicidal ideation and suicide attempts, after adjusting for comorbid major depression. The data are overall in favor of a low to moderate increase in suicide risk due to the presence of any minor mental disorder, but a comorbid major depression increases this risk dramatically (Hornig and McNally, 1995; Klein, et al., 2000; Rihmer, et al., 2002).

Several studies suggest that panic disorder patients are at an increased risk for committing suicide because of panic symptoms alone. The data from the National Institute of Mental Health (NIMH) Epidemiologic Catchment Area (ECA) study suggested that, although one-third of patients with panic attacks or social phobia were experiencing suicidal ideation, only 7% of panic patients without any comorbid disorder have a history of at least one attempt. Of more importance is the fact that panic attack in completed suicides is reported only in 1.2% of cases and, in these cases, comorbid major depression is present. Thus, the results of the NIMH-ECA study suggest that suicidal ideation in patients suffering from minor mental disorders is likely to be due to the co-existence of depressive symptoms (Cox, et al., 1994; Hornig and McNally, 1995). The results from the National Comorbidity Survey pointed to the same conclusion (Goodwin and Roy-Byrne, 2006; Sareen, et al, 2005b; Vickers and McNally, 2004). It is possible that, although anxiety symptoms could be associated with suicidal ideation, alone they are unlikely to lead to a suicidal attempt (Friedman, et al., 1999; Schmidt, et al., 2001). A 5-year follow-up study of 498 patients with panic disorder reported a 6% probability of suicidal behavior during this time-frame, but the authors concluded that panic disorder is not associated with suicidal behavior in the absence of other risk factors (Warshaw, et al., 2000).

Because the severity of depression is an important risk factor for suicide in such patients (Rihmer, 2007), it is not surprising that pure dysthymia (i.e., dysthymic disorder without lifetime major depression) carries a relatively low risk of suicide. A prospective, longitudinal follow-up study of 86 outpatients with early-onset dysthymic disorder versus 39 outpatients with episodic major depressive disorder suggested a 5-year recovery rate from dysthymic disorder equal to 52.9% and a relapse rate of 45.2%. But what is of prime importance was that patients with dysthymic disorder exhibited significantly greater levels of symptoms and lower functioning and were significantly more likely to attempt suicide and to be hospitalized than were patients with episodic major depressive disorder. The risk of having a first lifetime major depressive episode during follow up was 76.9% (Klein, et al., 2000). This prospective follow-up study also supports the strong clinical relationship between dysthymic disorder and major depression (Akiskal, 2001; Rihmer, 1999) and is in a good agreement with the findings of psychological autopsy studies that pure dysthymic disorder is very rare among suicides. (Henriksson, et al., 1993; Rihmer, 2007; Rihmer, et al., 2002).

Some data suggest that not all minor mental disorders and not all kinds of anxious symptomatology relate to suicidality in the same way or act toward the same direction. The problem with this is, of course, that comorbity confounds the results. However there are some data suggesting that panic symptoms relate positively to suicidal ideation while, in contrast, social phobia symptoms may have a negative relationship after controlling for depression (Valentiner, et al., 2002).

Another important possibility is that comorbid panic attacks in major depression increase the risk to commit suicide than in major depression alone (Pilowsky, et al., 2006). Consistent with this are data from the Netherlands Mental Health Survey and Incidence Study which suggest that, after adjusting for sociodemographic factors and comorbid mental disorders, the presence of any anxiety disorder was significantly associated with suicidal ideation and suicide attempts in both cross-sectional analyses and longitudinal analyses, but also the presence of a comorbid mood disorder was associated with an even higher suicidal risk (Sareen, et al., 2005a). A comorbid cluster B or C personality disorder also seems to increase the suicidal risk (Starcevic, et al., 1999). These findings are supported also by data from the primary care (Goodwin, et al., 2001).

In accord with the above, the meta-analysis of the US Food and Drug Administration (FDA) database data of recent clinical trials revealed that overall, among 20,076 participating anxious patients, 12 (0.06%) committed suicide and 28 (0.14%) attempted suicide. Although this constitutes a relatively high rate, since the duration of studies was relatively short, a major limitation for the conclusions is the fact that clinical trial data come from a highly selected, non-representative sample of the clinical population, and so conclusions are difficult to generalize. In addition, clinical trials typically exclude suicidal patients and are not designed to assess suicide risk (Khan, et al., 2002).

There are a few large population-based studies suggesting a relationship between anxiety and suicidality in children and adolescents. The study of a community-based sample of 1,580 13-14-year-old adolescents suggested that adolescents with panic attacks were three times more likely to have expressed suicidal ideation and two times more likely to have made suicide attempts than were adolescents without panic attacks (Pilowsky, et al., 1999). Another study of 1,285 randomly selected children and adolescents, aged 9 to 17 years, of whom 42 had attempted suicide and 67 had expressed suicidal ideation, suggested that mood, anxiety, and substance abuse or dependence disorders independently increased the risk of suicide attempts, after controlling for sociodemographic characteristics (Gould, et al., 1998). Since there are other studies of equal power suggesting that there is no relationship, the conclusion is rather that the study of younger populations has so far produced mixed and inconclusive results. A study of a large sample of 1,979 patients aged 5 to 19 years, of whom 817 were non-suicidal, 768 were having suicidal ideation and 394 had attempted suicide, gave no conclusive results on the relation between pediatric anxiety disorder and suicidal ideation and attempts (Strauss, et al., 2000). In another large population-based study of adolescent female twins, the conclusion was that, while the lifetime prevalence of social phobia was 16.3 %, comorbidity with major depression was the main predictive factor for a substantially elevated risk of suicidal ideation (Nelson, et al., 2000).

Early Identification, Management and Outcome of Suicidal Behavior in Minor Mental Disorders

Early identification and early intervention is a recommendation and rule in medicine in general and psychiatry in particular. There are many reports suggesting that most suicides had asked for professional help concerning their mental health problems before committing suicide and were either not correctly diagnosed or not properly treated. Most GPs who had examined these patients a few months prior to their completed suicide had prescribed antifatigue agents (such as vitamins) instead of psychotropic medication for their treatment (Rutz, 1992). Unfortunately, although it seems that early identification might be possible, data suggest that management and treatment are suboptimal, if not poor.

Antidepressants, along with some forms of psychotherapy, constitute the core of treatment for all minor mental disorders and for comorbid major depression which is present most cases. Concomittant use of benzodiazepines in the first few weeks of the treatment significantly speeds up the response to antidepressants, at least in patients with major depressive disorder (Furukawa, et al., 2001). Although there are no controlled studies to support an anti-suicidal effect for antidepressants, since suicidal patients are typically excluded from clinical trials because of ethical reasons, common sense suggests that antidepressants possess an anti-suicidal effect when used properly (Balazs, et al., 2006). What is of prime importance, however, is the fact that recently the Food and Drug Administration issued a warning concerning the use of antidepressants in children and adolescents and possibly in all age groups (FDA, 2006). This warning concerned the possible induction of suicidality (suicidal ideation and attempts but not completed suicide) by antidepressants. This is possibly due to the presence of unrecognized pseudo-unipolar or subthreshold bipolar patients (Balazs, et al., 2006) among patients suffering from panic disorder, social phobia or dysthymia, the majority of whom later develop a major depressive episode. In clinical practice it is common to diagnose these disorders as comorbid conditions or as the sole current diagnosis in patients suffering from bipolar disorder, especially when the bipolar disorder is not the classic type. In these patients, as well as in overtly bipolar patients, antidepressant monotherapy may induce, not only rapid cycling, but also mixed states, characterized by agitation, irritability, hostility and impulsivity, and in this state, suicidal ideation may emerge (Balazs, et al., 2006).

How the Management of Minor Mental Disorders Can Influence Suicide

Patients suffering from minor mental disorders and especially those with high levels of anxiety may frustrate the therapist. The management and therapy of these patients is often difficult and prolonged. Many physicians are afraid to tackle the delicate issue of thoughts of death and suicide, especially in patients who are demanding, complicated and suffer from a variety of existential dilemmas, because they are afraid of triggering this type of symptomatology. In fact, however, there is no basis for this common belief that inquiring about suicide provokes such behavior. On the contrary, patients are often relieved that the physician is able to understand the magnitude of their suffering, and the inquiry may enhance their commitment to treatment.

The proper use of antidepressants, after a careful diagnostic evaluation which should verify that the patient does not suffer from a bipolar illness or does not belong to the wider bipolar spectrum, is important. Early detection and appropriate treatment of minor mental disorders substantially decrease the risk of subsequently developing major depression (Davidson, 2003; den Boer, 2000; Goodwin, et al., 2001; Rihmer, 1999; Schmitt, et al., 2005; Sheehan, 2002) and decreases the risk of further complications, including suicide. The therapist should have in mind the FDA warning for the use of antidepressants in non-typically unipolar patients (FDA, 2006).

Any physician who accepts patients with minor mental disorders, and especially non-psychiatrists and GPs who see the vast majority of these patients, should have in mind that it has been reported that nearly 20% of suicides had visited a physician the very day they committed suicide, 40% within the last week, and 66% within the last 3 months before suicide (Rihmer, et al., 2002). These rates are disturbing since the same data suggest that most suicides received no proper treatment. An astonishingly low 3% received antidepressants in adequate dosages and 7% psychotherapy (Isometsa, et al., 1994). Knowledge and subtle changes in everyday clinical practice and attitude may result in a huge difference in suicide prevention. They can make the difference between failure and success. Today the majority of suicides happen outside psychiatric services although they are likely to suffer from a mental disorder. This remains a huge challenge for both medicine and society.

References

Akiskal, H. S. (2001). Dysthymia and cyclothymia in psychiatric practice a century after Kraepelin. *Journal of Affective Disorders*, 62, 17-31.

Alonso, J., Angermeyer, M. C., Bernert, S. et al. (2004). Disability and quality of life impact of mental disorders in Europe: results from the European Study of the Epidemiology of Mental Disorders (ESEMeD) project. *Acta Psychiatrica Scandinavica*, Supplement, 38-46.

Balazs, J., Benazzi, F., Rihmer, Z. et al. (2006). The close link between suicide attempts and mixed (bipolar) depression: implications for suicide prevention. *Journal of Affective Disorders*, 91, 133-138.

Baldwin, D. S. and Polkinghorn, C. (2005). Evidence-based pharmacotherapy of generalized anxiety disorder. *International Journal of Neuropsychopharmacology*, 8, 293-302.

Bernal, M., Haro, J. M., Bernert, S. et al. (2007). Risk factors for suicidality in Europe: results from the ESEMED study. *Journal of Affective Disorders*, 101, 27-34.

Bienvenu, O. J. (2006). Lifetime prevalence of panic disorder is about 5% in the USA. *Evidence-Based Mental Health*, 9, 114.

Blanco, C., Raza, M. S., Schneier, F. R. et al. (2003). The evidence-based pharmacological treatment of social anxiety disorder. *International Journal of Neuropsychopharmacology*, 6, 427-442.

Bondy, B., Buettner, A. and Zill, P. (2006). Genetics of suicide. *Molecular Psychiatry*, 11, 336-351.

Brown, G. and Goodwin, F. (1984). Diagnostic, clinical and personality characteristics of aggressive men with low 5-HIAA. *Clinical Neuropharmacology*, 7, S408-S409.

Chioqueta, A. P. and Stiles, T. C. (2003). Suicide risk in outpatients with specific mood and anxiety disorders. *Crisis*, 24, 105-112.

Coccaro, E. (1989). Central serotonin and impulsive aggression. *British Journal of Psychiatry*, 155, 52-62.

Cox, B. J., Direnfeld, D. M., Swinson, R. P. et al. (1994). Suicidal ideation and suicide attempts in panic disorder and social phobia. *American Journal of Psychiatry*, 151, 882-887.

Davidson, J. R. (2003). Pharmacotherapy of social phobia. *Acta Psychiatrica Scandinavica*, Supplement, 65-71.

Den Boer, J. A. (2000). Social anxiety disorder/social phobia: epidemiology, diagnosis, neurobiology, and treatment. *Comprehensive Psychiatry*, 41, 405-415.

Depue, R. and Spoont, M. (1986). Conceptualizing a serotonin trait: a behavioral dimension of constraint. *Annals of the New York Academy of Sciences*, 487, 47-62.

FDA (2006). http://www.fda.gov/cder/drug/antidepressants/default.htm. (accessed 16 October 2006).

Friedman, S., Smith, L. and Fogel, A. (1999). Suicidality in panic disorder: a comparison with schizophrenic, depressed, and other anxiety disorder outpatients. *Journal of Anxiety Disorders*, 13, 447-461.

Furukawa, T. A., Streiner, D. L. and Young, L. T. (2001). Is antidepressant-benzodiazepine combination therapy clinically more useful? A meta-analytic study. *Journal of Affective Disorders*, 65, 173-177.

Gabbard, G. (2005). *Psychodynamic psychiatry in clinical practice*. Washington, DC: American Psychiatric Press.

Goodwin, R. and Olfson, M. (2001). Treatment of panic attack and risk of major depressive disorder in the community. *American Journal of Psychiatry*, 158, 1146-1148.

Goodwin, R., Olfson, M., Feder, A. et al. (2001). Panic and suicidal ideation in primary care. *Depression and Anxiety*, 14, 244-246.

Goodwin, R. D. and Roy-Byrne, P. (2006). Panic and suicidal ideation and suicide attempts: results from the National Comorbidity Survey. *Depresion and Anxiety*, 23, 124-132.

Gould, M. S., King, R., Greenwald, S. et al. (1998). Psychopathology associated with suicidal ideation and attempts among children and adolescents. *Journal of the American Academy of Child and Adolescent Psychiatry*, 37, 915-923.

Henriksson, M. M., Aro, H. M., Marttunen, M. J. et al. (1993). Mental disorders and comorbidity in suicide. *American Journal of Psychiatry*, 150, 935-940.

Hornig, C. D. and McNally, R. J. (1995). Panic disorder and suicide attempt: a reanalysis of data from the Epidemiologic Catchment Area study. *British Journal of Psychiatry*, 167, 76-79.

Iancu, I., Dannon, P. N., Poreh, A. et al. (2001). Alexithymia and suicidality in panic disorder. *Comprehensive Psychiatry*, 42, 477-481.

Isometsa, E. T., Henriksson, M. M., Aro, H. M. et al. (1994). Suicide in major depression. *American Journal of Psychiatry*, 151, 530-536.

Keck, M. E. and Strohle, A. (2005). Challenge studies in anxiety disorders. *Handbook of Experimental Pharmacology*, 169, 449-468.

Kessler, R. C., Andrade, L. H., Bijl, R. V. et al. (2002). The effects of co-morbidity on the onset and persistence of generalized anxiety disorder in the ICPE surveys. International Consortium in Psychiatric Epidemiology. *Psychological Medicine*, 32, 1213-1225.

Khan, A., Leventhal, R. M., Khan, S. et al. (2002). Suicide risk in patients with anxiety disorders: a meta-analysis of the FDA database. *Journal of Affective Disorders*, 68, 183-190.

Klein, D. N., Schwartz, J. E., Rose, S. et al. (2000). Five-year course and outcome of dysthymic disorder: a prospective, naturalistic follow-up study. *American Journal of Psychiatry*, 157, 931-939.

Klein, D. N., Shankman, S. A. and Rose, S. (2006). Ten-year prospective follow-up study of the naturalistic course of dysthymic disorder and double depression. *American Journal of Psychiatry*, 163, 872-880.

Lima, M. S. and Moncrieff, J. (2000). Drugs versus placebo for dysthymia. *Cochrane Database of Systematic Reviews*, CD001130.

Markowitz, J. C., Kocsis, J. H., Bleiberg, K. L. et al. (2005). A comparative trial of psychotherapy and pharmacotherapy for "pure" dysthymic patients. *Journal of Affective Disorders*, 89, 167-175.

Mathew, S. J., Coplan, J. D. and Gorman, J. M. (2001). Management of treatment-refractory panic disorder. *Psychopharmacology Bulletin*, 35, 97-110.

Merikangas, K. (2005). Anxiety disorders: epidemiology. In B. Sadock and V. Shadock (Eds.) *Comprehensive textbook of psychiatry*, pp. 1720-1728. Philadelphia: Lippincott Williams and Wilkins.

Nelson, E. C., Grant, J. D., Bucholz, K. K. et al. (2000). Social phobia in a population-based female adolescent twin sample: co-morbidity and associated suicide-related symptoms. *Psychological Medicine*, 30, 797-804.

Nordstrom, P., Samuelsson, M., Asberg, M. et al. (1994). CSF 5-HIAA predicts suicide risk after attempted suicide. *Suicide and Life-Threatening Behavior*, 24, 1-9.

Ormel, J., VonKorff, M., Ustun, T. B. et al. (1994). Common mental disorders and disability across cultures: results from the WHO Collaborative Study on Psychological Problems in General Health Care. *Journal of the American Medical Association*, 272, 1741-1748.

Ozer, O. A., Kutanis, R., Agargun, M. Y. et al. (2004). Serum lipid levels, suicidality, and panic disorder. *Comprehensive Psychiatry*, 45, 95-98.

Pilowsky, D. J., Olfson, M., Gameroff, M. J. et al. (2006). Panic disorder and suicidal ideation in primary care. *Depression and Anxiety*, 23, 11-16.

Pilowsky, D. J., Wu, L. T. and Anthony, J. C. (1999). Panic attacks and suicide attempts in mid-adolescence. *American Journal of Psychiatry*, 156, 1545-1549.

Regier, D. A., Narrow, W. E., Rae, D. S. et al. (1993). The de facto US mental and addictive disorders service system: epidemiologic catchment area prospective 1-year prevalence rates of disorders and services. *Archives of General Psychiatry*, 50, 85-94.

Rihmer, Z. (1999). Dysthymic disorder: implications for diagnosis and treatment. *Current Opinion in Psychiatry*, 12, 69-75.

Rihmer, Z. (2007). Suicide risk in mood disorders. *Current Opinion in Psychiatry*, 20, 17-22.

Rihmer, Z., Belso, N. and Kiss, K. (2002). Strategies for suicide prevention. *Current Opinion in Psychiatry*, 15, 83-87.

Roy-Byrne, P. P., Craske, M. G. and Stein, M. B. (2006). Panic disorder. *Lancet*, 368, 1023-1032.

Rutz, W. (1992). Prevention of suicide. *Lancet*, 340, 1233-1234.

Sakai, Y., Kumano, H., Nishikawa, M. et al. (2005). Cerebral glucose metabolism associated with a fear network in panic disorder. *Neuroreport*, 16, 927-931.

Samuelsson, M., Jokinen, J., Nordstrom, A. L. et al. (2006). CSF 5-HIAA, suicide intent and hopelessness in the prediction of early suicide in male high-risk suicide attempters. *Acta Psychiatrica Scandinavica*, 113, 44-47.

Sareen, J., Cox, B. J., Afifi, T. O. et al. (2005a). Anxiety disorders and risk for suicidal ideation and suicide attempts: a population-based longitudinal study of adults. *Archives of General Psychiatry*, 62, 1249-1257.

Sareen, J., Houlahan, T., Cox, B. J. et al. (2005b). Anxiety disorders associated with suicidal ideation and suicide attempts in the National Comorbidity Survey. *Journal of Nervous and Mental Disease*, 193, 450-454.

Schmidt, N. B., Woolaway-Bickel, K. and Bates, M. (2001). Evaluating panic-specific factors in the relationship between suicide and panic disorder. *Behavior Research and Therapy*, 39, 635-649.

Schmitt, R., Gazalle, F. K., Lima, M. S. et al. (2005). The efficacy of antidepressants for generalized anxiety disorder: a systematic review and meta-analysis. *Revista Brasileira de Psiquiatria*, 27, 18-24.

Sheehan, D. V. (2002). The management of panic disorder. *Journal of Clinical Psychiatry*, 63, Supplement 14, 17-21.

Starcevic, V., Bogojevic, G., Marinkovic, J. et al. (1999). Axis I and axis II comorbidity in panic/agoraphobic patients with and without suicidal ideation. *Psychiatry Research*, 88, 153-161.

Strauss, J., Birmaher, B., Bridge, J. et al. (2000). Anxiety disorders in suicidal youth. *Canadian Journal of Psychiatry*, 45, 739-745.

Strohle, A. and Holsboer, F. (2003). Stress responsive neurohormones in depression and anxiety. *Pharmacopsychiatry*, 36 Supplement 3, S207-214.

Szadoczky, E., Vitrai, J., Rihmer, Z. et al. (2000). Suicide attempts in the Hungarian adult population: their relation with DIS/DSM-III-R affective and anxiety disorders. *European Psychiatry*, 15, 343-347.

Tripodianakis, J., Markianos, M., Sarantidis, D. et al. (1998). Platelet MAO activity in patients with dysthymic disorder. *Psychiatry Research*, 78, 173-178.

Valentiner, D. P., Gutierrez, P. M. and Blacker, D. (2002). Anxiety measures and their relationship to adolescent suicidal ideation and behavior. *Journal of Anxiety Disorders*, 16, 11-32.

Vickers, K. and McNally, R. J. (2004). Panic disorder and suicide attempt in the National Comorbidity Survey. *Journal of Abnormal Psychology*, 113, 582-591.

Waraich, P., Goldner, E. M., Somers, J. M. et al. (2004). Prevalence and incidence studies of mood disorders: a systematic review of the literature. *Canadian Journal of Psychiatry*, 49, 124-138.

Warshaw, M. G., Dolan, R. T. and Keller, M. B. (2000). Suicidal behavior in patients with current or past panic disorder: five years of prospective data from the Harvard/Brown Anxiety Research Program. *American Journal of Psychiatry*, 157, 1876-1878.

Weissman, M. M., Bland, R. C., Canino, G. J. et al. (1996). The cross-national epidemiology of social phobia: a preliminary report. *International Clinical Psychopharmacology*, 11, Supplement 3, 9-14.

In: Suicide from a Global Perspective: Psychiatric Approaches ISBN: 978-1-61942-267-4
Editors: A. Shrivastava, M. Kimbrell, and D. Lester © 2012 Nova Science Publishers, Inc.

Chapter 14

SUICIDE, PSYCHOSIS AND SEVERE MENTAL DISORDERS

Ajit Avasthi and Anindya Banerjee

INTRODOUCTION

Suicide is a silent epidemic of giant proportions and is an important cause of death among the productive, young population. Psychiatric disorders and suicide are closely related. In various studies, 93%-98% of all individuals who died of suicide were found to have mental illness (Henriksson, et al., 1993; Barraclough, et al., 1974). All major psychiatric illnesses are associated with a higher rate of suicide compared to the general population. There is limited consensus regarding the term "severe mental illness." Although there is agreement regarding the inclusion of psychotic disorders in this group and the exclusion of neurotic and stress-related disorders, affective disorders lie in the penumbra zone. Some studies (Birkenaes, et al., 2006; Bhugra, 2006) have included psychotic disorders (schizophrenia, schizoaffective and bipolar disorder) whereas others (Heikkila, et al., 2004; Rossler, et al., 2006) have also included severe depression and multiple diagnoses as well within the ambit of severe mental disorders. A broad definition would include people with a diagnosis of schizophrenia, major depression, bipolar disorder and some of the personality disorders (Hansson, 2006). However, most research related to severe mental illness is focused on patients with schizophrenia and psychotic disorders. In this review, all psychotic disorders and disorders which are potentially psychotic (bipolar disorder and severe depression) are considered to be part of the severe mental disorders group. These disorders are associated with a significant increase in mortality and lowered life expectancy compared to general population (Rossler, et al., 2005; Angst, et al., 2002).

Key Questions

The key questions which need to be addressed are:

1. How is suicide related to severe mental disorders?
2. What are the distinctive features of suicidal behavior in severe mental disorders?
3. What are the predictors of suicidal behavior in severe mental disorders?
4. What are the cultural differences relevant to suicidal behavior in this group?
5. What are the strategies to prevent suicide in this high-risk group?
6. What should be the role of health professionals and mental health professionals?
7. What are the areas for further research?

CURRENT STATUS

Schizophrenia

The estimates of lifetime suicidal attempt in patients with schizophrenia range from 18% to 55% (Radomsky, et al., 1999). Between 20%-50% of all suicide attempts in these patients result in death, and a history of previous suicide attempts is found in 40% to 61% of cases in patients with schizophrenia who die by suicide (Roy, 1986; Taiminen & Kujari, 1994).

Earlier reviews have reported lifetime rates of completed suicide in schizophrenia between 10%-13%, with a Standardized Mortality Ratio (SMR) of 8.45 (Miles, 1977; Harris & Barraclough, 1998). Recent data indicates that the rate of suicide in schizophrenia has increased over the years (Healy, et al., 2006). More recent studies, using cohort-based curve-fitting techniques have yielded lower lifetime suicide rates of 4%-5% (Inskip, et al., 1998; Palmer, et al., 2005). However, suicide continues to be the chief cause of premature death among individuals with schizophrenia and a significant contributor to the increased mortality and low life expectancy in this group of patients.

Acute Transient Psychosis (ATP)

In a cohort study, 11.3% of patients with early psychosis displayed suicidal behavior over two years, with most occurring in the first year (Verdoux, et al., 2001). However, in another study, in patients participating in an early psychosis program, only 2.9% made an attempt in the year after program entry and 0.4% completed suicide (Addington, et al., 2004).

Very few studies are available specifically on acute transient psychosis. In a prospective 5-year follow up study of patients with ATP, diagnosed as per ICD-10, with comparison groups of schizophrenia and schizoaffective disorder patients, the prevalence of suicidal behavior during the entire course of illness was 35.7%. The rates did not differ from that of schizophrenia and schizoaffective disorder after controlling for the duration of illness (Pillman, et al., 2003).

Mood Disorders

Although it is well accepted that mood disorders are associated with higher risk of suicide and a vast majority of suicides occur in the depressed state, there is no consensus regarding which form of depression (unipolar versus bipolar) is associated with a higher risk of suicide. Most of the earlier studies reported higher suicide rates in unipolar depression compared to bipolar depression (Angst, et al., 2002; Harris & Barraclough, 1997). However, this finding has been challenged of late. Earlier studies indicating higher rates in unipolar depression have been criticized for failing to control for a change in diagnosis during the follow-up from unipolar depression to bipolar disorder. Reviews (e.g., Harris & Barraclough, 1997) also did not consider the bipolar–II category separately. In the light of new data and a broadening of the bipolar spectrum to include many cases which would have been previously classified as unipolar, it appears that patients with bipolar disorders are at higher risk of attempted and completed suicide than patients with unipolar major depression. After pooling the data from six studies, the lifetime prevalence of attempted suicide was 17% in bipolar disorder-I and 24% in bipolar disorder-II as opposed to 12% in unipolar depression (Rihmer & Kiss , 2002). Moreover, the high lethality of suicidal acts in bipolar disorder patients is indicated by a much lower ratio of attempts to suicide (approximately 3:1) than in the general population (approximately 30:1) (Baldessarini, et al., 2006). However, since overall prevalence of unipolar depression is about fivefold more than bipolar depression, unipolar depression remains the single major contributor to suicide numerically.

DETERMINANTS OF SUICIDE IN SEVERE MENTAL ILLNESS

Schizophrenia and Psychotic Disorders

The question that has intrigued physicians and mental health professionals is which patient with psychosis is going to commit suicide? Unfortunately, there is no clear answer. Researchers have tried to answer this question through risk factor determination, mostly on patients with schizophrenia. The risk factors for suicide in schizophrenia have been well researched. Many are similar to those in the general population, but some are specific to the disease (Table 14-1).

In one longitudinal follow-up study of 163 patients with schizophrenia, the 13 patients who died by suicide were predominantly male and had a later onset of illness, less chronic illness, better premorbid functioning, greater ability for abstract and conceptual thinking and fewer negative symptoms but more severe delusions and suspiciousness (Dingman & McGlashan, 1986). Other high risk factors include living alone, single status, white male patients with chronic symptoms, a relatively high IQ, and a gradual onset of illness (Reid, 1998).

When compared to other illnesses, suicide in schizophrenia can occur at any point during the course and over a large age range. Significant life events were seen less often before suicide in individuals with schizophrenia than in those with other diagnoses (46% vs 83%, respectively). Life events in the form of recent losses were associated with suicide risk, but the effect does not appear to be disease-specific.

Table 14.1. Risk factors for suicide in schizophrenia

General risk factors
1. Male
2. Depression, hopelessness
3. Suicidal ideation and history of suicide attempts
4. Poor social support
5. Recent loss
6. Current or past substance abuse
7. Family history of suicide

Disease-specific risk factors
1. Recent discharge, poor functioning at discharge
2. Awareness of illness and disability
3. Motor restlessness
4. Depressed mood and hopelessness
5. Prominent positive symptoms

In one study, the combination of depression, younger age and traumatic stress explained 38 % of the variance in suicidality ratings in a general prediction model (Schwartz & Cohen, 2000).

In a recent review, Hawton, et al. (2005) affirmed that affective symptoms, agitation or motor restlessness and awareness of disability are more important determinants of suicide in schizophrenia than the core psychotic symptoms.

The majority of schizophrenic patients who commit suicide were previously hospitalized in a psychiatric ward. In one study, this proportion was found to be 96.7% (Heilä, et al., 1997). A significant proportion of patients commit suicide while hospitalized. Approximately 25% of schizophrenic patients who committed suicide do so while still hospitalized (Roy, 1986). Patients with schizophrenia who were admitted recently are at higher risk for suicide (Pompili, et al., 2005). However, the majority of suicides (60%-75%) in psychotic patients take place outside hospital, indicating that limiting safeguards to inpatient services is not enough.

Suicide is often unexpected and occurs with greater aggression and lethality. Suicide is most often performed with methods such as jumping in front of trains, trams or road traffic, jumping off buildings, hanging and drowning (Shah & Ganesvaran, 1999). In inpatients, hanging is most common method of suicide (comprising 53%), followed by jumping (17%). Outside hospital, in the West, use of guns constitutes the largest group (43%), followed by hanging (15%), poison (11%) and jumping (10%). Firearms as agents of suicide are rare in developing nations owing to limited availability. Hanging and poisoning are the usual measures adopted (Pompili, et al., 2005).

There is a marked reduction in suicidal behavior with recovery, so that suicidal behavior is greatest during the acute episode and decreases significantly with a reduction in psychotic symptomatology (Tarrier, et al., 2006). Suicidal ideation in psychosis appears to be an understandable, mood-driven process, often related to the distress of positive symptoms, rather than being of irrational or psychotic origin (Fialko, et al., 2006).

Few studies have examined suicidality separately in schizoaffective disorders. In one study, out of the 159 patients with schizoaffective disorder, 43% and 27% reported suicide attempts and suicidal ideation, respectively, which was greater than that in the schizophrenia group of 454 patients (27% and 26%, respectively) (Radomsky, et al., 1999). As in schizophrenia, depression was closely associated with suicide. The high suicide rate may be explained by the concomitant depression which is an integral part of the schizo-depressive episodes.

Effect of Symptom Domains of Schizophrenia

It has long been thought that command hallucinations constitute an important risk factor for suicide in schizophrenia. However, research is divided in this regard. Available studies have small samples, making it difficult to detect differences in rates of suicide or suicide attempts between patient groups. Moreover, the role of command hallucinations can be determined only in cases where suicide attempts have not resulted in death. There is research which has supported its role as a trigger for suicides (Zisook, et al., 1995; Juninger, 1995; Kasper, et al., 1996), whereas other research has refuted this on grounds that patients rarely obey commands and the association with suicide risk is at best weak.

Several studies have reported that a significant number of individuals (44%) obey the hallucinations, especially when they recognize the voice. In one study, 80% of those who experienced command hallucinations had made at least one attempt in response to the hallucinations. (Harkavy-Friedman, et al., 2003). Hence, there seems to be wisdom in the traditional teaching which implicates command hallucinations as a harbinger of suicidal behavior.

The most consistent finding regarding suicide in schizophrenia is the presence of depression around the time of suicidal act. Among the depressive symptoms, a sense of worthlessness (or low self-esteem) and hopelessness were specifically associated with elevated suicide risk. Agitation (or motor restlessness) was also a significant risk factor. It was not possible to distinguish between depressive symptoms that were part of the schizophrenic illness from that of post-schizophrenic depression or comorbid major depressive episode. The importance of depression as a risk factor is further supported by the positive association of risk with a family history of affective disorders (Hawton, et al., 2005).

Negative symptoms, when present as a prominent component of the illness, are associated with a significantly lower long-term risk of suicide among patients with schizophrenia. This is consistent with the much lower risk of suicide in deficit schizophrenia. On the other hand, two positive symptoms (suspiciousness and delusions) are associated with elevated long-term risk for suicide (Fenton, et al., 1997). Insight into the nature of the illness is not associated with suicide and is not a reliable predictor of suicide attempts (Hawton, 2005; Yen, et al., 2002).

Schizophrenia: Suicide Risk and Subtypes

The paranoid subtype of schizophrenia, where positive symptoms prevail and negative symptoms are few, is associated with a suicide risk that is three times greater than that associated with nonparanoid subtypes and eight times greater than the risk associated with the deficit subtype (Pompili, et al., 2005).

Two profiles of high risk inpatients have been identified. The first is that of an acutely psychotic, agitated suicidal patient who suffers from schizophrenia with a deteriorating course of illness. This patient is likely to commit suicide during the early part of the hospital stay. In contrast, the second type of patient is seen as less acutely ill, has strong depressive features and is believed to be a treatment-responder (Sharma, et al., 1998).

Another recent study has suggested two subtypes of "suicidal schizophrenia" identified according to suicidal motivation: psychotic motivation and depressive motivation. At one-year follow-up, the subgroup of "depressive motivation" showed comparatively higher depression and hopelessness scores (Acosta, et al., 2006).

First-Episode Psychosis and Early Psychosis

Predictors of suicide in early psychosis include a history of parasuicide before admission, substance misuse, fewer positive and negative symptoms and a longer duration for the first admission (Verdoux, et al., 2001). Suicidal behavior in acute psychosis is associated with the acute episode as opposed to schizophrenia where it is spread throughout the course of the illness (Pillman, et al., 2003).

Mood Disorders

Bipolar Disorder

Suicidal acts often occur early in the illness course and mostly in association with severe depressive and mixed phases of illness, especially following repeated episodes of severe depression (Tondo, et al., 2003). Psychotic symptoms are not associated with suicide risk in bipolar disorder. This is understandable as psychotic symptoms are more often associated with mania than depression, and suicide in the manic phase is rare. Even in depressed patients (bipolar and unipolar), the association between suicide risk and psychotic symptoms is not well established.

A family history of suicide is stronger in bipolar disorder compared to unipolar depression and strongest in the bipolar disorder-II group. When compared with bipolar I patients, bipolar II patients had a higher rate of family history of suicide in first-degree relatives, a higher rate of previous suicide attempts, a higher number of previous suicide attempts per patient, and a higher rate of completed suicide during follow-up (Rihmer & Kiss, 2002).

Within bipolar I disorder, rapid cycling bipolar disorder is characterized by less severe psychotic and suicidal features (Serretti et al, 2002). When compared with patients with major depression, suicide attempters with bipolar disorder reported higher levels of aggression and impulsivity but less hopelessness (Zalsman, et al., 2006).

In a study which used regression analysis to determine the predictors of suicide in bipolar disorder, a history of suicide attempt in bipolar disorder was associated with greater recent suicidal ideation, more psychiatric hospitalizations, more lifetime aggressive traits and an earlier age at onset of a first mood episode (Grunebaum, et al., 2006).

Hostility, a family history of suicide, early onset, extent and severity of depressive symptoms, mixed state, rapid cycling, comorbid Axis I disorders and substance abuse were correlates of non-fatal suicide attempts. Fatal suicidal attempts in bipolar disorder were associated with previous suicidal attempts and hopelessness (Hawton, et al., 2005; Galfalvy, 2006).

In summary, suicidal acts are common in bipolar disorders and typically occur early in the course and in association with severe depressive or mixed states.

The diagnostic category of bipolar II disorder (depression with hypomania but not with mania) carries the maximum risk. The available evidence indicates that aggressive traits, early treatment of mood disorders, especially major depressive and mixed episodes, and substance abuse are potential targets for suicide prevention in bipolar disorder.

Severe Major Depression

Suicidal ideation and attempted suicide are important indicators of the severity of depression. Similarly, psychotic depression is also accepted as a severe form of depression. However, the relationship between psychotic symptoms and suicidal behavior in depression is controversial. Several studies have supported a relationship between psychotic symptoms and suicidality in depression (Roose, et al., 1983; Johnson, et al., 1991; Hori, et al., 1993; Thakur, et al., 1999) whereas many others have failed to find such a link (Fawcett, et al., 1987; Black, et al., 1988; Malone, et al., 1995; Lykouras, et al., 2002).

Isometsä et al. (1994) carried out a psychological autopsy study of major depressive suicides. No differences emerged between the psychotic and nonpsychotic subgroups in sociodemographic features, comorbidity, clinical history or communication of suicide intent. However, the psychotic suicides were more likely to have used violent suicide methods. Suicide risk in patients with major depressive disorder is highest immediately after hospital discharge (Buchholtz-Hansen, et al., 1993).

Psychomotor retardation, a common concomitant of severe depression, can be a confounding factor in the assessment of suicidal behavior. Retardation may preclude suicidal behavior temporarily, thus giving rise to an apparent rise in suicidality after partial improvement in depression. However, psychomotor retardation is unlikely to mask suicidal ideation.

Assessment

The need for detailed clinical evaluation for suicidal ideation and suicidal behavior must be a part of every psychiatric evaluation and cannot be overemphasized. When assessing a patient with psychosis, in addition to a general enquiry, special attention should be given to risk factors such as depression, positive symptoms, agitation, hostility and command hallucinations.

The disease specific instruments available for assessment of suicidal ideation in psychosis include the Schizophrenia Suicide Risk Scale (SSRS) (Taiminen, et al., 2001) and the InterSePT Scale for Suicidal Thinking (ISST) (Lindenmayer, et al., 2003). Generic suicide assessment scales like the Beck Scale for Suicide Ideation has been validated for use in schizophrenia, schizoaffective disorders and bipolar disorders (Pinninti, et al., 2002). In a systematic review of suicide rating scales in schizophrenia, ISST was considered to be the only scale based on sound methodology and having clinical relevance (Preston & Hansen, 2005).

Management

The management of a suicidal patient with severe mental illness begins with a thorough clinical assessment, risk stratification and institution of appropriate management, usually in an inpatient setting. Empirical short-term interventions effective for all mental disorders for managing acute suicidal risk include close clinical supervision, rapid hospitalization, and electroconvulsive therapy (Baldessarini, et al., 2006). The following discussion will focus mainly on long-term management strategies and prevention.

Schizophrenia and Schizoaffective Disorders

A multi-center, randomized, international, parallel group study comparing the risk for suicidal behavior treated with clozapine versus olanzapine was conducted on 980 patients with schizophrenia or schizoaffective disorder. In this study, clozapine emerged as superior to olanzapine in preventing suicide attempts. This effect was independent of concomitant psychotropic medications and differences in the frequency of clinical contact (Glick, et al., 2004; Meltzer, et al., 2003).

The potential decrease in suicide among schizophrenic patients treated with clozapine is estimated to be as high as 85%. Treatment with clozapine is cost-effective, and the significant decrease in the risk of suicide far outweighs the very low risk of mortality from agranulocytosis. Clozapine should be considered for treatment of both neuroleptic-resistant and neuroleptic-responsive patients with schizophrenia and schizoaffective disorder who have persistent suicidal thoughts or behavior (Meltzer, 1998).

Treatment of depression in schizophrenia is of paramount importance. Antidepressants should be used when the depressive symptoms fulfill the criteria for a diagnosis of depressive syndrome. Some concerns were raised regarding an increase in suicide risk with the selective serotonin reuptake inhibitors (SSRIs), but there is no evidence to show that suicide or suicidality is increased by treatment with specific types of antidepressants in patients with depression (American Psychiatric Association, 2003).

Typical antipsychotics may also be associated with adverse effects, including extrapyramidal neurological side effects and possible worsening of depression as a result of the induction of akathisia (Meltzer, et al., 2003, Shear, et al., 1983). Atypical antipsychotics are devoid of such side-effects and are more efficacious than classical neuroleptics in treating depressive symptoms (Moller, 2005).

Early Psychosis: Can Early Intervention Prevent Suicide?

A recent study reported on the impact of a prevention program focusing on the early detection of psychosis and treatment engagement. Melle et al. (2006) concluded that the rate and severity of suicidal behavior were decreased with this early detection program relative to communities without this program.

In another study, whereas 15.1% of the sample had attempted suicide prior to entry into an early psychosis program, only 2.9% made an attempt in the year after program entry and 0.4% completed suicide (Addington, et al., 2004). These findings imply that programs may reduce the suicidal behavior in this high-risk population. However, the findings are difficult to generalize as the prevalence of suicide in the program patients was low. Harkavy-Friedman (2006) emphasized that, when people are educated about psychosis, they are more likely to seek treatment early, which in turn may lead to decreased morbidity and mortality, including suicide.

Bipolar Disorders

There is strong evidence that long-term maintenance treatment with lithium is associated with major reductions in the risk of both suicide and suicide attempts in patients with bipolar disorder, and there is moderate evidence for similar risk reductions in patients with recurrent major depressive disorder (American Psychiatric Association, 2003). A recent meta-analysis of available studies of suicide rates with versus without long-term lithium maintenance treatment found a statistically significant decrease in suicidal acts (i.e., suicide or suicide attempts) of almost 14-fold. For suicide, lithium maintenance treatment was associated with an 80%–90% decrease in risk, whereas the reduction in suicide attempt rates was more than 90% and was also associated with lower lethality (increased attempt/suicide ratio) (Baldessarini, et al., 2003).

Specific anticonvulsants, such as valproate and lamotrigine, have been shown to be efficacious in treating episodes of mania and bipolar depression, respectively, but there is no clear evidence that any anticonvulsant (valproate, carbamazepine, lamotrigine) alters the rates of suicide or suicidal behaviors (Baldessarini, et al., 2006).

Major Depression

There is equivocal evidence regarding the efficacy of antidepressants in preventing suicide in patients with major depression. Indirect evidence supporting the role of antidepressants in suicide prevention include decreasing suicide rates associated with increasing prescription rates of antidepressants in several countries (Mann, et al., 2005). However, whether such decrease can be attributed to the use of antidepressants alone is doubtful. Meta-analyses of randomized controlled trials have failed to detect any benefit for suicidal behavior in studies of antidepressants in mood disorders (Fergusson, et al., 2005; Gunnel, et al., 2005; Khan, et al., 2003).

The Role of Electroconvulsive Therapy

ECT may be used in patients who are acutely suicidal, in depressive disorders as well as in suicidal patients with schizophrenia, schizoaffective disorder and mixed or manic episodes of bipolar disorder, as it reduces short-term suicidal ideation (Kellner, et al., 2005; Prudic, et al., 1999). It may also be used in suicidal individuals during pregnancy. Since there is no evidence of a long-term reduction of suicide risk with ECT, continuation or maintenance treatment with pharmacotherapy or with ECT is recommended after a course of ECT (American Psychiatric Association, 2003).

Psychosocial Interventions

In suicidal patients, means restriction has met with success in many parts of the world. Although substitution is prevalent, a pragmatic approach towards means restriction may be an effective measure, particularly against the use of lethal methods. Similarly, alcohol restriction is also a useful strategy in reducing the risk of suicide.

It is important to provide more intensive support in the high-risk periods such as following a loss, hospital discharge, conflict with family and failure in life or during post-psychotic depression. There are a few studies that have used structured psychotherapy for the prevention of suicide in psychosis. In one such study, no beneficial effect was reported with cognitive behavior therapy or supportive therapy on suicidal behavior in recent-onset patients with schizophrenia (Tarrier et al., 2006).

Cultural Perspectives: Transcultural Studies

Several studies have shown that cultural variables have a significant impact on the epidemiology of suicide. In a comparison of rates of suicidal behavior in psychotic patients of Caribbean and British White origin, patients of Caribbean origin had a lower risk of suicidal behavior than British Whites. However, the difference was not significant in those under 35 years of age, suggesting that the protective effect of Caribbean origin is disappearing in younger generations (McKenzie, et al., 2003). A study from China (Philips, et al., 2004) demonstrated that cultural differences have a significant impact on the epidemiological pattern of suicide. Contrary to what is observed elsewhere, the prevalence of both schizophrenia and suicide in China was higher in women than in men.

In an Indo-USA joint study of patients with schizophrenia or schizoaffective disorder, a diagnosis of schizoaffective disorder, a history of depression, pattern of symptoms and educational status were significantly associated with suicide attempts in the American sample but not in the Indian sample. Suicide rates were significantly lower in the Indian sample, mirroring the pattern in the general population (Bhatia, et al., 2006).

However, not all studies have found cultural differences in determinants of suicide. In a population-based case-control study from India employing the psychological autopsy technique, it was found that presence of an Axis I disorder, a family history of psychopathology and recent life events were all found to be significant risk factors. This suggests that risk factors for completed suicide are universal across countries and cultures (Vijaykumar, et al., 1999).

Suicide rates in Asia are low compared to Western countries, and this effect is carried over to severe mental disorders as well. However, a part of this gap may be due to the underreporting of suicide owing to the intense stigma associated with it. In China, such underestimation may be more common in rural populations and in males (Ran & Chen, 2004).

The above findings indicate that cultural differences exist in suicidal behavior and the determinants and have implications for suicide prevention. Findings from one culture cannot be reliably generalized to other cultures.

This also points out the need for more research from developing nations, as policy makers there have to depend largely on Western data while framing measures to tackle the problem of suicide. While some universal strategies can be implemented (e.g., treatment of Axis I disorders and increased surveillance after stressful life events), cultural needs and mores should be considered while framing policies to counter suicide.

The Role of Professionals

Most patients with suicidal ideation report their ideations to physicians, most commonly primary care physicians. Several studies (Anderson, 1973; Fenton, 1992; Roy, et al., 1986) have found that a high percentage of patients with schizophrenia who complete suicide were seen by an apparently unsuspecting clinician a few days just prior to death (Fenton, et al, 1997).

Hence, if the physician is sensitive to the risk and can assess and intervene adequately, most suicides can be averted. Intervention may consist of identification and treatment of the mental illnesses, identification of high-risk groups, and addressing specific problems through pharmacological and non-pharmacological interventions or referral to a specialist.

Health professionals also have an important role to play in crisis intervention and helplines where they can act as leaders, trainers or contact persons. Other intermediate-term measures include promoting education about suicide with an emphasis on preventability, reducing the stigma of mental illness through adequate treatment, rehabilitation and education, and advocacy of legal enforcement regarding the availability of medications and substances with high lethality, firearms and drugs of abuse.

In the long run, health professionals, lay counselors and teachers need to be adequately trained and sensitized to deal with mental illness and identify risk factors for suicide. They need to act as watchdogs for the media which often sensationalizes suicide or portrays effective treatment measures like ECT in a poor light. Finally, undergraduate curricula in medical and nursing training should be such that professionals are equipped to deal with suicide.

FUTURE RESEARCH

The Neurobiology of Suicide

Although substantial work has been done focusing on the neurobiology of psychosis as well as suicide, there are no consistent data to suggest a common substrate. More research is warranted in this area.

Early Psychosis and Other Psychotic Disorders

More research is needed on acute transient psychosis, schizoaffective disorder and subtypes of schizophrenia. Initial studies on the impact of early detection and intervention programs in psychosis on suicide have yielded promising results. They need to be replicated in larger samples and across cultures.

Risk Factors and Protective Factors

More data are needed on determining factors that are associated with modifying short-term risk (days to weeks), rather than intermediate or lifetime risk. Researchers should also address the effect of co-existence of multiple risk factors - whether they have an additive or a synergistic effect? Emphasis should be on modifiable risk factors and protective factors (factors reducing risk).

Treatment

In drugs with demonstrated efficacy (lithium and clozapine), streamlining efficacious blood levels is necessary. Newer and safer agents need to be tried and tested in clinical trials. Long-term treatment after ECT needs further research. More studies are required on the application of psychotherapies alone and in combination with pharmacotherapy in the prevention of suicide in severe mental illness.

Conclusion

Suicide is more prevalent in patients with severe mental disorders as compared with the general population and is the major cause of premature death in these patients. The main predictors of risk of suicide in patients with psychosis are affective symptoms or syndromes, suicidal thoughts, threats or behavior, poor adherence to treatment, fear of the impact of illness on mental functioning, and drug misuse. Prevention of suicide is, therefore, likely to result from active treatment of affective symptoms and syndromes, improving adherence to treatment, use of medications such as clozapine and lithium or treatments such as ECT that may have special anti-suicidal effects, and maintaining special vigilance in patients with risk factors. Understanding cultural variations in suicidal behavior and tailoring prevention strategies to suit the target population is likely to be fruitful. Primary health-care physicians can have a tremendous impact through the early detection of suicidal ideation and timely intervention. Mental health professionals have an important role in education, training, decreasing stigma, and managing difficult to treat cases.

Further studies should be conducted in the areas of neurobiology and genetics of suicidal behavior, suicide in psychotic disorders other than schizophrenia and in early psychosis, short-term predictors of suicide risk, protective factors in suicide, and the components of psychological therapies effective in preventing suicide.

References

Acosta, F. J., Aguilar, E. J., Cejas, M. R., et al. (2006). Are there subtypes of suicidal schizophrenia? A prospective study. *Schizophrenia Research*, 86, 215–220.

Addington, J., Williams, J., Young, J., et al. (2004). Suicidal behaviour in early psychosis. *Acta Psychiatrica Scandinavica*, 109, 116–120.

American Psychiatric Association (APA). (2003). Practice guideline for the assessment and treatment of patients with suicidal behaviours. APA. http://www.psych.org/psych_pract/treatg/pg/prac_guide.cfm

Anderson, N. P. (1973). Suicide in schizophrenia. *Perspectives in Psychiatric Care,* 11, 106-112.

Angst, F., Stassen, H. H., Clayton, P. J., et al. (2002). Mortality of patients with mood disorders: follow-up over 34–38 years. *Journal of Affective Disorders*, 68,167–181.

Baldessarini, R. J., Tondo, L., Davis, P., et al. (2006). Decreased risk of suicides and attempts during long-term lithium treatment: a meta-analytic review. *Bipolar Disorders*, 8, 625–639.

Baldessarini, R .J., Tondo, L., Hennen, J., et al. (2003). Lithium treatment and suicide risk in major affective disorders: update and new findings. *Journal of Clinical Psychiatry*, 64 (supplement 5), 44–52.

Baldessarini, R. J., Pompili, M., Tondo, L., et al. (2006). Suicide in bipolar disorder: risks and management. *CNS*, 11, 465-471.

Barraclough, B., Bunch, J., Nelson, B., et al. (1974). A hundred cases of suicide: clinical aspects. *British Journal of Psychiatry*, 125, 355–373.

Bhatia, T., Thomas, P., Semwal, P., et al. (2006). Differing correlates for suicide attempts among patients with schizophrenia or schizoaffective disorder in India and USA. *Schizophrenia Research,* 86, 208–214.

Bhugra, D. (2006). Severe mental illness across cultures. *Acta Psychiatrica Scandinavica*, 113(Supplement 429), 17–23.

Birkenaes, A. B., Sogaard, A. J., Engh, J. A., et al. (2006). Sociodemographic characteristics and cardiovascular risk factors in patients with severe mental disorders compared with the general population. *Journal of Clinical Psychiatry*, 67, 425-433.

Black, D. W., Winokur, G., Nasrallah, A., et al. (1988). Effect of psychosis on suicide risk in 1593 patients with unipolar and bipolar affective disorders. *American Journal of Psychiatry,* 145, 849–852.

Buchholtz-Hansen, P. E., Wang, A. G., Kragh-Sorensen, P., et al. (1993). Mortality in major affective disorder: relationship to subtype of depression. *Acta Psychiatrica Scandinavica*, 87, 329–335

Dingman, C. W., & McGlashan, T. H. (1986). Discriminating characteristics of suicides: Chestnut Lodge follow-up sample including patients with affective disorder, schizophrenia and schizoaffective disorder. *Acta Psychiatrica Scandinavica*, 74, 91-97.

Fawcett, J., Scheftner, W., Clark, D., et al. (1987). Clinical predictors of suicide in patients with major affective disorders: a controlled prospective study. *American Journal of Psychiatry*, 144, 35–40.

Fenton ,W. S. (1992). The suicide of Maigold Perry: comment. *Suicide & Life Threatening Behavior*, 22, 402-405.

Fenton, W. S., McGlashan, T. H., Victor, B. J., et al. (1997). Symptoms, subtype, and suicidality in patients with schizophrenia spectrum disorders. *American Journal of Psychiatry,* 154, 199-204.

Fergusson, D., Doucette, S., Glass, K. C., et al. (2005). Association between suicide attempts and selective serotonin reuptake inhibitors: systematic review of randomised controlled trials. *British Medical Journal*, 330, 396.

Fialko, L., Freeman, D., Bebbington, P. E., et al. (2006). Understanding suicidal ideation in psychosis: findings from the Psychological Prevention of Relapse in Psychosis (PRP) trial. *Acta Psychiatrica Scandinavica*, 114, 177-186.

Galfalvy, H., Oquendo, M. A., Carballo, J. J., et al. (2006). Clinical predictors of suicidal acts after major depression in bipolar disorder: a prospective study. *Bipolar Disorders*, 8, 586-595.

Glick, I. D., Zaninelli, R., Hsu, C., et al. (2004). Patterns of concomitant psychotropic medication use during a 2-year study comparing clozapine and olanzapine for the prevention of suicidal behavior. *Journal of Clinical* Psychiatry, 65, 679-685.

Grunebaum, M. F., Ramsay, S. R., Galfalvy, H. C., et al. (2006). Correlates of suicide attempt history in bipolar disorder: a stress-diathesis perspective. *Bipolar Disorders*, 8, 551–557.

Gunnell, D., Saperia, J., Ashby, D., et al. (2005). Selective serotonin reuptake inhibitors (SSRIs) and suicide in adults: meta-analysis of drug company data from placebo controlled, randomised controlled trials submitted to the MHRA's safety review. *British Medical Journal,* 330, 385.

Hansson, L. (2006). Determinants of quality of life in people with severe mental illness. *Acta Psychiatrica Scandinavica*,113(Supplement 429), 46–50.

Harkavy-Friedman, J. M. (2006). Can early detection of psychosis prevent suicidal behavior? *American Journal of Psychiatry,* 163, 768-770

Harkavy-Friedman, J. M., Kimhy, D., Nelson, E. A., et al. (2003). Suicide attempts in schizophrenia: the role of command auditory hallucinations for suicide. *Journal of Clinical Psychiatry*, 64, 871–874

Harris, E. C., & Barraclough, B. (1997). Suicide as an outcome for mental disorders. *British Journal of Psychiatry*, 170, 205–228.

Harris, E. C., & Barraclough, B. (1998). Excess mortality of mental disorder. *British Journal of Psychiatry,* 173, 11–53

Hawton, K., Sutton, L., Haw, C., et al. (2005). Schizophrenia and suicide: systematic review of risk factors. *British Journal of Psychiatry*, 187, 9-20.

Healy, D., Harris, M., Tranter, R., et al. (2006). Lifetime suicide rates in treated schizophrenia: 1875-1924 and 1994-1998 cohorts compared. *British Journal of Psychiatry*, 188, 223-228

Heikkila, J., Karlsson, H., Taiminen, T., et al. (2004). Psychodynamic personality profile in first-episode severe mental disorders. *Acta Psychiatrica Scandinavica*, 109, 187–193.

Heila, H., Isometsa, E. T., Henriksson, M. M., et al. (1997). Suicide and schizophrenia: a nationwide psychological autopsy study on age- and sex-specific clinical characteristics of 92 suicide victims with schizophrenia. *American Journal of Psychiatry*, 154, 1235-1242.

Henriksson, M. M., Aro, H. M., Marttunen, M. J., et al. (1993). Mental disorders and comorbidity in suicide. *American Journal of Psychiatry*, 150, 935-940.

Hori, M., Shiraishi, H., Koizumi, J., et al. (1993). Delusional depression and suicide. *Japanese Journal of Psychiatry,* 47, 812–817.

Inskip, H. M., Harris, E. C., Barraclough, B., et al. (1998). Lifetime risk of suicide for affective disorder, alcoholism and schizophrenia. *British Journal of Psychiatry*, 172, 35–37.

Isometsa, E., Henriksson, M., Aro, H., et al. (1994). Suicide in major depression. *American Journal of Psychiatry*, 151, 530-536.

Isometsa, E., Henriksson, M., Aro, H., et al. (1994). Suicide in psychotic major depression. *Journal of Affective Disorders*, 31, 187-191.

Johnson, J., Horwath, E., Weissman, M., et al. (1991). The validity of major depression with psychotic features based on a community study. *Archives of General Psychiatry*, 48, 1075–1081.

Junginger J. (1990). Predicting compliance with command hallucinations. *American Journal of Psychiatry*, 147, 245–247.

Kasper, M. E., Rogers, R., Adams, P. A., et al. (1996). Dangerousness and command hallucinations: an investigation of psychotic inpatients. *Bulletin of the American Academy of Psychiatry & the Law*, 24, 219–224.

Kellner, C. H., Fink, M., Knapp, R., et al. (2005). Relief of expressed suicidal intent by ECT: a consortium for research in ECT study. *American Journal of Psychiatry*, 62, 77-82.

Khan, A., Khan, S., Kolts, R., et al. (2003). Suicide rates in clinical trials of SSRIs, other antidepressants, and placebo: analysis of FDA reports. *American Journal of Psychiatry*, 160, 90-92.

Lindenmayer, J. P ., Czobor, P., Alphs, L., et al. (2003). The InterSePT scale for suicidal thinking reliability and validity. *Schizophrenia Research,* 63, 161– 170.

Lykouras, L., Gournellis, R., Fortos, A., et al. (2002). Psychotic (delusional) major depression in the elderly and suicidal behaviour. *Journal of Affective Disorders*, 69, 225-229.

Malone, K. M., Haas, G. L., Sweeney, J. A., et al. (1995). Major depression and the risk of attempted suicide. *Journal of Affective Disorders*, 34, 173–185.

Mann, J. J., Apter, A., Bertolote, J., et al. (2005). Suicide prevention strategies: a systematic review. *Journal of American Medical Association* , 294, 2064-2074.

Mckenzie, K.,Van Os, J., Samele, C., et al. (2003). Suicide and attempted suicide among people of Caribbean origin with psychosis living in the UK. *British Journal of Psychiatry*, 183, 40-44.

Melle, I., Johannesen, J. O., Friis, S., et al. (2006). Early detection of the first episode of schizophrenia and suicidal behavior. *American Journal of Psychiatry*, 163, 800-804.

Meltzer, H. Y. (1998). Suicide in schizophrenia: risk factors and clozapine treatment. *Journal of Clinical Psychiatry*, 59(Supplement 3), 5-20.

Meltzer, H. Y., Alphs, L., Green, A. I., Altamura, A. C., et al. (2003). Clozapine treatment for suicidality in schizophrenia: International Suicide Prevention Trial (InterSePT). *Archives of General Psychiatry*, 60, 82-91.

Meltzer, H. Y. & Baldessarini, R. J. (2003). Reducing the risk for suicide in schizophrenia and affective disorders. *Journal of Clinical Psychiatry*, 64, 122-129.

Miles, C. P. (1977). Conditions predisposing to suicide: a review. *Journal of Nervous & Mental Disorders*, 164, 231–246.

Moller, H. J. (2005). Occurrence and treatment of depressive comorbidity/cosyndromality in schizophrenic psychoses: conceptual and treatment issues. *World Journal of Biological Psychiatry*, 6, 47-63.

Palmer, B. A., Pankratz, V. S.,Bostwick, J. M., et al. (2005). The lifetime risk of suicide in schizophrenia: a reexamination. *Archives of General Psychiatry*, 62, 247-253.

Phillips, M. R., Yang, G., Li, S., et al. (2004). Suicide and the unique prevalence pattern of schizophrenia in mainland China: a retrospective observational study. *Lancet*, 364, 1062-1068.

Pillmann, F., Balzuweit, S., Haring, A., et al. (2003). Suicidal behavior in acute and transient psychotic disorders. *Psychiatry Research*, 117, 99–209.

Pinninti, N., Steer, R. A., Rissmiller, D. J., et al. (2002). Use of the Beck Scale for Suicide Ideation with psychiatric inpatients diagnosed with schizophrenia, schizoaffective, or bipolar disorders. *Behaviour Research & Therapy*, 40, 1071–1079.

Pompilli, M., Mancinelli, I., Ruberto, A., et al. (2005). Where schizophrenic patients commit suicide: a review of suicide among inpatients and former inpatients. *International Journal of Psychiatry in Medicine*, 35, 171-190.

Preston, E., & Hansen, L. (2002). A systematic review of suicide rating scales in schizophrenia. *Crisis*, 2005, 26, 70-80.

Prudic, J., & Sackeim, H. A. (1999). Electroconvulsive therapy and suicide risk. *Journal of Clinical Psychiatry*, 60(Supplement 2), 104–110.

Radomsky, E. D., Haas, G. L., Mann, J. J., et al. (1999). Suicidal behavior in patients with schizophrenia and other psychotic disorders. *American Journal of Psychiatry*, 56, 590-595.

Ran, M. S. & Chen, E. Y. (2004). Suicide and schizophrenia in China. *Lancet,* 364, 1016.

Reid, S. (1998). Suicide in schizophrenia: a review of the literature. *Journal of Mental Health*, 4, 345-353.

Rihmer ,Z., & Kiss, K. (2002). Bipolar disorders and suicidal behaviour. *Bipolar Disorders*, 4(Supplement 1), 21–25.

Roose, S. P., Glassman, A. H., Walsh, B. T., et al. (1983). Depression, delusions, and suicide. *American Journal of Psychiatry*, 140, 1159–1162.

Rossler, W., Lauber, C., Sartorius, N., et al. (2006). Patients with severe mental illness: a most difficult-to-treat patient population. *Acta Psychiatrica Scandinavica*, 113(Supplement 429), 7–8.

Rossler, W., Salize, H.J., van, O.S. J., et al. (2005). Size of burden of schizophrenia and psychotic disorders. *European Neuropsychopharmacology*, 4, 399-409.

Roy, A. (1986). Suicide in schizophrenia In A. Roy (Ed.) *Suicide*, pp. 97-109. Baltimore: Williams & Wilkins.

Roy, A., Schreiber, J., Mazonson, A., et al. (1986). Suicidal behavior in schizophrenic patients. *Canadian Journal of Psychiatry,* 31, 737-740.

Schwartz, R. C. & Cohen, B. N. (2001). Risk factors for suicidality among clients with schizophrenia. *Journal of Counseling & Development*, 79, 314-319.

Serretti, A., Mandelli, L., Lattuada, E., et al. (2002). Rapid cycling mood disorder: clinical and demographic features. *Comprehensive Psychiatry,* 43, 336-343.

Shah, A., & Ganesvaran, T. (1999). Suicide among psychiatric in-patients with schizophrenia in an Australian mental hospital. *Medicine, Science, & the Law*, 39, 251-259.

Sharma, V., Persad, E., Kueneman, K., et al. (1998). A closer look at inpatient suicide. *Journal of Affective Disorders*, 47, 23-29.

Shear, M. K., Frances, A., Weiden, P., et al. (1983). Suicide associated with akathisia and depot fluphenazine treatment. *Journal of Clinical Psychopharmacology*, 3, 235–236.

Taiminen, T., Huttunena, J., Heila, H., et al. (2001). The Schizophrenia Suicide Risk Scale (SSRS): development and initial validation. *Schizophrenia Research*, 47, 199-213.

Taiminen, T. J. & Kujari, H., et al. (1994). Antipsychotic medication and suicide risk among schizophrenic and paranoid inpatients: a controlled retrospective study. *Acta Psychiatrica Scandinavica*, 90, 247-251.

Tarrier, N., Haddock, G., Lewis, S., et al. (2006). Suicide behaviour over 18 months in recent onset schizophrenic patients: the effects of CBT. *Schizophrenia Research*, 83, 15-27.

Thakur, M., Hays, J., Ranga, K., et al. (1999). Clinical, demographic and social characteristics of psychotic depression. *Psychiatry Research,* 86, 99-106.

Tondo, L., Isacsson, G., Baldessarini, R., et al. (2003). Suicidal behaviour in bipolar disorder: risk and prevention. *CNS Drugs*, 17, 491-511.

Verdoux, H., Liraud, F., Gonzales, B., et al. (2001). Predictors and outcome characteristics with suicidal behaviour in early psychosis: a two-year follow-up of first-admitted subjects. *Acta Psychiatrica Scandinavica*, 103, 347–354.

Vijayakumar, L., & Rajkumar, S. (1999). Are risk factors for suicide universal? A case-control study in India. *Acta Psychiatrica Scandinavica*, 99, 407-411.

Yen, C. F., Yeh, M. L., Chen, C. S., et al. (2002). Predictive value of insight for suicide, violence, hospitalization, and social adjustment for outpatients with schizophrenia: a prospective study. *Comprehensive Psychiatry,* 43, 443-447.

Zalsman, G., Braun, M., Arendt, M., Grunebaum, M. F., et al. (2006). A comparison of the medical lethality of suicide attempts in bipolar and major depressive disorders. *Bipolar Disorders*, 8, 558–565.

Zisook, S., Byrd, D., Kuck, J., et al. (1995). Command hallucinations in outpatients with schizophrenia. *Journal of Clinical Psychiatry*, 56, 462–465.

In: Suicide from a Global Perspective: Psychiatric Approaches ISBN: 978-1-61942-267-4
Editors: A. Shrivastava, M. Kimbrell, and D. Lester © 2012 Nova Science Publishers, Inc.

Chapter 15

SUICIDE IN UNIPOLAR MAJOR DEPRESSION

Konstantinos N. Fountoulakis, Xenia Gonda, and Zoltan Rihmer

INTRODUCTION

The understanding, prediction and prevention of suicidal behavior is one of the most challenging tasks in general, and for psychiatry in particular. Psychological autopsy studies of suicides in the general population has provided the bulk of our knowledge about why people commit suicide. The data have shown that over 90% of suicides have at least one current major (Axis I) mental disorder, often comorbid with others, and major depression (MD) is the mental disorder most related to the manifestation of suicidal behavior (Barraclough, et al., 1974; Henriksson, et al., 1993; Monkman, 1987; Rihmer, 2007; Rihmer, et al., 2002). However, estimates vary from 15% to 70%, and much of this discrepancy is due to differences in the way behaviors are registered, classified and reported, as well as treatment limitations at the time that the study took place (Badawi, et al., 1999; Rich & Runeson, 1992; Rich, et al., 1986; Runeson, 1992).

Most recent psychological autopsy studies using current diagnostic classifications and sound methodology indicate that the rate of current major depressive episode among unselected suicides from the general population is between 59% and 87% and, in spite of the frequent medical contact before the suicide, only a small minority of depressive suicides have received appropriate antidepressant pharmacotherapy, particularly those seen in primary care (Henriksson, et al., 1993; Isometsa, et al., 1994; Luoma, et al., 2002; Rihmer, et al., 2002). It is generally accepted that around 15% of major depressive patients will eventually die from suicide and, additionally, it is reported that close to 10% of patients with late-life depression complete suicide annually (Murphy, 1994).

In the last two decades, the national suicide rates of most European countries, as well as those of the USA and Canada, have declined substantially. This decrease is more pronounced in countries with traditionally high baseline suicide rates and in females, who have major depression more frequently than males and who more often seek medical help for their psychiatric disorders (Isometsa, Aro, et al., 1994b; Luoma, et al., 2002; Rihmer & Akiskal, 2006). The causes of these changes are not known at present, but the available data suggest that more widespread and more appropriate treatment of depressive disorders (which is reflected in the 4-8-fold increase in antidepressant prescriptions in most of these countries) is one of the main contributory factors (Akiskal, et al., 2005; Isometsa, et al., 1994b; Rihmer & Akiskal, 2006).

Research has focused on risk factors, and several have been identified. They include male gender, previous suicide attempt(s), major depression with comorbid mental disorders (especially personality disorders and substance abuse), permanent adverse life-situations and acute psychosocial stressors (Henriksson, et al., 1993; Rihmer, et al., 2002), but their predictive value is far from satisfactory. Although there is some national variation in prevalence, the risk factors for suicidality in depressed patients are reported to be consistent in European countries. They include comorbidity, especially with anxiety and personality disorders, as well as alcohol dependence, but also sociodemographic and psychosocial factors such as being younger, divorced or widowed and experiencing adverse life-situations (Bernal, et al., 2007; Rihmer, 2007; Rihmer, et al., 2002). Although the statistical relationship between the different psychosocial and demographic suicide risk factors and suicidal behavior is well-documented, they have limited value in predicting suicide in individual cases. However, the hierarchical classification of suicide risk factors, such as (1) primary (psychiatric-medical, e.g., depression), (2) secondary (psychosocial, e.g., adverse life-situations), and (3) tertiary (demographic, e.g., male gender), helps clinicians estimate the risk of suicide. The presence of secondary and tertiary suicide risk factors indicate high suicide risk only in the presence of primary risk factors (Rihmer, 2007; Rihmer, et al., 2002).

A large variation of suicide prevalence is observed within the different ethnic groups in the USA, with Puerto Ricans having higher suicide attempt rates compared with other groups (Whites, Blacks, Hispanics, Mexican Americans and Cuban Americans). However, it is important to note that a higher lifetime rate of suicide attempt in different ethnic groups is associated with more frequent lifetime rates of major depression (Oquendo, et al., 2004).

Although psychiatric care for depressed patients is provided in a variety of settings, from traditional large mental hospitals to community health centers, there are few data available concerning the differences between these settings in terms of the prevalence of suicide, the methods used for the suicidal act or its lethality. Much of the variation that is documented can be attributed to the differences in clinical characteristics of the populations in each setting, as well as the population's socio-demographic characteristics. Differences in the therapeutic methods available in each setting may also play a role. It is reported that significantly more suicides in psychiatric care than in medical care had communicated to therapists or staff their intent to commit suicide (59% vs. 19%). In terms of treatment, antidepressants were received by 60% of victims in psychiatric care, but only 16% in medical care (Isometsa, et al., 1994).

Psychopathological Understanding of Unipolar Depression

The traditional psychoanalytic approach recognises the strong relationship between depression and suicidal behavior and considers suicide to be murder or aggression turned inward upon the self. The motivations to commit suicide vary but may include wishes such as the wishes to kill, to be killed and to die, as well as a wish for a reunion with a lost loved one.

Some empirical data suggest that there is a statistically significant correlation between suicide and the anniversary of a parent's death.

Hopelessness is usually considered to be critical to an understanding of suicide in depressed individuals. Hopelessness as a result of continuous frustration because of rigidly held and unrealistic expectations may lead to suicide as the only way out that the individual has (Gabbard, 2005). Although hopelessness could lead to depression, this does not seem to hold true when controlling for the severity of depression, at least in the elderly. Patients who report moderate or severe depression are more likely to have suicidal ideation with increasing hopelessness, whereas hopelessness *per se* seems to have little effect on the level of ideation at mild or lower depression levels (Uncapher, et al., 1998). In other words, hopelessness, guilt and related suicidal behavior in major depression is a state-related, severity-dependent phenomenon, and the recurrence of suicidal ideation across depressive episodes shows a high consistency (Rihmer, 2007; Valtonen, et al., 2005; Williams, et al., 2006).

Apart from behaviors and overt suicidal attempts, thoughts of death and suicidal ideation are common symptoms in depressed patients, both before and after a suicidal attempt. These thoughts are neither simple nor concrete. Many patients may fear that they will die, but do not wish to die, while others seem determined to kill themselves. It is not clear whether these states constitute consecutive phases, or represent distinct symptoms and reflect a qualitatively different underlying psychopathology (Fountoulakis, et al., 2004).

There may be significant differences between males and females that point to different psychological mechanisms underlying suicide. Low social and family support and depersonalization may be associated with suicidal ideation in men, while depressive mood and anxiety may be associated with suicidal ideation in women (Yoshimasu, et al., 2006).

Biological Correlates of Suicide in Unipolar Depression

Studies of the cerebrospinal fluid (CSF) and brain receptors suggest that low brain serotonin activity might play a key role in suicidal behavior.

However, this is also true for depression in general, and research has not clarified this overlap. The precise biological substrate that distinguishes suicidal from nonsuicidal depressives is largely unknown, suggesting that other clinical (e.g., severity of major depression), personality (e.g., impulsiveness) and psychosocial (e.g., acute stressors) factors play an important role.

There are some data suggesting a predictive value for low concentrations of CSF 5-HIAA (Nordstrom, et al., 1994; Samuelsson, et al., 2006). In a recent study, it has been shown that depressed suicide attempters had lower CSF HVA levels compared to depressed non-attempters and to controls, while there was no difference between depressed non-attempters and controls. Thus, it seems that dopaminergic abnormalities might be associated with suicidality but not with depression (Sher, et al., 2006).

Suicidal behavior, like other psychiatric disorders, tends to run in families. Therefore, a family history of suicide in first-degree relatives is a clinically important suicide risk factor, particularly in patients with current major depression (Rihmer, 2007; Rihmer, et al., 2002). Twin and adoption studies have confirmed this, and genetic studies support the involvement of the tryptophan hydroxylase gene (LL and UL genotypes, especially for violent attempters) which is involved in serotonin synthesis (Roy, et al., 1999).

Research suggests that the level of emotional arousal is of prime importance for the expression of aggression towards the self or others. It seems that serotonin activity cannot be linked to aggression when an adequate level of emotional alertness is not present (Coccaro, 1989).

The problem may lay in the imbalance between the inhibition of behavior mediated through serotonin and the level of arousal mediated by catecholamines, particularly by acetylcholine (Brown & Goodwin, 1984; Depue & Spoont, 1986). It is possible that the inhibition of behavior is mediated by serotonin and its release by norepinephrine and dopamine (Depue & Spoont, 1986). This may be the case only for impulsive physical aggression and not for physical aggression in general (Brown, 1982; Coccaro, et al., 1990; Coccaro & Kavoussi, 1995; Mehlman & Higley, 1994).

Several studies have suggested that HPA-axis hyperactivity is a risk factor for suicide in patients with a major depressive disorder, but more recent prospective data from a large sample suggest that this may be true only for severely ill, previously hospitalized, major depressives (Coryell, et al., 2006).

Recent research suggests that low levels of omega-3-fatty acids (an important contributor to central serotonin synthesis) is inversely correlated with the lifetime prevalence of unipolar and bipolar depression (Parker, et al., 2006) and seems to be a powerful predictor of future suicidal behavior in patients with unipolar major depression (Sublette, et al., 2006).

Psychological and Social Correlates

The social and cultural environment plays an important role in the manifestation of suicidal behavior. Specific social parameters like social support networks and religion, may either promote or inhibit the manifestation of suicidal behavior, or modify its expression (Rihmer, et al., 2002).

Research suggests that low levels of social and family support are significantly associated with suicide in men, but not in women, whereas psychological factors, such as depersonalization and anxiety, may be more important for women (Yoshimasu, et al., 2006). A person may experience a variety of losses, including physical losses resulting from poor health, painful illness, sensory deficits, and cognitive decline, social losses such as the death of a spouse and loss of one's work role, and income losses associated with retirement and medical expenses.

These losses, along with chronic stress, may lead to social isolation and reduced social networks, and these in turn may worsen depression and trigger the development of suicidal ideation. This is especially true for the elderly (Osgood, 1982, 1991). The co-existence of a serious somatic disease, such as renal failure and cancer, represents an additional major risk factor for a well-planned suicide attempt (Heikkinen & Lonnqvist, 1995; Kishi, et al., 1996). In most countries, males are over-represented among suicides, and this is particularly true in old age. In younger patients, being divorced or widowed are associated with a higher prevalence of suicide ideation as well as attempts (Bernal, et al., 2007; Sokero, et al., 2005).

In multicultural populations, such as the USA, a difference in the prevalence of lifetime suicide attempts among ethnic groups has been observed. Although there is no clear answer concerning the causes of this, the relationship with lifetime major depression is obvious. However, it is also suggested that it may be a result of differences in the migration process, socioeconomic status, and acculturation (Oquendo, et al., 2004).

THE PREDICTION OF SUICIDE IN UNIPOLAR DEPRESSION

Unipolar depression is traditionally classified into two opposite poles, 'endogenous' and 'neurotic' depression, on the basis of severity, "cause" and impairment (Fountoulakis, et al., 1999a).

Today, the most advanced definition is that of the American Psychiatric Association concerning the 'melancholic' and the 'atypical' features, the presence of psychotic or catatonic symptoms, and seasonal patterns (APA, 1994) and that of the World Health Organization concerning the somatic syndrome (WHO, 1993).

Since the vast majority of unipolar depressives never commit suicide, and more than two-thirds of them never attempt suicide, specific (depression-related) and unspecific (psychosocial) suicide risk factors, must play an important role.

One of the most consistent findings of clinical studies is that psychotic depressed patients are more likely to have used violent suicide methods (guns, hanging or a fall from height) (Isometsa, et al., 1994a), and it has been reported that psychotic depressives have a higher risk for completed suicide than their nonpsychotic counterparts (Angst, et al, 2005). The net severity of depression and time spent in depressive episodes, rather than particular signs or symptoms, seems to correlate strongly with suicidal ideation and suicidal acts (Sokero, et al., 2005; Uncapher, et al., 1998).

Suicidality seems to be a stable feature across episodes independently of the presence or absence of other symptoms except hopelessness and guilt and, of course, the wish to die (Williams, et al., 2006).

A recent prospective follow-up study of 269 major depressives, most of them on antidepressants, showed that, among patients with suicidal ideation at baseline, the decline in suicidal ideation was predicted by earlier declines in the levels of both depressive symptoms and hopelessness (Sokero, et al., 2006).

A relatively newly recognized suicide risk factor in patients with a major depressive episode is the depressive mixed state (three or more simultaneously co-occurring intra-depressive hypomanic symptoms in patients with "unipolar depression").

This shows an overlap with agitated depression, and it has been well-documented that depressive mixed states and agitation increase substantially the risk both of attempted and completed suicide (Akiskal, et al., 2005; Balazs, et al., 2006; Isometsa, et al., 1994b; Rihmer, 2007; Rihmer & Akiskal, 2006).

However, although severity is reported to be one of the strongest correlates of suicide in patients with depressive episodes (Kessing, 2004; Rihmer, 2007), there is no satisfactory criterion for the severity of depression. Some rely on the number of symptoms.

A different approach would be to take into consideration the need for hospital admission and the degree of disability as an index of severity. But again, the definition of disability relates to specific symptoms such as suicidal ideation, anhedonia or fatigue, and so reasoning may be circular. It is difficult to search for syndromes or subtypes that correlate with suicidal ideation since suicidal ideation itself contributes to the definition of syndromes or subtypes, either directly or indirectly (Fountoulakis, et al., 1999b). The clinically most important suicide risk factors in unipolar depression (Rihmer, 2007; Sokero, et al., 2005) are listed in Table 15-1.

Table 15.1. Suicide risk factors in unipolar depression

- Prior suicide attempt
- Current suicidal ideation, wish to die, few reasons for living
- Severe symptomatology (hopelessness, guilt, psychotic features)
- Agitation/depressive mixed state
- Comorbid substance-use, personality disorder, serious somatic illness
- Permanent psychosocial stressors
- Recent (acute) adverse life situations
- Family history of suicide (in 1st and 2nd degree relatives)
- Lack of family/social and medical support.

Early Identification, Management and Outcome

Recent studies on suicides, who had asked for professional help concerning their mental health problem before completing suicide, found that the vast majority of GPs who had examined these patients a few months prior to their completed suicide had prescribed antifatigue agents (e.g., vitamins) and anxiolytics, instead of psychotropic medication (Rutz, 1992). Although early identification is possible, data suggest that the management and treatment of suicidal patients are suboptimal, if not poor (Oquendo, et al., 1999).

Therefore, promoting suicide prevention in patients with major depressive disorders requires an improvement in the training and skills of physicians, especially GPs, in recognizing and treating depression in medical and primary care settings (Isometsa, et al., 1994; Mann, et al., 2005).

Lithium is reported to have a robust anti-suicidal effect, in patients with either unipolar depression or bipolar disorders, and this was further supported after a systematic review of existing data on 32 trials including more than 3,400 patients (Cipriani, et al., 2005). Another comprehensive review of 34 studies involving more than 16,000 unipolar and bipolar patients, also showed a 21-fold risk-reduction for attempted and completed suicide in unipolar and bipolar patients with long-term lithium therapy (Baldessarini, et al., 2003). However, although it is clear that lithium is superior to antidepressants, there is some concern that there is an over-interpretation of data when comparing it to other agents (Connemann, 2006), and the usefulness of lithium use for preventing the recurrence of unipolar depression has not been adequately studied.

Antidepressant medication is the only well-established treatment for major depression, especially for the most severe cases. Proper treatment of depression minimizes the risk for suicide (Akiskal, et al., 2005; Rihmer & Akiskal, 2006; Yerevanian, et al., 2004). However, there are no controlled data to support an anti-suicidal effect for antidepressants, and this is largely because suicidal patients are typically excluded from randomized clinical drug trials because of ethical reasons. Common sense and "uncontrolled" long-term, real-life clinical follow-up studies, including the most severely suicidal unipolar depressives, suggest that antidepressants possess a marked anti-suicidal effect when used with unipolar depressive patients (Angst, et al., 2005; Yerevanian, et al., 2004). Recently, the U.S. Food and Drug Administration issued a warning concerning the use of antidepressants in children and adolescents and possibly in all age groups (FDA). This warning concerned the possible induction of suicidality (thinking and behavior, but not completed suicide) by antidepressants in adolescent depressive patients. This is possibly due to the presence of unrecognized pseudo-unipolar or subthreshold bipolar patients among unipolar patients (Akiskal, et al., 2005; Rihmer & Akiskal, 2006). In these particular patients, as well as in overtly bipolar patients, antidepressant monotherapy may result in, not only rapid cycling, but also mixed states, characterized by agitation, irritability, hostility and impulsivity and, in this state, suicidal ideation may emerge (Balazs, et al., 2006; Rihmer & Akiskal, 2006).

How the Management of Unipolar Depression Can Influence Suicide

Although many physicians are afraid to tackle the delicate issue of thoughts of death and suicide because they are afraid of triggering this type of symptomatology, there is no basis for the common belief that inquiring about suicide provokes such behavior. On the contrary, patients are often relieved that the physician appreciates the magnitude of their suffering.

After approaching the patient and establishing rapport, the most important issue that arises is the diagnosis. The therapist should clarify whether the patient suffers from unipolar depression or belongs to the wider bipolar spectrum. Having in mind the FDA warning for the use of antidepressants in non-typical unipolar patients (FDA, 2006), this diagnostic clarification is of prime importance (Rihmer & Akiskal, 2006).

After firmly establishing a diagnosis of unipolar depression, it is reasonable to accept that depression is causally related to suicide for a great number of suicides. The relationship between successful treatment of depression and a lower risk for suicide could be expected (Rihmer, 2007; Rihmer & Akiskal, 2006; Yerevanian, et al., 2004). However, in everyday clinical practice, the situation is more complex. Research suggests that about 75% of depressed suicides may have a history of psychiatric treatment at some point in their life, and 66% had psychiatric treatment during the last year, but only 50% were receiving psychiatric treatment at the time of suicide, and the rate of specific and adequate antidepressive pharmacotherapy is much lower. (Barraclough, et al., 1974; Henriksson, et al., 1993; Isometsa, et al., 1994a, 1994b, 1994c; Rihmer, et al., 2002; Rutz, 1992).

Regarding contact with the health service system, it has been reported that nearly 20% of suicides had visited a physician the day they committed suicide, 40% had visited him within the last week, and 66% within the last three months before the suicide. These rates are disturbing, since the same data suggest that most depressed suicides received no treatment. An astonishingly low 3% received antidepressants in adequate dosages, and 7% psychotherapy. Another disturbing fact was that there are significant sex differences in current and previous treatment and suicide methods. Males less frequently receive treatment and use violent suicide methods more often (Isometsa, et al., 1994b; Rutz, 1992; Suominen, et al., 1996).

Proper and aggressive treatment of major depression, aiming at achieving full remission, should be the target. Any residual symptoms increase the burden on the patients and their families and give the problem a chronic form which predisposes patients to demoralization and the manifestation of suicidal behavior. In spite of the fact that we can not prevent all suicides, more early identification and more effective acute and long-term treatment of depressive disorders is a key element in preventing suicide in these patients (Mann, et al., 2005).

REFERENCES

Akiskal, H. S., Benazzi, F., Perugi, G., et al. (2005). Agitated "unipolar" depression re-conceptualized as a depressive mixed state: implications for the antidepressant-suicide controversy. *Journal of Affective Disorders*, 85, 245-258.

Angst, J., Angst, F., Gerber-Werder, R., et al. (2005). Suicide in 406 mood-disorder patients with and without long-term medication: a 40 to 44 years' follow-up. *Archives of Suicide Research*, 9, 279-300.

APA. (1994). *Diagnostic and Statistical Manual of Mental Disorders, 4th Edition DSM-IV*. Washington, DC: American Psychiatric Association.

Badawi, M. A., Eaton, W. W., Myllyluoma, J., et al. (1999). Psychopathology and attrition in the Baltimore ECA 15-year follow-up 1981-1996. *Social Psychiatry & Psychiatric Epidemiology*, 34, 91-98.

Balazs, J., Benazzi, F., Rihmer, Z., et al. (2006). The close link between suicide attempts and mixed (bipolar) depression: implications for suicide prevention. *Journal of Affective Disorders*, 91, 133-138.

Baldessarini, R. J., Tondo, L., & Hennen, J. (2003). Lithium treatment and suicide risk in major affective disorders: update and new findings. *Journal of Clinical Psychiatry*, 64(Supplement 5), 44-52.

Barraclough, B., Bunch, J., Nelson, B., et al. (1974). A hundred cases of suicide: clinical aspects. *British Journal of Psychiatry*, 125, 355-373.

Bernal, M., Haro, J. M., Bernert, S., et al. (2007). Risk factors for suicidality in Europe: Results from the ESEMED study. *Journal of Affective Disorders*, 101, 27-34.

Brown, G., & Ebert, M (1982). Aggression, suicide and serotonin: relationships to CSF amine metabolites. *American Journal of Psychiatry*, 139, 741-746.

Brown, G., & Goodwin, F. (1984). Diagnostic, clinical and personality characteristics of aggressive men with low 5-HIAA. *Clinical Neuropharmacology*, 7, S408-S409.

Cipriani, A., Pretty, H., Hawton, K., et al. (2005). Lithium in the prevention of suicidal behavior and all-cause mortality in patients with mood disorders: a systematic review of randomized trials. *American Journal of Psychiatry*, 162, 1805-1819.

Coccaro, E. (1989). Central serotonin and impulsive aggression. *British Journal of Psychiatry*, 155, 52-62.

Coccaro, E., Gabriel, S., & Siever, L. (1990). Buspirone challenge: preliminary evidence for a role for central 5-HT1a receptor function in impulsive aggressive behavior in humans. *Psychopharmacological Bulletin*, 26, 393-405.

Coccaro, E., & Kavoussi, R. (1995). Relationship of prolactin response to d-fenfluramine and ipsapirone challenge correlate with indices of aggression in males with personality disorder. *International Clinical Psychopharmacology*, 10, 177-180.

Coccaro, E., & Kavoussi, R. (1997). Central serotonin activity and aggression: inverse relationship with prolactin response to d-fenfluramine, but not CSF 5-HIAA concentration in human subjects. *American Journal of Psychiatry*, 154, 1430-1435.

Connemann, B. J. (2006). Lithium and suicidality revisited. *American Journal of Psychiatry*, 163, 550..

Coryell, W., Young, E., & Carroll, B. (2006). Hyperactivity of the hypothalamic-pituitary-adrenal axis and mortality in major depressive disorder. *Psychiatry Research*, 142, 99-104.

Depue, R., & Spoont, M. (1986). Conceptualizing a derotonin trait: a behavioral dimension of Constraint. *Annals of the New York Academy of Sciences*, 487, 47-62.

FDA. (2006). http://www.fda.gov/cder/drug/antidepressants. (accessed 16 October 2006).

Fountoulakis, K., Iacovides, A., Nimatoudis, I., et al. (1999a). Comparison of the diagnosis of melancholic and atypical features according to DSM-IV and somatic syndrome according to ICD-10 in patients suffering from major depression. *European Psychiatry*, 14, 426-434.

Fountoulakis, K. N., Iacovides, A., Fotiou, F., et al. (2004). Neurobiological and psychological correlates of suicidal attempts and thoughts of death in patients with major depression. *Neuropsychobiology*, 49, 42-52.

Fountoulakis, K. N., Iacovides, A., Nimatoudis, I., et al. (1999b). Comparison of the diagnosis of melancholic and atypical features according to DSM-IV and somatic syndrome according to ICD-10 in patients suffering from major depression. *European Psychiatry*, 14, 426-433.

Gabbard, G. (2005). *Psychodynamic psychiatry in clinical practice*. Washington, DC: American Psychiatric Press.

Heikkinen, M., & Lonnqvist, J. (1995). Recent life events in elderly suicide: a nationwide study in Finland. *International Psychogeriatrics*, 7, 287-300.

Henriksson, M. M., Aro, H. M., Marttunen, M. J., et al. (1993). Mental disorders and comorbidity in suicide. *American Journal of Psychiatry*, 150, 935-940.

Isometsa, E. T., Aro, H. M., Henriksson, M. M., et al. (1994c). Suicide in major depression in different treatment settings. *Journal of Clinical Psychiatry*, 55, 523-527.

Isometsa, E., Henriksson, M., Aro, H., et al. (1994a). Suicide in psychotic major depression. *Journal of Affective Disorders*, 31, 187-191.

Isometsa, E. T., Henriksson, M. M., Aro, H. M., et al. (1994b). Suicide in major depression. *American Journal of Psychiatry*, 151, 530-536.

Kessing, L. V. (2004). Severity of depressive episodes according to ICD-10: prediction of risk of relapse and suicide. *British Journal of Psychiatry*, 184, 153-156.

Kishi, Y., Robinson, R., & Kosier, J. (1996). Suicidal plans in patients with stroke: comparison between acute-onset and delayed-onset suicidal plans. *International Psychogeriatrics*, 8, 623-634.

Luoma, J. B., Martin, C. E. & Pearson, J. L. (2002). Contact with mental health and primary care providers before suicide: a review of the evidence. *American Journal of Psychiatry*, 159, 909-916.

Mann, J. J., Apter, A., Bertolote, J., et al. (2005). Suicide prevention strategies: a systematic review. *Journal of the American Medical Association*, 294, 2064-2074.

Mehlman, P., & Higley, J. (1994). Low CSF 5-HIAA concentrations and severe aggression and impaired impulse control in nonhuman primates. *American Journal of Psychiatry*, 151, 1485-1491.

Monkman, M. (1987). Epidemiology of suicide. *Epidemiology Reviews*, 9, 51-62.

Murphy, E. (1994). The course and outcome of depression in late life. In L. Schneider, C. Reynolds, B. Lebowitz, et al. (Eds.) *Diagnosis and treatment of depression in late life: Results of the NIH Consensus Development Conference*, pp. 81-98. Washington DC: American Psychiatric Press.

Nordstrom, P., Samuelsson, M., Asberg, M., et al .(1994). CSF 5-HIAA predicts suicide risk after attempted suicide. *Suicide & Life-Threatening Behavior*, 24, 1-9.

Oquendo, M. A., Lizardi, D., Greenwald, S., et al. (2004). Rates of lifetime suicide attempt and rates of lifetime major depression in different ethnic groups in the United States. *Acta Psychiatrica Scandinavica*, 110, 446-451.

Oquendo, M. A., Malone, K. M., Ellis, S. P., et al. (1999). Inadequacy of antidepressant treatment for patients with major depression who are at risk for suicidal behavior. *American Journal of Psychiatry*, 156, 190-194.

Osgood, N. J. (1982). Suicide in the elderly: are we heeding the warnings? *Postgraduate Medicine*, 72, 123-130.

Osgood, N. J. (1991). Psychological factors in late-life suicide. *Crisis*, 12, 18-24.

Parker, G., Gibson, N. A., Brotchie, H., et al. (2006). Omega-3 fatty acids and mood disorders. *American Journal of Psychiatry*, 163, 969-978.

Rich, C. L., & Runeson, B. S. (1992). Similarities in diagnostic comorbidity between suicide among young people in Sweden and the United States. *Acta Psychiatrica Scandinavica*, 86, 335-339.

Rich, C. L., Young, D., & Fowler, R. C. (1986). San Diego suicide study: I. Young vs old subjects. *Archives of General Psychiatry*, 43, 577-582.

Rihmer, Z. (2007) Suicide risk in mood disorders. *Current Opinion in Psychiatry*, 20, 17-22.

Rihmer, Z., & Akiskal, H. (2006). Do antidepressants t(h)reat(en) depressives? Toward a clinically judicious formulation of the antidepressant-suicidality FDA advisory in light of declining national suicide statistics from many countries. *Journal of Affective Disorders*, 94, 3-13.

Rihmer, Z., Belso, N., & Kiss, K. (2002). Strategies for suicide prevention. *Current Opinion in Psychiatry*, 15, 83-87.

Roy, A., Nielsen, D., Rylander, G., et al. (1999). Genetics of suicide in depression. *Journal of Clinical Psychiatry*, 60(Supplement 2), 12-17.

Runeson, B. S. (1992). Youth suicides unknown to psychiatric care providers. *Suicide & Life-Threatening Behavior*, 22, 494-503.

Rutz, W. (1992). Prevention of suicide. *Lancet*, 340, 1233-1234.

Samuelsson, M., Jokinen, J., Nordstrom, A. L., et al. (2006). CSF 5-HIAA, suicide intent and hopelessness in the prediction of early suicide in male high-risk suicide attempters. *Acta Psychiatrica Scandinavica*, 113, 44-47.

Sher, L., Mann, J. J., Traskman-Bendz, L., et al. (2006). Lower cerebrospinal fluid homovanillic acid levels in depressed suicide attempters. *Journal of Affective Disorders*, 90, 83-89.

Sokero, P., Eerola, M., Rytsala, H., et al. (2006). Decline in suicidal ideation among patients with MDD is preceded by decline in depression and hopelessness. *Journal of Affective Disorders*, 95, 95-102.

Sokero, T. P., Melartin, T. K., Rytsala, H. J., et al. (2005). Prospective study of risk factors for attempted suicide among patients with DSM-IV major depressive disorder. *British Journal of Psychiatry*, 186, 314-318.

Sublette, M. E., Hibbeln, J. R., Galfalvy, H., et al. (2006). Omega-3 polyunsaturated essential fatty acid status as a predictor of future suicide risk. *American Journal of Psychiatry*, 163, 1100-1102.

Suominen, K., Henriksson, M., Suokas, J., et al. (1996). Mental disorders and comorbidity in attempted suicide. *Acta Psychiatrica Scandinavica*, 94, 234-240.

Uncapher, H., Gallagher-Thompson, D., Osgood, N. J., et al. (1998). Hopelessness and suicidal ideation in older adults. *Gerontologist*, 38, 62-70.

Valtonen, H., Suominen, K., Mantere, O., et al. (2005). Suicidal ideation and attempts in bipolar I and II disorders. *Journal of Clinical Psychiatry*, 66, 1456-1462.

WHO. (1993). *The ICD-10 classification of mental and behavioural disorders: Diagnostic criteria for research.* Geneva, Switzerland: WHO.

Williams, J. M., Crane, C., Barnhofer, T., et al. (2006). Recurrence of suicidal ideation across depressive episodes. *Journal of Affective Disorders*, 91, 189-194.

Yerevanian, B., Koek, R., Feusner, J., et al. (2004). Antidepressants and suicidal behaviour in unipolar depression. *Acta Psychiatrica Scandinavica*, 110, 452-458.

Yoshimasu, K., Sugahara, H., Tokunaga, S., et al. (2006). Gender differences in psychiatric symptoms related to suicidal ideation in Japanese patients with depression. *Psychiatry & Clinical Neuroscience*, 60, 563-569.

In: Suicide from a Global Perspective: Psychiatric Approaches ISBN: 978-1-61942-267-4
Editors: A. Shrivastava, M. Kimbrell, and D. Lester © 2012 Nova Science Publishers, Inc.

Chapter 16

SUICIDE AND BIPOLAR DISORDERS

Judit Balázs and Zoltán Rihmer

INTRODUCTION

Suicidal behavior is neither a "normal" response to the levels of stress experienced by many people, nor a direct consequence of major mental disorders. Suicide and suicide attempts are very complex, multi-caused human behaviors with numerous biological, psychosocial and cultural determinants and with several risk and protective factors (Hawton & van Heeringen, 2000; Rihmer, et al., 2002). Suicide is a major health problem everywhere in the world, and its prediction and prevention receives increasing attention. Scientific literature on this topic shows that more than 90% of suicide attempters or completers have (mainly untreated or unsuccessfully treated) major mental disorders. The most common Axis I diagnoses preceding suicide or suicide attempts have consistently been found to be affective disorders (30%-90%), followed by substance-related disorders (19%-60%) and schizophrenia (2%-14%). Comorbid anxiety and personality disorders are also frequently present, but they are quite rare as principal (or only) diagnoses (Henriksson, et al., 1993; Isometsä, et al., 1994; Cheng, et al., 2000; Beautrais, et al., 1996; Conwell, et al., 1996; Suominen, et al., 1996; Hawton & van Heeringen, 2000; Balazs, et al., 2003; Rihmer, 2005; Rihmer, et al., 2006).

The term "suicidality" or "suicidal behavior" is a heterogenous concept involving suicidal ideation, suicide attempts with different levels of lethality, and completed suicide. The aim of this chapter is to review the complex relationship between the two most pronounced and frequently overlapping forms of suicidal behavior (suicide attempt and completed suicide) and bipolar disorder. We will also discuss the well-established, as well as the newly recognized, suicide risk factors in bipolar disorder. As the risk factors for attempted and completed suicide show only a few differences, and as a suicide attempt is among the most powerful predictors of completed suicide (Goodwin & Jamison, 1990; Beautrais, et al., 1996; Hawton & van Heeringen, 2000; Rihmer, et al., 2002; Balázs, et al., 2003; Angst, et al., 2005; Rihmer, et al., 2006), the risk factors for attempted and completed suicide are not discussed separately in this review. The biological aspects of suicidal behavior in bipolar disorder is also outside of the scope of this chapter and it is discussed in detail elsewhere (Goodwin & Jamison, 1990; Hawton & van Heeringen, 2000).

AFFECTIVE DISORDERS AND SUICIDAL BEHAVIOR

The classification systems (DSM-IV [American Psychiatric Association, 1994] and ICD-10 [World Health Organization, 1992]) split affective disorders into depressive disorder and bipolar disorder. Bipolar disorder is divided into bipolar I (BP-I) disorder and bipolar II (BP-II) disorder. BP-I disorder is defined by having manic and major/minor depressive episodes, while BP-II disorder is characterized by hypomanic (but not manic) and major depressive episodes. In contrast to manic episodes of BP-I patients, the hypomanic episodes of BP-II patients should not require hospital care for this condition and should not cause marked impairment of function.

While the unipolar-bipolar distinction of major mood disorders has been well accepted for decades, several studies also supported the clinical and biological validity of the distinction between BP-I and BP-II disorder (Akiskal, 1981; Rihmer, et al., 1984; Akiskal, et al., 1995; Goodwin & Jamison, 1990; Duffy, et al., 2000). However, looking at the nosological position of BP-II illness in the wide unipolar-bipolar mood disorder spectrum, most recent findings show that BP-II disorder takes an intermediate position between BP-I disorder and unipolar major depression (Akiskal, et al., 1995; Benazzi, 2006). In spite of the significance of bipolar disorder (suicidal behavior, loss of productivity, secondary substance-related disorders, and increased somatic morbidity and mortality), it is still under-referred, under-diagnosed and under-treated.

As mentioned above, patients with untreated or unsuccessfully treated major mood disorders are at particularly high risk of attempted or completed suicide. The life of patients with major mood disorders is shortened by about ten years, and this is mainly ascribable to suicide. Studies consistently show that 9%-19% of depressed patients die by suicide (Goodwin & Jamison, 1990; Bostwick & Pankratz, 2000; Angst, et al., 2005).

Earlier studies, performed more than 30 years ago, did not consider BP-II disorder separately and could not provide a separate estimate of the true suicide risk in the three major clinical phenotypes of affective disorders (unipolar depression and BP-I and BP-II disorders). In addition to this, a high proportion of patients originally diagnosed as having major depressive disorder changed their diagnosis during the follow-up to BP-I or BP-II disorder (Goodwin & Jamison, 1990; Akiskal, et al., 1995; Angst, et al., 2005). By considering the BP-II diagnosis as a distinct diagnostic subtype, recent studies clearly indicate that the risk of attempted and completed suicide in bipolar patients is higher than previously believed (Rihmer, et al., 1990; 1995; Balázs, et al., 2003; Rihmer, et al., 2006).

SUICIDAL BEHAVIOR IN BIPOLAR I AND BIPOLAR II DISORDERS

Several studies have confirmed the importance of bipolar disorder as a risk factor for suicide. A very striking data is that almost one-fifth of bipolar patients' deaths are due to suicide, and more than half of them attempt suicide at least once in their lifetime (Goodwin & Jamison, 1990; Isometsä, et al., 1994b; Angst, et al., 2005; Rihmer, 2005). As the lifetime prevalence of bipolar (I+II) disorder in the adult population is between 2% and 5 % (Angst, 1998; Szádóczky, et al., 1998), the problem of suicidality, related to bipolar disorder, affects a substantial proportion (around 1%-2%) of the general public. The fact that suicidal behavior in major mood disorder patients occurs mostly during major depressive episode (70%-79%), less frequently during mixed affective episode and dysphoric mania (11%-20%), and practically never (0%-1%) during euphoric mania and euthymia (Rouillon, et al., 1991; Isometsa, et al., 1994; Tondo, et al., 1999) strongly supports the routine clinical observation that suicidal behavior vanishes after the clinical recovery from acute mood episodes, that is, suicidal behavior in major mood disorder patients is a "state-dependent" phenomenon.

Investigating the relative distribution of current unipolar major depression, BP-I and BP-II disorder among depressed suicides, two studies have reported that bipolar patients in general, and BP-II patients in particular, are relatively over-represented among consecutively investigated suicides with a major depressive episode at the time of the suicide (Rihmer, et al., 1990, 1995). Similar findings have been found in two independent studies on consecutively investigated suicide attempters (Balázs, et al., 2003; Rihmer, et al., 2006) (see Table 16-1). In the contrast, a recently published, large-scale, prospective study has found that much higher rate of unipolar (14%) than the bipolar (I+II) patients (8%) committed suicide during a 40-44 year follow-up period, while the rate of suicide attempts were quite similar in both diagnostic groups. Excluding the patients with a predominantly manic course (mania only or mania and minor depression) from the BP-I subgroup, the risk of completed suicide remained about two-fold higher in unipolar than in bipolar patients (Angst, et al., 2005).

Table 16.1. Relative distribution of unipolar major depression, BP-I and BP-II disorder among suicides/attempters with current major depressive episode

Study population	Unipolar depression	BP-I disorder	BP-II disorder	Authors
100 depressed suicides	53 %	1 %	46 %	Rihmer, et al., 1990
25 depressed suicides	56 %	8 %	36 %	Rihmer, et al., 1995
69 depressed suicide attempters	65 %	7 %	28 %	Balazs, et al., 2003
85 depressed suicide attempters	69%	14%	17%	Rihmer, et al., 2006

Other studies also support the findings of a higher risk of suicidal behavior in bipolar disorder patients than in unipolar depression patients. Modestin and Kopp (1988) compared the clinical diagnoses of 75 inpatient depressed suicides and 50 depressed inpatient clinical controls. The rate of unipolar major depression was the same in the two groups (45% vs 44%), while the proportion of bipolar disorder (BP- I and BP-II combined) was significantly higher among the suicides (20% vs 6%).

It has been demonstrated that 9%-30% of unipolar depressed patients and up to 61% of bipolar patients attempt suicide at least once in their life (Goodwin & Jamison, 1990; Rihmer, 2005), while the lifetime prevalence rate of suicide attempt in the general population is between 3% and 5% (Weissman, et al., 1999; Szádóczky, et al., 2000). Community-based epidemiological studies from the USA (Chen & Dilsaver, 1996; Kessler, et al., 1999) and from Hungary (Szádóczky, et al., 2000) also show that the lifetime rate of prior suicide attempts was 1.5-2.5 times higher in bipolar (I+II) disorder than in unipolar major depression.

Examining 100 consecutive nonviolent suicide attempters in Hungary, we also found that BP-II disorder was relatively over-represented and that, for 60% of the patients diagnosed with major depressive episode at the time of their suicide attempt, it was their first depressive episode in their life (Balázs, et al., 2003). Another recent Hungarian study using the same diagnostic procedure and patient-setting found very similar results (Rihmer, et al., 2006) (see Table 16-1).

Investigating the clinical profile of 230 inpatients with recurrent major depressive episode, Bulik, et al. (1990) also found that BP-II diagnosis was significantly more frequent among the 67 patients who attempted suicide (19%) than in the 163 who had not attempted suicide (9%). Considering only the ten independent studies (including 3,187 patients) in which unipolar, BP-I and BP-II patients were analyzed separately and summarizing the results, it has been found that the rate of prior suicide attempts in unipolar, BP-I and BP-II patients are 13%, 26%, and 33%, respectively (Rihmer, 2005).

Males with bipolar disorder (I+II) make more serious and more lethal suicide attempts than female bipolar patients, but this is not the case among patients with unipolar major depressive disorder (Zalsman, et al., 2006). Vieta, et al. (1997) reported a similar rate of prior suicide attempts in BP-I and BP-II patients, although BP-II patients made significantly more violent and significantly more lethal attempts than did BP-I patients. The findings of the two studies, mentioned above, can explain, at least in part, why bipolar depressives are relatively over-represented among consecutively investigated suicides (Rihmer, et al., 1990, 1995). However, since repeated suicide attempters frequently change their suicide method from nonviolent/nonlethal to violent/lethal, but the opposite is rare (Rihmer, et al., 1995; Isometsa & Lönnqvist, 1998), nonviolent suicide attempts should be also considered seriously.

Well-Recognized Suicide Risk and Protective Factors among Bipolar Patients

Suicidal behavior is associated with a number of psychiatric (e.g., current major mental disorders), psychosocial (e.g., adverse life situations) and demographic (e.g., male gender) risk factors of varying prognostic utility (Rihmer, et al., 2002). As suicidal behavior is very rare in the absence of current major mental disorder, psychiatric suicide risk factors are the most powerful and clinically useful predictors of suicide, particularly if the psychosocial and demographic suicide risk factors are also present.

Since the majority of bipolar patients never commit suicide (and almost half of them never attempt suicide), other risk factors for suicidal behavior in bipolar disorder must play a contributory role (Conwell, et al., 1996, Cheng, et al., 2000; Hawton & van Heeringen, 2000; Bush, et al., 2003; Rihmer, 2005).

Attempted suicide is one of the most powerful clinical predictors of completed suicide, particularly in the presence of major depressive episode and other psychiatric (comorbid disorders) and psychosocial (adverse life situations) suicide risk factors (Goodwin & Jamison, 1990; Isometsä, et al., 1994; Nordstrom, et al., 1995; Cheng, et al., 2000; Rihmer, 2005).

Several authors have suggested that one of the important sources of suicide risk in BP-II patients is a high rate of comorbid anxiety disorder (Akiskal, 1981; Rihmer, et al., 2001; Balazs, et al., 2003; Rihmer, 2005) and substance use and personality disorders (Akiskal, 1981, 1985; Vieta, et al., 1997; Tondo, et al., 1999; Rihmer, 2005).

Studies have found that early onset of the bipolar disorder (Goodwin & Jamison, 1990; Rihmer, 2005), agitated depression (Szádóczky, et al., 2000; Bush, et al., 2003; Maj, et al., 2003) and mixed affective episode or dysphoric mania (Isometsa, et al., 1994; Rihmer, 2005), as well as severe depressive episodes (Bostwick & Pankratz, 2000; Rihmer, 2005) and psychotic features (Angst et al, 2005), also increase the risk of both attempted and completed suicide.

It has been found that bipolar patients with a positive family history of suicide in first-degree relatives (Dunner, et al., 1976; Tondo, et al., 1988) were significantly more likely to attempt and complete suicide, and a positive family history of completed suicide seems to be much higher in BP-II than in unipolar and BP-I patients (Dunner, et al., 1976; Tondo, et al., 1998).

Table 16.2. Clinical predictors of suicidal behaviour in bipolar disorder

Clinical predictors of suicidal behaviour in bipolar disorder
Early onset of the illness
Bipolar II diagnosis
Prior suicide attempt
Severe depression, guilt, hopelessness, agitation (depressive mixed state), psychotic features
Current suicidal ideation/plan
Comorbid anxiety/substance-use/personality disorder
Family history of suicide (first-degree relatives)
Adverse life situations (including serious medical illness)
Lack of social and medical support
Mixed affective episode/dysphoric mania

In contrast to the fact that men are markedly over-represented in unselected samples of suicides (Goodwin & Jamison, 1990; Hawton & van Heeringen, 2000), male gender is not a suicide risk factor in patients with bipolar disorder. Adverse life events, such as childhood psychosocial stressors (parental loss, physical, emotional and sexual abuse) and recent negative life situations (death of a relative, loss of job and other acute psychosocial stressors), as well as permanent stressors (such as chronic unemployment) have been shown to be risk factors for attempted and completed suicide (Goodwin & Jamison, 1990; Isometsä, et al., 1994; Rihmer, et al., 2002). However, life events can also be the consequences of bipolar disorder, since hypomanic and manic episodes lead easily to aggressive and antisocial behavior and to financial and sexual extravagance, generating interpersonal conflicts and difficult life situations, resulting in marital breakdown and job loss, all of which have a negative impact on the further course of the illness. These adverse situations can trigger suicidal behavior during the next major depressive episode (Akiskal, 1981; Goodwin & Jamison, 1990; Rihmer, et al., 2002). The most important and clinically explorable suicide risk factors in bipolar disorder are listed in Table 16-2. Although it has not been scientifically tested, it is obvious that a higher number of these risk factors in a given patient indicates a higher risk for future suicidal behavior. However, good family and social support, pregnancy, having many children and holding strong religious beliefs are protective factors for both attempted and completed suicide (Hawton & van Heeringen, 2000; Rihmer, et al., 2002).

The rate of appropriate pharmacotherapy among bipolar suicides and attempters is less than 20%, which is disturbingly low (Ismometsa, et al., 1994; Rihmer, et al., 1990; Balázs, et al., 2003). Appropriate acute and long-term pharmacotherapy has well-documented anti-suicidal effect in such patients (Kallner, et al., 2000; Ahrens & Müller-Oerlinghausen, 2001; Baldessarini, et al., 2003; Angst, et al., 2005). Therefore, adequate medical care should be also considered protective factor in this population.

Depressive Mixed States as a Newly Recognized Suicide Risk Factor in Bipolar Disorder

According to Kraepelin's unitary view of mood disorders, manic-depressive insanity (illness) is one disorder manifesting in both unipolar and bipolar forms, and it has different clinical presentations, such as mania, hypomania, depression, mixed states ("excited depression") and mood temperaments (Kraepelin, 1921). Weygandt, Kraepelin's pupil, was the first to use the term "agitated depression," referring to a mixed state characterized by a depressed mood, psychomotor agitation and flight of ideas (Weygandt, 1899; Benazzi, 2006).

Table 16.3. Comparison of the risk of suicidal behavior of bipolar patients with and without long-term pharmacotherapy

	Suicidal behavior of bipolar patients with long-term lithium therapy compared with untreated patients	**Authors**
Retrospective study of bipolar (I+II) patients (n=405): the rate of suicides	1.8 – fold lower	Kallner, et al., 2000
40-44-year-long naturalistic follow-up study bipolar (I+II) patients (n=220) [x]: the rate of suicides	2.5 – fold lower	Angst, et al., 2005
Meta-analyses of 9 studies on bipolar (I+II) patients (n=2580): the rate of suicide attempts	21 –fold lower	Baldessarini, et al., 2003

[x] = lithium and/or antidepressants, antipsychotics.

Psychomotor agitation is an important risk factor for both completed and attempted suicide (Szádóczky, et al., 2000; Bush, et al., 2003; Akiskal, et al., 2005), and recent studies have demonstrated that depressive mixed state (DMX) (a major depressive episode plus three or more co-occurring intra-depressive non-euphoric hypomanic symptoms) and agitated depression are greatly overlapping conditions, suggesting that agitated depression is a variant of mixed depression (Akiskal & Benazzi, 2003a, 2003b; Maj, et al., 2003; Akiskal & Benazzi, 2005; Akiskal, et al., 2005). The frequency of DMX was found to be around 60% in BP-II, 19%-29% in BP-I and 30% in unipolar untreated depressed patients (Akiskal, et al., 2003a; Maj, et al., 2003; Benazzi, 2005, 2006), and the bipolar nature of DMX has been validated with several clinical variables, including a family history of bipolar disorder, DSM-IV atypical features, bipolar transformation during the long-term course and early onset of the illness (Akiskal & Benazzi, 2003b; Benazzi, 2003, 2006; Akiskal, et al., 2005).

It has been proposed recently that DMX (like agitated depression) increases the risk of all forms of suicidal behavior in both unipolar and bipolar depression, as the frequency of past suicide attempts and current suicidal ideation has been reported to be much higher among mixed/agitated than nonmixed/nonagitated unipolar and bipolar major depressive patients (Perugi, et al., 2001; Benazzi, 2003, 2005; Maj, et al., 2003; Sato, et al., 2003; Cassano, et al., 2004; Akiskal, et al., 2005). In our most recent study, we used the opposite strategy. We analyzed the frequency and clinical characteristics of depressive mixed states among 100 consecutively investigated, nonviolent suicide attempters in Budapest, Hungary (Balázs, et al., 2006). Eighty-seven patients have had current major depression, and 71% of them have had DMX. Irritability, distractibility, psychomotor agitation and more talkativeness were the most common intra-depressive non-euphoric hypomanic symptoms. The rate of DMX was significantly higher among the 29 bipolar (I+II) depressive attempters, than in the 60 unipolar depressive attempters (90% and 62%, respectively). These figures are about two times higher than the same rates (59% and 27%, respectively) that were previously reported among 241 BP-II and 164 unipolar nonsuicidal outpatients with a current major depressive episode (Benazzi & Aksikal, 2003). These findings suggest that depressive suicide attempters come primarily from mixed bipolar and unipolar depressives and support the role of DMX in the development of suicidal behavior (Balázs, et al., 2006).

In their retrospective study, Olgiati, et al. (2006) examined the co-occurrence of agitation, bipolar features and suicide ideation in 314 patients with a major depressive episode. Although a retrospective clinical analysis could not confirm the significant association between agitated depression and bipolar family history, the results supported the strong relationship of agitation with intra-depressive hypomanic symptoms and suicidal thoughts reported previously in both unipolar and bipolar depression (Benazzi, 2003, 2005; Akiskal, et al., 2005). Investigating more than 240 adolescent outpatients with current major depressive episode (100 of them have had BP-I or BP-II disorder), a close link between suicidality and bipolar mixed depression has also been observed, but only for girls. Out of the 82 patients with mixed major depression, girls had almost four times the risk of having made a suicide attempt compared with patients having nonmixed major depression (Dilsaver, et al., 2005). These results clearly suggest that the correct identification of the "covert" bipolar nature of a given depressive episode, as reflected in mixed/agitated clinical picture, is crucial for selecting the most appropriate pharmacological treatment.

The possible causes of extremely high suicidality in BP-II disorder is not exactly known at present, and this problem seems to be quite complex. Beside the familial-genetic factors (Dunner, et al., 1976; Tondo, et al., 1998), several important clinical characteristics, such as very frequent anxiety/substance-use/personality disorder comorbidity, as well as the much higher rate of DMX/agitation in BP-II than in BP-I and unipolar depression (Akiskal, 1981; Vieta, et al., 1997; Tondo, et al., 1999; Rihmer, et al., 2001; Balázs, et al., 2003; Benazzi,

2005, 2006), and more serious/more lethal suicide attempts in BP-II than in BP-I and unipolar major depressive patients (Vieta, et al., 1997; Zalsman, et al., 2006), can also play a significant role. The lack of identification of the bipolar nature of major depressive episode in BP-II patients can also be an important factor. Misdiagnosis of BP-II disorder as unipolar depression routinely results in inadequate pharmacotherapy, and antidepressant monotherapy without the concomitant use of mood stabilizers, the standard treatment of unipolar depression, frequently worsens the long-term course of BP-II disorder by inducing DMX, "treatment resistance" and rapid cycling (Ghaemi, et al., 2003; Akiskal & Benazzi, 2005; Benazzi, 2005; Rihmer & Akiskal, 2006).

PREVENTION OF SUICIDAL BEHAVIOR IN BIPOLAR DISORDER

The diagnosis and treatment of depressive disorders in general, and the better identification of BP-II disorder in particular, are only one (although important) aspect in the recognition and management of suicidal patients. As has been discussed above, patients with affective disorders attempt or complete suicide mainly during their major depressive episodes (pure but mostly mixed depression), mixed affective episodes (meeting the full syndrome criteria for mania and major depression in the same time) and dysphonic mania, but almost never during euthymia. Therefore, treating acute major mood episodes effectively and stabilizing the period of euthymia is fundamental in preventing suicide in such patients. One-third of suicides have made one or more suicide attempts previously, which also means that two-thirds of them die as a result of their first attempt (Goodwin & Jamison, 1990; Hawton & van Heeringen, 2000; Rouillon, et al., 1991; Rihmer, et al., 2002; Isometsa & Lönnqvist, 1998). Therefore, it is important to detect suicide risk factors in bipolar patients as early as possible and intervene prior to the patient making the first suicide attempt.

Research shows that the risk of attempted and completed suicide in bipolar patients during long-term lithium treatment is much lower (on average, 6-fold), than without lithium therapy (Kallner, et al., 2000; Angst, et al., 2005; Baldessarini, et al., 2003). The marked anti-suicidal effect of prophylactic lithium therapy seems to be more than the simple result of its prophylactic effect, as it has been demonstrated that during the long-term lithium therapy of unipolar and bipolar mood disorder patients with at least one prior suicide attempt, a significant reduction in the number of suicide attempts was found not only in the excellent responders (93%), but also in moderate responders (83%) and in nonresponders (49%) (Ahrens & Müller-Oerlinghausen, 2001).

Two recent reviews (Ghaemi, et al., 2003; Rihmer & Aksikal, 2006) have summarized knowledge on the use of antidepressant therapy in bipolar depression. Antidepressants often induce rapid mood-cycling. Antidepressants have not been shown to definitively prevent completed suicide and reduce mortality, whereas lithium has, and antidepressants have not been shown to be more effective than mood stabilizers in acute bipolar depression, They have been shown to be less effective than mood stabilizers in preventing depressive relapse in bipolar disorder. It has been also demonstrated that antidepressant monotherapy (unprotected by mood stabilizers, anxiolytics and aypical antipsychotics) can result in treatment resistance and can worsen bipolar depression via inducing/worsening DMX and, therefore, in a few cases "provoking" suicidal behavior (Rihmer & Akiskal, 2006). In other words, the rarely observed antidepressant-suicidality link seems to be mediated by agitated, excited mixed depressive states, and recent data suggest that concomitant use of mood stabilizers, atypical antipsychotics or benzodiazepines in such cases could prevent the newly developing suicidality in this high-risk population (Akiskal, et al., 2005; Akiskal & Benazzi, 2005; Benazzi, 2005; Rihmer & Akiskal, 2006).

Antidepressants (always in combination with mood stabilizers) should be reserved for severe cases of acute bipolar depression and should be discontinued after recovery from the depressive episode, and maintained only in those who repeatedly relapse after antidepressant discontinuation (15%–20% of bipolar depressed patients) (Ghaemi, et al., 2003).

In the last two decades, more and more effective psychosocial interventions for bipolar disorder have been developed mainly for patients with no response or partial response to pharmacotherapy, who cannot tolerate the drugs or who are noncompliant with the psycho-pharmacological treatments (Rucci, et al., 2002; Michalak, et al., 2004). These psychosocial treatments (such as psychoeducation, cognitive-behavioral therapy and lifestyle modification) specifically designed for relapse/recurrence prevention in bipolar patients, are effective either alone or in combination with mood stabilizers. These psychosocial inter-ventions, while reducing relapse or recurrence, may indirectly reduce the risk of suicidal behavior. Rucci, et al. (2002) investigated the lifetime rates of suicide attempts among BP-I patients during a two-year period of intensive prophylactic pharmacotherapy (lithium, carbamazepine or valproate) and an adjunctive psychosocial intervention. The authors found that the patients experienced a three-fold reduction in the rate of suicide attempts during the acute treatment phase and an 18-fold reduction during the two-year long maintenance phase.

The detailed review of suicide prevention strategies in bipolar disorder is outside of the scope of this chapter. However, it should be noted that early and precise clinical diagnosis, adequate pharmacotherapy, and careful acute and long-term care of the patients, as well as implementation of targeted psychosocial interventions, are the most important elements in this work.

Conclusion

Attempted and completed suicide are relatively rare events in the general population, but they are quite common in patients with major mood disorders and particularly in patients with bipolar disorder. Considering our present knowledge on the risk and protective factors in bipolar patients reviewed above, the early detection and appropriate acute and long-term treatment of bipolar disorder in general, and BP-II in particular, as well as depressive "pseudo-unipolar" (bipolar) mixed subgroups, are of great public health significance for suicide prevention. The careful and systematic exploration of suicide risk factors in bipolar patients, as well as the correct identification of soft bipolarity in patients with major depressive episode, helps clinicians identify potential suicidal individuals. Considering all the above, in the majority of patients with bipolar disorder, suicidal behavior is predictable. Of course, we are unable to prevent all suicides. However, our present theoretical knowledge and treatment strategies are sufficient to prevent many of them.

References

Ahrens, B., & Müller-Oerlinghausen B. (2001). Does lithium exert an independent antisuicidal effect? *Pharmacopsychiatry*, 34, 132-136.

Akiskal, H. S. (1981). Subaffective disorders: dysthymic, cyclothymic and bipolar II disorders in the 'borderline' realm. *Psychiatric Clinics of North America*, 4, 25–46.

Akiskal, H. S., Maser, J. D., Zeller, P. J., et al. (1995). Switching from 'unipolar' to bipolar II: an 11-year prospective study of clinical and temperamental predictors in 559 patients. *Archives of General Psychiatry*, 52, 114–123.

Akiskal, H. S., & Benazzi, F. (2003a). Delineating depressive mixed states: their therapeutic significance. *Clinical Approaches in Bipolar Disorders*, 2, 41-47.

Akiskal, H. S., & Benazzi, F., (2003b). Family history validation of the bipolar nature of depressive mixed states. *Journal of Affective Disorders*, 73, 113-122.

Akiskal, H.S., & Benazzi, F. (2005). Psychopathologic correlates of suicidal ideation in major depressive outpatients: is it all due to unrecognized (bipolar) depressive mixed states? *Psychopathology*, 38, 273-280.

Akiskal, H. S., Benazzi, F., Perugi, G., et al. (2005). Agitated "unipolar" depression re-conceptualized as a depressive mixed state: implications for the antidepressant-suicide controversy. *Journal of Affective Disorders*, 85, 245-268.

American Psychiatric Association. (1994). *Diagnostic and Statistical Manual of Mental Disorders Fourth Edition (DSM-IV)*. Washington, DC: American Psychiatric Association.

Angst, J. (1998). The emerging epidemiology of hypomania and bipolar II disorder. *Journal of Affective Disorders*, 50, 143–151.

Angst, J., Angst ,F., Gerber-Werder, R., et al. (2005). Suicide in 406 mood-disorder patients with and without long-term medication: a 40 to 44 years' follow-up. *Archives of Suicide Research*, 9, 279-300.

Balazs, J., Lecrubier, Y., Csiszer, N., et al. (2003) Prevalence and comorbidity of affective disorders in persons making suicide attempts in Hungary: importance of the first depressive episodes and of bipolar II diagnoses. *Journal of Affective Disorders*, 76, 113-119.

Balazs, J., Benazzi, F., Rihmer, Z., et al. (2006). The close link between suicide attempts and mixed (bipolar) depression: implications for suicide prevention. *Journal of Affective Disorders*, 91, 133-138.

Baldessarini, R .J., Tondo, L., & Hennen, J. (2003). Lithium treatment and suicide risk in major affective disorders: update and new findings. *Journal of Clinical Psychiatry*, 64(Supplement 5), 44-52.

Beautrais, A. L., Joyce, P. R., Mulder, R. T., et al. (1996). Prevalence and comorbidity of mental disorders in persons making serious suicide attempts: a case-control study. *American Journal of Psychiatry*, 153, 1009-1014.

Benazzi, F. (2003). Depression with racing thoughts. *Psychiatry Research*, 120, 273-282.

Benazzi, F. (2005). Suicidal ideation and depressive mixed states. *Psychotherapie, Psychosomatik, Medizinische Psychologie*, 74, 61-62.

Benazzi, F. (2006). Mood patterns and classification in bipolar disorder. *Current Opinion in Psychiatry*, 19, 1-8.

Benazzi, F., & Aksikal, H. S. (2003). Clinical and factor-analytic validation of depressive mixed states: a report from the Ravenna-San Diego collaboration. *Current Opinion in Psychiatry*, 16(Supplement 2), 71-78.

Bostwick, J. M., & Pankratz, V. S. (2000). Affective disorders and suicide risk: a re-examination. *American Journal of Psychiatry*, 157, 1925–1932.

Bulik, C. M., Carpenter, L. L., Kupfer, D. L., et al. (1990). Features associated with suicide attempts in recurrent major depressive disorder. *Journal of Affective Disorders*, 18, 29-37.

Busch, K. A., Fawcett, J., & Jacobs, D. G. (2003). Clinical correlates of inpatient suicide. *Journal of Clinical Psychiatry*, 64, 14-19.

Cassano, G. B., Rucci, P., Frank, E., et al. (2004). The mood spectrum in unipolar and bipolar disorder: arguments for unitary approach. *American Journal of Psychiatry*, 161, 1264-1269.

Chen, Y. W., & Dilsaver, S. C. (1996). Lifetime rates of suicide attempts among subjects with bipolar and unipolar disorders relative to subjects with other axis I disorders. *Biological Psychiatry*, 39, 896–899.

Cheng, A. T. A., Chen, T. H. H., Chen, C. C., et al. (2000). Psychological and psychiatric risk factors for suicide: case–control psychological autopsy study. *British Journal of Psychiatry*, 177, 360–365.

Conwell, Y., Duberstein, P. R., Cox, C., et al. (1996). Relationships of age and Axis I diagnoses in victims of completed suicide: a psychological autopsy study. *American Journal of Psychiatry*, 153, 1001-1008.

Dilsaver, S. C., Benazzi, F., Rihmer, Z., et al. (2005). Gender, suicidality and bipolar mixed states in adolescents. *Journal of Affective Disorders*, 87, 11-16.

Duffy, A., Grof, P., Robertson, C., et al. (2000). The implications of genetics studies of major mood disorders for clinical practice. *Journal of Clinical Psychiatry*, 61, 630-637.

Dunner, D. L., Gershon, E. S., & Goodwin, F. K. (1976). Heritable factors in the severity of affective illness. *Biological Psychiatry*, 11, 31-42.

Ghaemi, S. N., Hsu, D. J., Soldani F., et al. (2003). Antidepressants in bipolar disorder: the case for caution. *Bipolar Disorders*, 5, 421-433.

Goodwin, F. K., & Jamison, K. R. (1990). *Manic-depressive illness.* New York: Oxford University Press.

Hawton, K., & van Heeringen, C. (Eds.) (2000). *International handbook of suicide and attempted suicide*. Chichester, UK: Wiley.

Henriksson, M. M., Aro, H. M., Martutunen, M .J., et al. (1993). Mental disorders and comorbidity in suicide. *American Journal of Psychiatry*, 150, 935-940.

Isometsä, E. T., Henriksson, M. M., Aro, H. M., et al. (1994). Suicide in bipolar disorder in Finland. *American Journal of Psychiatry*, 151, 1020–1024.

Isometsa, E. T., & Lönnqvist, J. K. (1998). Suicide attempts preceding completed suicide. *British Journal of Psychiatry*, 173, 531-533.

Kallner, G., Lindelius, R., Petterson, U., et al. (2000). Mortality in 497 patients with affective disorders attending a lithium clinic or after having left it. *Pharmacopsychiatry*, 33, 8-13.

Kessler, R. C., Borges, G., & Walters, E. E. (1999). Prevalence of and risk factors for lifetime suicide attempts in the National Comorbidity Survey. *Archives of General Psychiatry*, 56, 617–626.

Kraepelin, E. (1921). *Manic-depressive insanity and paranoia*. Edinburgh: E. & S. Livingstone

Maj, M., Pirozzi, R., Magliano, L., et al. (2003). Agitated depression in bipolar I disorder: prevalence, phenomenology, and outcome. *American Journal of Psychiatry*, 160, 2134-2140.

Michalak, E. E., Yatham, L. N., & Lam, R. W. (2004). The role of psychoeducation in the treatment of bipolar disorder: a clinical perspective. *Clinical Approaches in Bipolar Disorders*, 85, 233-242.

Modestin, J., & Kopp, W. (1988). Study on suicide in depressed inpatients. *Journal of Affective Disorders*, 15, 157–162.

Nordstrom, P., Asberg, M., Aberg-Wistedt, A., et al. (1995). Attempted suicide predicts suicide risk in mood disorders. *Acta Psychiatrica Scandinavica*, 92, 345–350.

Olgiati, P., Serretti, A., & Colombo, C. (2006). Retrospective analysis of psychomotor agitation, hypomanic symptoms, and suicidal ideation in unipolar depression. *Depression & Anxiety*, 23, 389-397.

Rihmer, Z. (2005). Prediction and prevention of suicide in bipolar disorder. *Clinical Neuropsychiatry*, 2, 48-54.

Rihmer, Z., Bagdy, G., & Arató, M. (1984). Serum dopamine-beta-hydroxylase activity in manic-depressive female patients. *Biological Psychiatry*, 19, 423-427.

Rihmer, Z., Barsi, J., Arato, M., et al. (1990). Suicide in subtypes of primary major depression. *Journal of Affective Disorders*, 18, 221–225.

Rihmer, Z., Belso, N., & Kiss, K. (2002). Strategies for suicide prevention. *Current Opinion in Psychiatry*, 15, 83-87.

Rihmer, A., Rihmer, Z., Jekkel, É., et al. (2006). Psychiatric characteristics of 100 nonviolent suicide attempters in Hungary. *International Journal of Psychiatry in Clinical Practice*, 10, 69-72.

Rihmer, Z., Rutz, W., & Pihlgren, H. (1995). Depression and suicide on Gotland: an intensive study of all suicides before and after a depression-training programme for general practitioners. *Journal of Affective Disorders*, 35, 147–152.

Rihmer, Z., Szadoczky, E., Furedi, J., et al. (2001). Anxiety disorders comorbidity in bipolar I, bipolar II and unipolar major depression: results from a populationbased study in Hungary. *Journal of Affective Disorders*, 67, 175–179.

Rihmer, Z., & Aksikal, H. S. (2006). Do antidepressants t(h)reat(hen) depressives? Toward a clinically judicious formulation of the antidepressant-suicidality FDA advisory in light of declining national suicide statistics from many countries. *Journal of Affective Disorders*, 94, 3-13.

Rouillon, F., Serrurier, D., Miller, H. D., et al. (1991). Prophylactic efficacy of maprotiline on unipolar depression relapse. *Journal of Clinical Psychiatry*, 40, 971-974.

Rucci, P., Frank, E., Kostelnik, B., et al. (2002). Suicide attempts in patients with bipolar I disorder during acute and maintenance phases of intensive treatment with pharmacotherapy and adjunctive psychotherapy. *American Journal of Psychiatry*, 159, 1160-1164.

Sato, T., Bottlender, R., Schröter, A., et al. (2003). Frequency of manic symptoms during a depressive episode and unipolar "depressive mixed state" as bipolar spectrum. *Acta Psychiatrica Scandinavica*, 107, 268-274.

Suominen, K., Henriksson, M., Suokas, J., et al. (1996). Mental disorders and comorbidity in attempted suicide. *Acta Psychiatrica Scandinavica*, 94, 234-240.

Szadoczky, E., Papp, Z., Vitrai, J., et al. (1998). The prevalence of major depressive and bipolar disorders in Hungary. *Journal of Affective Dis*orders, 50, 153–162.

Szadoczky, E., Vitrai, J., Rihmer, Z., et al. (2000). Suicide attempts in the Hungarian adult population: their relation with DIS/DSM-III-R affective and anxiety disorders. *European Psychiatry*, 15, 343-347.

Tondo, L., Baldessarini, R. J., Hennen, J., et al. (1998). Lithium maintenance treatment of depression and mania in bipolar I and bipolar II disorders. *American Journal of Psychiatry*, 155, 638–645.

Tondo, L., Baldessarini, R. J., Hennen, J., et al. (1999). Suicide attempts in major affective disorder patients with comorbid substance use disorders. *Journal of Clinical Psychiatry*, 60(Supplement 2), 63–69.

Vieta, E., Benabarre, A., Colom, F., et al. (1997). Suicidal behaviour in bipolar I and bipolar II disorder. *Journal of Nervous & Mental Disorders*, 185, 407–409.

Weissman, M. M., Bland, R. C., Canino, G. J., et al. (1999). Prevalence of suicide ideation and suicide attempts in nine countries. *Psychological Medicine*, 29, 9-17.

Weygandt, W. (1899). *Ueber die Mischzustaende des manisch-depressiven Irreseins*. Munich: Lehmann.

World Health Organization. (1992). *The ICD-10 classification of mental and behavioural disorders, clinical description and diagnostic guidelines*. Geneva, Switzerland: WHO.

Zalsman, G., Braun, M., Arendt, M., et al. (2006). A comparison of the medical lethality of suicide attempts in bipolar and major depressive disorders. *Bipolar Disorders*, 8, 558-565.

In: Suicide from a Global Perspective: Psychiatric Approaches ISBN: 978-1-61942-267-4
Editors: A. Shrivastava, M. Kimbrell, and D. Lester © 2012 Nova Science Publishers, Inc.

Chapter 17

SUICIDE IN SCHIZOPHRENIA

Merete Nordentoft

INTRODUCTION

Suicide in relation to schizophrenia is an important clinical and public health problem. Reviews of suicide risk in schizophrenia are presented and risk factors are reviewed. Suicide risk in schizophrenia decreased with the same speed as the decrease in the general population and, in Denmark, the suicide risk in schizophrenia was halved from 1981 to 1997. Danish population registers were used to identify high risk periods for suicide, and two sharp peaks for suicide risk in schizophrenia were identified: shortly after admission and shortly after discharge. Increased attention should be paid to assessing suicide risk in these two high-risk periods, and to measures that can hopefully influence the high risk. Assessment of suicide risk and outpatient treatment immediately after discharge is of particular importance. Randomized clinical trials aiming to reduce suicidal behaviour are sparse and often inconclusive due to small sample size.

Much attention has been paid to the risk of suicide in schizophrenia. Miles (1977) estimated that the risk of suicide was 10%, and this figure has been repeated many times in reviews and comments. However, to give a true estimate of suicide risk in schizophrenia, it is necessary to base the estimates on follow-up of first-episode schizophrenia patients. Estimating the suicide risk in first-episode schizophrenia also depends on the diagnostic criteria, on the setting, and on the age limits in the sampling. The gender distribution in the sample might also play an important role.

In a recent review, Palmer, et al. (2005) identified all first-episode studies and estimated the lifetime risk of suicide to be 5.6%. Their meta-analysis was split into an evaluation of mixed samples and of first-episode studies. From their review, it can be concluded that most studies are of small samples, and that the two largest studies are Danish and Swedish register-based studies (Mortensen & Juel, 1993; Osby, et al., 2000a) These two large studies estimated a case fatality rate of 6% and 5% after a follow-up period of nine and 14 years, respectively. High case fatality rates due to suicide were mostly found in smaller studies. In their estimation of lifetime risk of suicide in various disorders, Inskip, et al. (1998) estimated the lifetime risk in schizophrenia to be 4%. Thus, it seems reasonable to conclude that case fatality due to suicide will not reach as high as 10% since suicide risk is highest the first years after first admission. It is more likely that the true case fatality is between 5% or 6%.

However, estimating the lifetime suicide risk is very complicated and also susceptible to change along with changes in the treatment support offered to the patient group and in the general features of the society. It is likely that large prospective studies of first-onset cases with a long follow-up period will provide a better estimate of the suicide risk, but an inherent problem with such studies is that, by the time the results of such studies become available, the risk for new first-episode patients may have changed because of changes in treatment and other factors.

Studies also should be reviewed with regard to age of onset, since cases with early onset have worse outcomes than cases with later onset. The risk of suicide is much higher among patients with schizophrenia than in the never-admitted population and, as in the general population, the risk of suicide increases with increasing age. However, the excess of risk of suicide is higher among young patients with schizophrenia compared to the never-admitted population (see Figure 1).

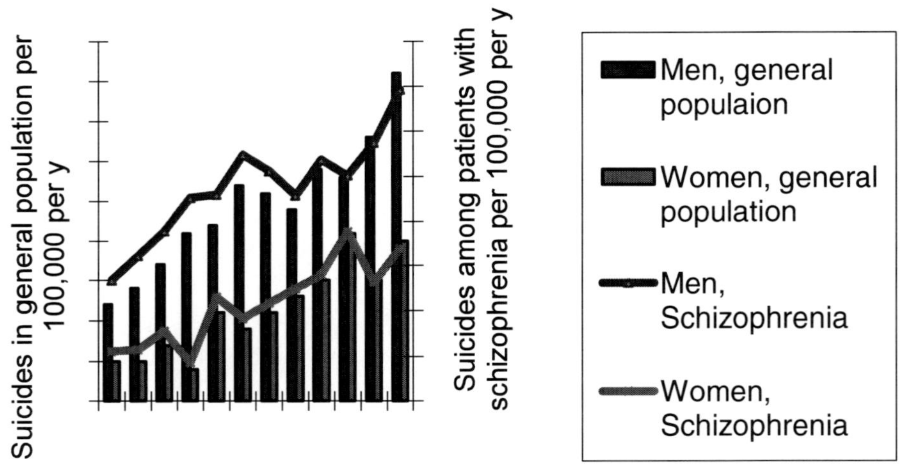

Figure 1. Age-specific suicide rates in the general population and estimated rates among patients with schizophrenia, men and women, 1997.

RISK FACTORS FOR SUICIDE IN SCHIZOPHRENIA

Many factors associated with suicide in schizophrenia have been identified, but attempts to identify high-risk patients have so far produced too many false positives to be clinically useful (Caldwell & Gottesman, 1990). Risk factors for schizophrenia have been the subject of several studies. Some studies were case-control studies, while others were prospective studies. Even though schizophrenia is a high-risk condition for suicide, suicide is still a rare event in schizophrenia. Therefore, a large sample size and a long follow-up are needed in prospective studies. For this reason, case-control studies might be more powerful in identifying risk factors for suicide in schizophrenia.

In a review of studies evaluating risk of suicide in schizophrenia, Caldwell and Gottesman (1990) retrieved a long list of studies of first-episode and mixed samples. They concluded that a range of studies found that young age, male gender, white race, social isolation, depressed mood, a past history of suicide attempt, a family history of suicide, unmarried, unemployed, deteriorating health, recent loss, limited external support, family stress or instability, chronic illness with numerous exacerbations, high level of psychopathology and functional impairment, fear of deterioration, and loss of faith in treatment were risk factors. Hawton, et al. (2005) recently published a systematic review of risk factors and identified 29 eligible studies. They found robust evidence of increased risk of suicide in schizophrenia for depressive disorders, previous suicide attempts, drug misuse, agitation and motor restlessness, fear of mental disintegration, poor adherence to treatment and recent loss. Some of the studies were based solely on information from registers and, in these studies, clinical characteristics can be included only if they are reported as a comorbid diagnosis, such as depression or substance abuse. Other predictors that have been investigated were male gender, young age, substance abuse, and in some cases previous suicide attempts. The studies that included more detailed information about clinical characteristics are often smaller as the practical work involved in clinical assessment is substantial.

Three large Danish register-based studies of suicide risk in patients with schizophrenia indicate that male gender, young age, short duration of illness, many admissions during the last year, current inpatient status, a short time since discharge and co-morbid depression were independent risk factors (Mortensen & Juel, 1993; Nordentoft, et al., 2004; Rossau & Mortensen, 1997)

Since some of the clinical studies have small sample sizes, some risk factors might not be identified because of a lack of power. Previous suicide attempts are taken into consideration in almost all clinical studies but, apart from that, since different studies evaluate different risk factors, it cannot be concluded that not mentioning a risk factor in a specific study excludes this risk factor from being a significant predictor of suicide. The information extracted from the clinical studies identify the following risk factors as the most important and frequently observed predictors: previous suicide attempts, co-morbid depression, drug misuse, poor compliance with medication, poor adherence to treatment, high IQ and suicidal ideation.

The results of analyses of psychotic symptoms as risk factors for suicide are contradictory, and results are reported using different categories. In a meta-analysis of risk factors for suicide in schizophrenia, Hawton concluded that the pooled odds ratio for suicide for positive symptoms was not significantly different from 1.0 but, when symptoms were divided into hallucinations and delusions, both hallucinations and delusions seemed to be protective (delusions: OR= 0.53 (95% CI 0.28-1.01); hallucinations: OR=0.5 (95% CI 0.35-0.71)).

A number of studies have found that the active and exacerbated phase of the illness and the presence of psychotic symptoms are associated with a high risk of suicide (Heila, et al., 1997; Westermeyer, Harrow & Marengo, 1991). Several studies have reported that negative symptoms were protective but, in the meta-analysis by Hawton, et al. (2005), this turned out to be nonsignificant.

Haw, et al. (2005) conducted a systematic review of schizophrenia and deliberate self-harm and identified past or recent suicidal ideation, previous deliberate self-harm, past depressive episodes, drug abuse or dependence and a high number of psychiatric admissions as risk factors for deliberate self-harm among patients with schizophrenia.

Biology

As noted by Tsai and Lee (2006), the search for biological factors affecting schizophrenic suicide is just beginning. Since serotonergic dysfunction has been implicated in the pathogenesis of both schizophrenia and suicidal behaviors, most studies of schizophrenic suicide have focused on the serotonergic system. A review of these studies suggests that schizophrenic patients with a history of suicide attempts also show lower levels of serotonin neurotransmission, as do other psychiatric populations, although genetic studies of the serotonergic system are generally negative. In postmortem studies, aberrant 5-HT1 and 5-HT2 manifestations in the hippocampal and prefrontal cortex have been revealed. Tsai and Lee discussed only serotonin's role in schizophrenic suicide, but other neurotransmitters may also be involved in suicidal behavior.

Schizophrenia and Suicide Risk around the Time of Admission

In a recent Danish register-based study by Qin and Nordentoft (2005), we found that, for patients with schizophrenia and related disorders, there were two sharp peaks in suicide risk, the first immediately after admission and the second shortly after discharge (see Figures 2 and 3). Approximately one-third of suicides in schizophrenia occur during admission or the first week after discharge and, from a preventive perspective, that is useful to know because it identifies important risk periods on which preventive interventions should focus. Suicide among patients with schizophrenia currently admitted or discharged within last week accounts for almost 3% of all suicides in Denmark. Other authors have identified the same risk periods (Appleby, et al., 1999; Goldacre, Seagroatt & Hawton, 1993; Lawrence, et al., 1999; Mortensen & Juel, 1993; Rossau & Mortensen, 1997).

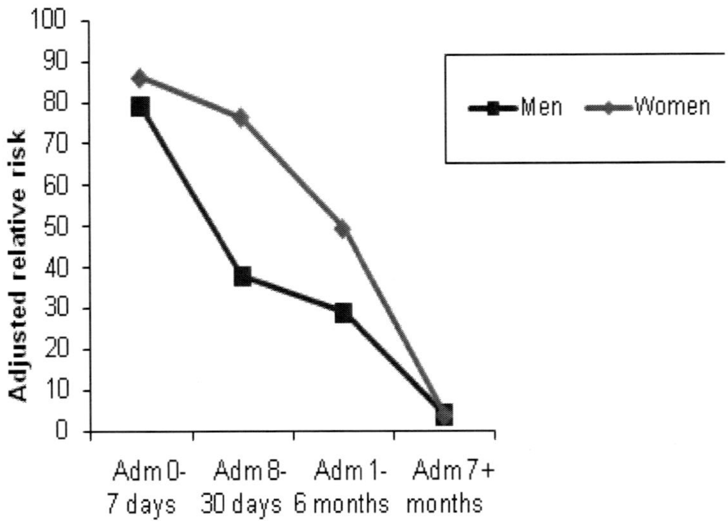

Figure 2. Suicide during admission. Patients with schizophrenia compared to the never admitted population.

DECREASING TIME TRENDS IN SUICIDE RISK IN SCHIZOPHRENIA

Several papers have reported an increasing risk of suicide in schizophrenia (Osby, et al., 2000b; Wolfersdorf, et al., 1988). It is a very complicated task to evaluate time trends in suicide risk in schizophrenia as sample compositions might change over time. To give a valid answer about time changes, it is necessary to have access to large case registers with a sufficiently long follow-up period and to be able to control for differences in sample composition, with controls for calendar year, time since first admission, age of first admission, etc. This is possible in only very few countries in the world.

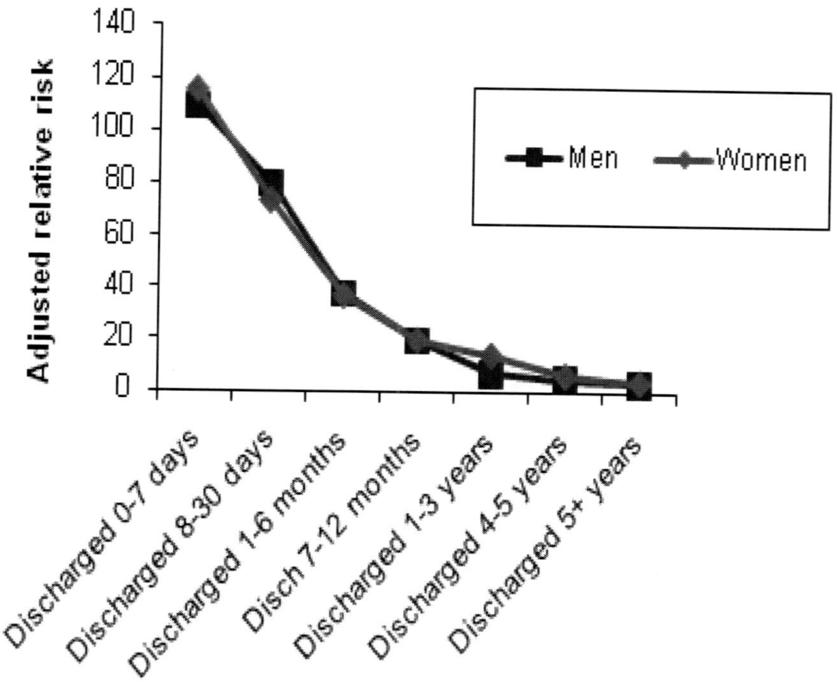

Figure 3. Suicide after discharge. Patients with schizophrenia compared to the never admitted population.

Since increasing suicide risk has been connected with deinstitutionalization, we wanted to examine this development carefully in the Danish population. We were able to combine four longitudinal population-based registers and follow the development in suicide rates for patients with schizophrenia and related disorders. In 1980, the suicide rate in Denmark peaked and reached a level that was among the highest in the world, with 34 suicides per 100,000 inhabitants. After 1980, the number of suicides decreased each year and, in 1997, the rate was 15, a 56% reduction in the suicide rate during the period 1980-1997. In Denmark, approximately half of the persons who die from suicide have previously been admitted to psychiatric departments, and more than one-fourth have been admitted during the last year (Mortensen, et al., 2000; Qin, et al.,2003). We found that, although the risk of suicide among patients with schizophrenia and related disorders is almost 20 times higher than among never-admitted persons in the general population, the suicide rate among patients with schizophrenia and related disorders in Denmark declined by a half from 1981 to 1997. The change in the suicide rate among these patients was the same as the change among never-admitted persons in the general population (Nordentoft, et al., 2004).

Thus, our data do not support the notion that deinstitutionalization in Denmark has led to an increased suicide rate. It is unknown whether this finding can be replicated in other countries.

RECOMMENDATIONS

Much more attention should be paid to the risk of suicide in schizophrenia, such as co-morbid depressive disorders, previous suicide attempts, drug misuse, agitation and motor restlessness, fear of mental disintegration, poor adherence to treatment and recent loss.

To evaluate an intervention, the best method is a large randomized clinical trial that includes a representative sample of the target group. However, due to the low base rate, the trials must include several thousand participants in order to reduce the risk of type II error (Pocock, 1996). Randomized clinical trials large enough to provide evidence of effectiveness of suicide preventive measures in risk groups are difficult to organize, and practical, political and ethical considerations may make such trials impossible. It is seldom possible to carry out such large trials. They necessitate multi-center trials, which are associated with methodological difficulties in ensuring that the same interventions are carried out at different sites. Meta-analyses of randomized clinical trials can compensate to some extent for the trials being under-powered, but often the trials included in meta-analyses are different with regard to the population group included, duration and intensity of treatment.

As suicide attempts are much more common than suicides, many investigators have chosen to use suicide attempts as an outcome measure instead suicide. If suicide attempt is chosen as the outcome measure, it is possible to establish randomized studies with sufficient power to examine a potential effect of preventive measures. Even though risk factors for suicide and suicide attempt are not completely the same, it is likely that preventive efforts effective in reducing frequency of suicide attempts are also effective in preventing suicide.

The number needed in a randomized trial is a function of both the expected rate of repetition (compared to the control group) and the size of the difference. If the predicted rate were 10% in the experimental group versus 15% in the control group, with the level of significance (alpha) set at 0.05 and required power (beta) set at 0.90, 913 subjects would be required in each treatment group. If the rates were 20% and 30%, respectively, 388 subjects would be required in each group (Hawton, et al., 1998; Pocock, 1996).

If suicide is the outcome, a much larger sample size is needed. If for instance an experimental intervention reduced suicide rate from 4% to 2%, 1,522 participants would be needed in each treatment group to detect with a power (beta) of 0.90 and a significance level (alpha) of 0.05 (Pocock, 1996).

For patients with schizophrenia, there are no large studies investigating the effect on suicide of psychosocial interventions. The Danish OPUS-trial examined whether the risk of suicide and suicide attempt could be reduced by offering intensive treatment to patients with first contact because of disorders in schizophrenia spectrum. Among the patients who received the intensive treatment, one of the 275 committed suicide during the first two-years of treatment, while four of the 272 patients in standard treatment committed suicide (Petersen, et al., 2005). The intensive treatment was not associated with a reduced risk of suicide attempt (Nordentoft, et al., 2002). Examination of risk factors for attempted suicide among the patients included in the OPUS-trial revealed that suicidal plans and suicidal thoughts reported at baseline and one-year follow-up interviews were predictive of suicide attempt the following year.

In schizophrenia, no randomized controlled trial of specific antipsychotic drugs has a proven effect on suicide (Meltzer, 2002). However, a recent study indicates that clozapine is superior to olanzapine with regard to reducing the risk of deliberate self-harm (Meltzer, et al., 2003). Based on current evidence, clozapine is the only pharmacological treatment for schizophrenia with an established specific effect on reducing suicidal behaviour. There is preliminary but ultimately inconclusive evidence that other atypical antipsychotic agents may also be beneficial in reducing this risk. The introduction of traditional neuroleptics does not appear to have reduced rates of suicide compared to those of the pre-neuroleptic era. The effects of antidepressant or mood stabilizer augmentation of antipsychotic drugs on suicide risk in schizophrenia have not been systematically investigated. (Meltzer & Bobo, 2006). It is necessary, therefore, to conduct further studies of the possible anti-suicidal effects of pharmacological and psychosocial treatment.

In many cases, it is not possible to carry out a randomized clinical trial of factors likely to play a role in decreasing suicide rates among patients with schizophrenia. In such cases, it is necessary to carry out naturalistic, individually-based, observational studies or ecological studies. Individually-based naturalistic studies can identify prognostic factors. Naturalistic studies include prospective cohort studies, nested case-control studies and case-control studies. Nested case-control studies have an advantage over case-control studies, since selecting controls from a large database permits matching on several relevant factors and for adjusting estimates of risk for possible confounders. However, naturalistic studies of any kind carry a risk of interchanging cause and effect.

Randomized clinical trials cannot be carried out to evaluate healthcare reforms. Observational studies cannot provide the same strong evidence as randomized clinical trials. Nevertheless, there are numerous areas where recommendations for practice will have to rely on weaker evidence.

In the Danish Action Plan for Prevention of Suicide and Suicide Attempts, it was recommended that outpatient care immediately after discharge should be intensified, and that it should be set as a standard that all patients should have an outpatient appointment within one week after discharge. The importance of this intervention is underlined by the finding that one-third of all suicides in schizophrenia occur during admission or shortly after discharge. In the Danish national quality development project (National Indicator Project, schizophrenia), the standard is that all patients discharged from psychiatric department with a diagnosis of schizophrenia should be carefully interviewed and assessed with regard to risk of suicide. The British Action Plan also contains the same kind of elements. Such initiatives should be extended to other countries.

References

Appleby, L., Shaw, J., Amos, T., McDonnell, R., Harris, C., McCann, K., Kiernan, K., Davies, S., Bickley, H., & Parsons, R. (1999). Suicide within 12 months of contact with mental health services: national clinical survey. *British Medical Journal*, 318, 1235-1239.

Caldwell, C. B., & Gottesman, I. I. (1990). Schizophrenics kill themselves too: a review of risk factors for suicide. *Schizophrenia Bulletin*, 16, 571-589.

Goldacre, M., Seagroatt, V., & Hawton, K. (1993). Suicide after discharge from psychiatric inpatient care. *Lancet*, 342, 283-286.

Haw, C., Hawton, K., Sutton, L., Sinclair, J., & Deeks, J. (2005). Schizophrenia and deliberate self-harm: a systematic review of risk factors. *Suicide & Life-Threatening Behavior*, 35, 50-62.

Hawton, K., Arensman, E., Townsend, E., Bremner, S., Feldman, E., Goldney, R., Gunnell, D., Hazell, P., Van Heeringen, K., House, A., Owens, D., Sakinofsky, I., & Traskman-Bendz, L. (1998). Deliberate self harm: systematic review of efficacy of psychosocial and pharmacological treatments in preventing repetition. *British Medical Journal*, 317, 441-447.

Hawton, K., Sutton, L., Haw, C., Sinclair, J., & Deeks, J. J. (2005). Schizophrenia and suicide: systematic review of risk factors. *British Journal of Psychiatry*, 187, 9-20.

Heila, H., Isometsa, E. T., Henriksson, M. M., Heikkinen, M. E., Marttunen, M. J., & Lonnqvist, J. K. (1997). Suicide and schizophrenia: a nationwide psychological autopsy study on age- and sex-specific clinical characteristics of 92 suicide victims with schizophrenia. *American Journal of Psychiatry*, 154, 1235-1242.

Inskip, H. M., Harris, E. C., & Barraclough, B. (1998). Lifetime risk of suicide for affective disorder, alcoholism and schizophrenia. *British Journal of Psychiatry*, 172, 35-37.

Lawrence, D. M., Holman, C. D., Jablensky, A. V., & Fuller, S. A. (1999). Suicide rates in psychiatric in-patients: an application of record linkage to mental health research. *Australian & New Zealand Journal of Public Health*, 23, 468-470.

Meltzer, H. Y. (2002). Suicidality in schizophrenia: a review of the evidence for risk factors and treatment options. *Current Psychiatry Reports*, 4, 279-283.

Meltzer, H. Y., Alphs, L., Green, A. I., Altamura, A. C., Anand, R., Bertoldi, A., Bourgeois, M., Chouinard, G., Islam, M. Z., Kane, J., Krishnan, R., Lindenmayer, J. P., & Potkin, S. (2003). Clozapine treatment for suicidality in schizophrenia: International Suicide Prevention Trial (InterSePT). *Archives of General Psychiatry*, 60, 82-91.

Meltzer, H. Y. & Bobo, V. W. (2006). Pharmacological management of suicide risk in schizophrenia. In R. Tatarelli, M. Pompili, & P. Girardi (Eds.) *Suicide in schizophrenia*. Hauppauge, NY: Nova Science.

Miles, C. P. (1977). Conditions predisposing to suicide: a review. *Journal of Nervous & Mental Disease*, 164, 231-246.

Mortensen, P. B., Agerbo, E., Erikson, T., Qin, P., & Westergaard-Nielsen, N. (2000). Psychiatric illness and risk factors for suicide in Denmark. *Lancet*, 355, 9-12.

Mortensen, P. B. & Juel, K. (1993). Mortality and causes of death in first admitted schizophrenic patients. *British Journal of Psychiatry*, 163, 183-189.

Nordentoft, M., Jeppesen, P., Abel, M., Kassow, P., Petersen, L., Thorup, A., Krarup, G., Hemmingsen, R., & Jorgensen, P. (2002). OPUS study: suicidal behaviour, suicidal ideation and hopelessness among patients with first-episode psychosis: one-year follow-up of a randomised controlled trial. *British Journal of Psychiatry*, 43(Supplement), S98-S106.

Nordentoft, M., Laursen, T. M., Agerbo, E., Qin, P., Hoyer, E. H., & Mortensen, P. B. (2004). Change in suicide rates for patients with schizophrenia in Denmark, 1981-97: nested case-control study. *British Medical Journal*, 329, 261-266.

Osby, U., Correia, N., Brandt, L., Ekbom, A., & Sparen, P. (2000a). Mortality and causes of death in schizophrenia in Stockholm county, Sweden. *Schizophrenia Research*, 45, 21-28.

Osby, U., Correia, N., Brandt, L., Ekbom, A., & Sparen, P. (2000b). Time trends in schizophrenia mortality in Stockholm county, Sweden: cohort study. *British Medical Journal*, 321, 483-484.

Palmer, B. A., Pankratz, V. S., & Bostwick, J. M. (2005). The lifetime risk of suicide in schizophrenia: a reexamination. *Archives of General Psychiatry*, 62, 247-253.

Petersen, L., Jeppesen, P., Thorup, A., Abel, M. B., Ohlenschlaeger, J., Christensen, T. O., Krarup, G., Jorgensen, P., & Nordentoft, M. (2005). A randomised multicentre trial of integrated versus standard treatment for patients with a first episode of psychotic illness. *British Medical Journal*, 331, 602.

Pocock, S. J. (1996). *Clinical trials: A practical approach.* New York: Wiley.

Qin, P., Agerbo, E., & Mortensen, P. B. (2003). Suicide risk in relation to socioeconomic, demographic, psychiatric, and familial factors: a national register-based study of all suicides in Denmark, 1981-1997. *American Journal of Psychiatry*, 160, 765-772.

Qin, P. & Nordentoft, M. (2005). Suicide risk in relation to psychiatric hospitalization: evidence based on longitudinal registers. *Archives of General Psychiatry*, 62, 427-432.

Rossau, C. D. & Mortensen, P. B. (1997). Risk factors for suicide in patients with schizophrenia: nested case-control study. *British Journal of Psychiatry*, 171, 355-359.

Tsai, S. J. & Lee, T. W. (2006). Schizophrenia, suicide, and the role of the serotonergic system. In R. Tatarelli, M. Pompili, & P. Girardi (Eds.) *Suicide in Schizophrenia.* Hauppauge, NY: Nova Science.

Westermeyer, J. F., Harrow, M., & Marengo, J. T. (1991). Risk for suicide in schizophrenia and other psychotic and nonpsychotic disorders. *Journal of Nervous & Mental Disease*, 179, 259-266.

Wolfersdorf, M., Keller, F., & Schmidt-Michel, P. O. (1988). Are hospital suicides on the increase? A survey of reports on hospital suicides in the psychiatric literature of the 19th and the 20th century. *Social Psychiatry & Psychiatric Epidemiology*, 23, 207-216.

In: Suicide from a Global Perspective: Psychiatric Approaches ISBN: 978-1-61942-267-4
Editors: A. Shrivastava, M. Kimbrell, and D. Lester © 2012 Nova Science Publishers, Inc.

Chapter 18

SUICIDE AND SUBSTANCE ABUSE

Donald M. Dougherty**, *Charles W. Mathias, Dawn M. Marsh, and Michael A. Dawes

INTRODUCTION

Drug abuse, impulsivity, serotonin dysregulation, and stressful life events are associated with suicide. Impulsivity and serotonin (5-HT) function are linked to previous suicidal behaviors and drug abuse. The relationships between impulsivity and 5-HT, while often included in theories of suicide, have not been firmly established. Little is known about how the combination of factors (e.g., impulsivity, 5-HT, and stressful life events) affects the developmental trajectories of drug abuse and suicidal behaviors or what is the predictive validity of these factors to determine the dual outcomes of drug abuse and suicidal behaviors. Future studies should include prospective examination of (a) the role of impulsivity in suicidal behaviors and drug abuse; (b) how biological mechanisms predict these relationships; and (c) how suicidality and drug abuse interrelate longitudinally. Knowledge gained from prospective study of these variables will provide insights into the state and trait characteristics and biological mechanisms present in adolescents at risk for suicide and substance abuse, thereby enabling the characterization of clinical subgroups within this heterogeneous high-risk population. The knowledge gained from these studies should be used to inform the development of multimodal treatment and prevention programs that take into account the specific needs of each subgroup.

Most researchers and clinicians would agree that there is a high rate of co-occurrence between suicidal behaviors and substance use disorders. For instance, the rapid escalation of drug abuse that began during the 1960's in the United States was followed by a 300% increase in adolescent suicidal behaviors over the next twenty years (Goldsmith, et al., 2002). A national epidemiological survey (SAMHSA, 2002) found that adolescents reporting illicit drug use (except marijuana) were nearly three times more likely to be at risk for suicidal behaviors compared to non-drug using adolescents. Furthermore, 29% of the adults admitted

* E-mail address: ddougher@wfubmc.edu. Phone: 210-567-2726. Fax: 210-567-2732. Address all correspondence to: Donald M. Dougherty, Ph.D., Professor and Vice Chair of Research.

to drug-abuse treatment centers reported histories of suicidal ideation, and 22% reported histories of suicide attempts (Wines, et al., 2004). During the two years following discharge from treatment, significant percentages continued to report suicidal ideation and further attempts (20% and 7%, respectively, [Wines, et al., 2004]). Finally, data from the South Carolina Youth Risk Behavior Survey indicated that the progression of drug use severity was related to corresponding increases in the severity of suicidal behaviors (Garrison, et al., 1993). Although a relationship between drug abuse and suicidality appears clear, the underlying mechanisms responsible for this relationship remain largely undetermined.

Interaction of Factors Increasing Risk for Suicidal Behavior and Substance Abuse

There are a number of risk factors that have been proposed as leading to suicide, substance abuse, and their co-occurrence. One possibility is that stressful life events trigger suicidal behaviors or substance abuse in an attempt to relieve or reduce stress. Various studies report that suicide attempts or substance abuse are often attributed to a need to escape negative feelings or obtain relief from life's circumstances (Boergers, et al., 1998; Hawton, et al., 1982; Kienhorst, et al., 1995). Similarly, drug users often report using drugs to self-medicate or escape (Hufford, 2001; Khantzain, 1997). This relief/escape mechanism may result in the co-occurrence of suicidal and drug use behaviors. For example, suicidal ideation is associated with high levels of stress, and the anxiolytic effect of substance use is one alternative for reducing that stress (Light, et al., 2003). Alternatively, substance abuse can also trigger suicidal behavior by contributing to increased psychological distress and aggressiveness (Hufford, 2001), as well as developmental failures, such as school difficulties or expulsion, and problematic interaction with peers (Conner & Goldston, 2007). Furthermore, drug use may lower inhibitions and provide the means for attempting suicide (Schuckit & Schuckit, 1989), as well as significantly impairing judgment which can restrict the use of alternative coping strategies and "help to propel suicidal ideation into action" (Hufford, 2001, p. 803).

While there is ample evidence for risk factors that appear to lead to suicidal and drug use behaviors, there are also behavioral mechanisms that may act as links between suicidality and drug use. For example, impulsivity is an important behavioral mechanism that contributes to both suicide and substance abuse behaviors. The predisposition for impulsivity can substantially increase the likelihood of acting on suicidal thoughts (Mann, et al., 1999). Impulsivity has also been shown to be an independent predictor of suicidal behaviors, separate from the contribution of other known risk factors like depression (Kingsbury, et al., 1999). Similarly, impulsivity is a central mechanism in substance abuse as evidenced by the fact that: (1) substance abusers are more impulsive on self-report and laboratory behavioral measures; (2) impulsive groups have a higher incidence of substance abuse; (3) impulsivity is both a risk factor for the development of substance abuse, as well as a consequence of that abuse; (4) impulsivity predicts attrition from substance abuse treatment programs; and (5) treatments for impulsivity are accompanied by reduced substance use (Moeller, et al., 2001). Thus, cross-sectional research seems to indicate that impulsivity is independently related to both substance abuse and suicidal behavior.

The complexity of the relationships among suicide, substance abuse and impulsivity makes identification of causal mechanisms difficult. Which of these behaviors happens first, and how might the progression to co-occurrence of suicidality and drug abuse occur? Are these relationships different depending on individual circumstances? One perspective has been that substance abuse increases impulsivity, which then increases the risk for suicide (Mann, et al., 1999; Putnins, 1995). Conversely, impulsivity may lead to the initiation of substance abuse (Chambers, et al., 2003) and ultimately suicide. Alternatively, substance abuse may be initiated to cope with a failed suicide attempt, which then leads to increased impulsive behavior. In addition, perhaps a trigger for any or all of these behaviors is some combination of stressful life events and a psychiatric state (Mann, et al., 1999). All of these perspectives are likely to be correct, depending on individual circumstances and biological predisposition. However, determining the underlying causal mechanisms and the directional relationships among impulsivity, substance abuse and suicidality will require prospective, longitudinal research designs that concurrently examine potential biological, behavioral and psychosocial attributes of these behaviors.

The Role of Serotonin in Suicidal Behavior and Substance Abuse

One biological approach that has been examined as a potential causal mechanism underlying the individual behaviors of impulsivity (Dougherty, et al., 2004; Walderhaug, et al., 2002), substance abuse (e.g., Javors, et al., 2005), and suicidality (Mann, 1999) is the serotonin neurotransmitter system. However, the question of how serotonin may link these behaviors remains unclear. One prominent line of thought is that disruptions of serotonin function may lead to increased impulsivity and, ultimately, suicidal acts, or there may be a bi-directional relationship between substance abuse and disruptions in serotonin function that together lead to increased impulsivity and, ultimately, suicidal acts (Mann, et al., 1999).

A number of methodological approaches that examine peripheral indicators of serotonergic functioning have been used in cross-sectional studies of both suicidality and drug abuse. Low concentrations of the major metabolite of serotonin (5-hydroxyindoleacetic acid) have been related to both suicide and drug abuse (Linnoila & Virkkunen, 1992). Low plasma concentrations of the serotonin precursor, L-tryptophan, have been shown to correlate negatively with past suicidal behaviors (Capuron, et al., 2002) and positively with cocaine dependence (Van der Does, 2001). Functional disruptions in peripheral platelet measures of serotonin have been shown in substance abusers like alcoholics (Javors, et al., 2005), and this disruption has been thought to be the result of variants of the serotonin transporter gene. Recent findings have shown that these genetic variants interact with stressful life events in a dose-response manner to predict suicidality (Caspi, et al., 2003; Eley, et al., 2004; Gibb, et al., 2006) and the quantity and frequency of substance use (Covault, et al., 2007; Olsson, et al., 2005). Collectively, the results of these studies suggest that disruptions of serotonergic function contribute to increases in suicidality and drug abuse, and these disruptions may act as a link that increases the co-occurrence of these behaviors.

Accounting for the Heterogeneity of Suicidal and Substance Abuse Populations

An important consideration in the study of the relationship between suicide and substance abuse is the heterogeneity of populations expressing these behaviors. There is a wide range of substance abuse behaviors that are defined by the developmental time course of substance abuse, the drug class, and the level of impairment. Similarly, suicidal behaviors also represent a continuum of behaviors ranging from ideation to suicide attempts and death by suicide. These share some overlap, but also have a unique relationship with substance use disorders. Complicating this picture is the fact that efforts to distinguish or characterize groups have generally focused on suicidality or drug use status at a single time point, such as time of treatment. However, individuals' drug use or suicidal behavior may change over time. Little research has focused on characterizing the high-risk individuals' course of suicidal and drug use behaviors prospectively, distinguishing between individuals with different long-term courses, or identifying the risk and protective factors associated with these different trajectories. However, latent class models are a new and promising tool that has the potential to clarify the relationship among these heterogeneous behaviors.

Latent growth curve modeling is a statistical method for understanding growth patterns over time. More recently, an approach has been developed that combines latent class analysis and latent growth modeling (Muthén, 2001). Under this model, latent trajectory classes are derived that represent subgroups with similar growth trajectories or developmental patterns. The combined approaches are advantageous since they allow classes to be defined based on their patterns of responses over time (Muthén, 2001). Such methods could be applied to identify groups with differing trajectories of suicidal and drug use behaviors, and have been suggested by the Institute of Medicine as an alternative method for analyzing suicidal behaviors (Goldsmith, et al., 2002). This approach of latent class modeling prospective data on suicidal behaviors and substance abuse should be a priority for future research.

Future Directions to Advance the Field

Taken in combination, behavioral and biological studies have each attempted to determine underlying contributors to suicidality and drug use behaviors and the potential mechanisms that may increase the co-occurrence of these behaviors. Most studies, however, have relied on cross-sectional, retrospective research methods to develop unitary treatment and prevention programs for suicidality and drug use. It is notable that most interventions that have been developed, especially those developed for adolescents, have not focused on individual differences, but rather have been predicated on the notion that a single approach might be useful for all individuals. It is important to recognize that the co-occurrence of suicidal and drug use behaviors may result from different developmental patterns. Prospective, longitudinal designs offer a more powerful indication of what factors are associated with the co-occurrence of these behaviors, and when and how these factors influence future risk for suicide or drug use. Using prospective measurement to characterize the developmental time course of suicidal and drug use behaviors could lead to the identification of specific temporal combinations of risk factors and mechanisms which would have the potential to lead to treatments that could be specifically designed for different developmental trajectories and, thereby, increase the efficacy of those treatment programs.

The current state of the field has been to study what factors are associated with substance abuse and suicidal behaviors, but what is needed at this stage is research that can push the boundaries of our knowledge of *when* and *how* factors interact to influence the expression of suicidal behaviors and initiation of substance abuse. Specific recommendations to address these questions include: (1) determining the interaction between behavioral and biological factors and the dual outcomes of suicidal and substance use behaviors; (2) testing the neurobiological mechanisms that contribute to the co-occurrence of suicidal and drug use behaviors using cellular and neurochemical methods; (3) using longitudinal studies to examine when and how other risk factors, such as impulsivity and substance abuse, influence suicidality; and (4) using an interdisciplinary approach which will be more likely to produce results that may better inform treatment and result in reduced suicidality. The knowledge gained from research that addresses these questions will provide insights regarding the state and trait characteristics, the interaction of life-events, impulsivity and the role of serotonin in suicidal behaviors and substance abuse which will enable the field to better distinguish subgroups among this heterogeneous, high-risk population. In turn, this knowledge will be used to inform the future development of treatment and prevention programs for youths with suicidal and drug use behaviors and will allow for multiple treatment approaches to be designed that take into account the specific needs of the various subgroups.

REFERENCES

Boergers, J., Spirito, A., & Donaldson, D. (1998). Reasons for adolescent suicide attempts: associations with psychological functioning. *Journal of the American Academy of Child & Adolescent Psychiatry*, 37, 1287-1293.

Capuron, L., Ravaud, A., Neveu, P. J., et al. (2002). Association between decreased serum tryptophan concentrations and depressive symptoms in cancer patients undergoing cytokine therapy. *Molecular Psychiatry*, 7, 468-473.

Caspi, A., Sugden, K., Moffitt, T. E., et al. (2003). Influence of life stress on depression: moderation by a polymorphism in the 5-HTT gene. *Science*, 18, 386-389.

Chambers, R. A., Taylor, J. R., & Potenza, M. N. (2003). Developmental neurocircuitry of motivation in adolescence: a critical period of addiction vulnerability. *American Journal of Psychiatry*, 160, 1041-1052.

Conner, K., & Goldston, D. B. (2007) Rates of suicide among males increase steadily from age 11 to 21: proposed causes and implications for prevention. *Aggression & Violent Behavior*, 12, 193-207.

Covault, J., Tennen, H., Armeli, S., et al. (2007) Interactive effects of the serotonin 5-HTTLPR polymorphism and stressful life events on college drinking and drug use. *Biological Psychiatry*, 61, 609-616.

Dougherty, D. M., Marsh, D. M., Mathias, C. W., et al. (2004). Impulsive behavioral differences following combined alcohol and L-tryptophan depletion/loading manipulation. *Journal of Psychopharmacology*, 18, A32.

Eley, T. C., Sugden, K., Corsico, A., et al. (2004). Gene-environment interaction analysis of serotonin system markers with adolescent depression. *Molecular Psychiatry*, 9, 908-915.

Garrison, C., McKeown, R., Valois, R., et al. (1993). Aggression, substance use, and suicidal behaviors in high school students. *American Journal of Public Health*, 83, 179-184.

Gibb, B. E., McGeary, J. E., Beevers, C. G., et al. (2006). Serotonin transporter (5-HTTLPR) genotype, child abuse, and suicide attempts in adults psychiatric inpatients. *Suicide & Life-Threatening Behavior*, 36, 687-693.

Goldsmith, S. K., Pellmar, T. C., Kleinman, A. M., et al. (2002). *Reducing suicide: A national imperative*. Washington, DC: National Academy Press.

Hawton, K., Osborn, M., O'Grady, J., et al. (1982). Classification of adolescents who take overdoses. *British Journal of Psychiatry*, 140, 124-131.

Hufford, M. R. (2001). Alcohol and suicidal behavior. *Clinical Psychology Review*, 21, 797-811.

Javors, M. A., Seneviratne, C., Roache, J. D., et al. (2005). Platelet serotonin uptake and paroxetine binding among allelic genotypes of the serotonin transporter in alcoholics. *Progress in Neuro-Psychopharmacology & Biological Psychiatry*, 29, 7-13.

Khantzian, E. (1997). The self-medication hypothesis of substance use disorders: a reconsideration and recent applications. *Harvard Review of Psychiatry*, 4, 231-244.

Kienhorst, I., DeWilde, E., Diekstra, R., et al. (1995). Adolescents' image of their suicide attempt. *Journal of the American Academy of Child & Adolescent Psychiatry*, 34, 623-628.

Kingsbury, S., Hawton, K., Steinhardt, K., et al. (1999). Do adolescents who take overdoses have specific psychological characteristics? A comparative study with psychiatric and community controls. *Journal of the American Academy of Child & Adolescent Psychiatry*, 38, 1125-1131.

LeMarquand, D., Benkelfat, C., Pihl, R. O., et al. (1999). Behavioral disinhibition induced by tryptophan depletion in nonalcoholic young men with multigenerational family histories of paternal alcoholism. *American Journal of Psychiatry*, 156, 1771-1779.

Light, J. M., Grube, J. W., Madden, P. A., et al. (2003). Adolescent alcohol use and suicidal ideation: a nonrecursive model. *Addictive Behaviors*, 28, 705-724.

Linnoila, M., & Virkkunen, M. (1992). Biologic correlates of suicidal risk and aggressive behavior traits. *Journal of Clinical Psychopharmacology*, 12(Supplement), 19-20.

Mann, J. J., Waternaux, C., Haas, G. L., et al. (1999). Toward a clinical model of suicidal behavior in psychiatric patients. *American Journal of Psychiatry*, 156, 181-189.

Moeller, F. G., Barratt, E. S., Dougherty, D. M., et al. (2001). Psychiatric aspects of impulsivity. *American Journal of Psychiatry*, 158, 1783-1793.

Muthén, B. (2001). Latent variable mixture modeling. In G. Marcoulides and R. Schumacker (Eds.) *New Developments and Techniques in Structural Equation Modeling*, pp. 1-33. Mahaw, NJ: Lawrence Erlbaum Associates.

Olsson, C. A., Byrnes, G. B., Lofti-Miri, M., et al. (2005). Association between 5-HTTLPR genotypes and persisting patterns of anxiety and alcohol use: results from a 10-year longitudinal study of adolescent mental health. *Molecular Psychiatry*, 10, 868-876.

Putnins, A. L. (1995). Recent drug use and suicidal behaviour among young offenders. *Drug & Alcohol Review*, 14, 151-158.

Schuckit, M. A., & Schuckit, J. J. (1989). Substance use and abuse: a risk factor in youth suicide. In *Report of the Secretary's task force on youth suicide, Volume 2: Risk factors for youth suicide*. Washington, DC: U.S. Government Printing Office.

Substance Abuse and Mental Health Services Administration (SAMHSA). (2002). *Substance use and the risk of suicide among youths: National household survey on drug abuse report.* Retrieved January 19, 2007 from http://www.oas.samhsa.gov/ 2k2/suicide/suicide.htm

Walderhaug, E., Lunde, H., Nordvik, J.E., et al. (2002). Lowering of serotonin by rapid tryptophan depletion increases impulsiveness in normal individuals. *Psychopharmacology*, 164, 385-391.

Wines, J. D., Saitz, R., Horton, N. J., et al. (2004). Suicidal behavior, drug use and depressive symptoms after detoxification: a 2-year prospective study. *Drug & Alcohol Dependence*, 76s, 21-29.

Van der Does, A. J. (2001). The effects of tryptophan depletion on mood and psychiatric symptoms. *Journal of Affective Disorders*, 64, 107-119.

In: Suicide from a Global Perspective: Psychiatric Approaches ISBN: 978-1-61942-267-4
Editors: A. Shrivastava, M. Kimbrell, and D. Lester © 2012 Nova Science Publishers, Inc.

Chapter 19

What Is the Relationship between Suicide and Eating Disorders?

Ida F. Dancyger, Victor M. Fornari, and Jennie Goldstein

Introduction

This chapter reviews the literature regarding the relationship between eating disorders (EDs) and suicide (both attempters and completers). Several investigators have suggested that suicide is the major cause of death among patients with anorexia nervosa (AN), refuting the assumption that inanition generally threatens the life of these patients). The implications for assessment and treatment of individuals with an ED who have a history of suicidal ideation, a serious suicide plan or a history of suicide attempts, require special consideration. The prevention of suicide in individuals with an ED remains a major focus of clinical care, often underestimated by the clinician treating the individual patient and under-reported in the literature.

An overview of the literature of the past 15 years highlights the importance that all clinicans treating patients with an ED must be keenly aware of the serious risks of suicidal behavior and of suicide in this population.

Epidemiology

Most studies regarding the mortality rate, including death by suicide, in patients with ED, have varied in a number of important ways, and different researchers have reported a wide range of findings. This variability in outcome can be understood by examining the particular characteristics of each study sample.

As in other psychiatric epidemiological surveys, the methodological variables, such as age of onset of the ED, age of patients at time of study, co-morbid psychopathology and length of follow-up, have all contributed to different findings. In this review, as seen in Table 19-1, the following conclusions can be drawn. The suicide rates reported for patients specifically with AN range from 2.2% (Emborg, 1999; Harris & Barraclough, 1997) to a high of 15% (Crisp, et al., 1992); rates for patients with bulimia nervosa (BN) range from 0.4% (Keel, et al., 2003) to 2.2% (Harris & Barraclough, 1997); and suicide rates for patients with EDs are higher for males than for females (Powers & Spratt, 1994).

The range of years at follow-up was 5 to 23 years (Pompili, et al., 2004) to 1.7 to 33.0 years (Sullivan, 1995), with a mean of 22 years for the St. George cohort and 21.8 years for the Aberdeen cohort (Crisp, et al., 1992).

The Sullivan (1995) study had the largest number of patients as it was a meta-analysis of forty-two other studies and reported that 27% of the patients, who had died after a median follow-up of 7.6 years, had completed suicide. Other findings indicate a difference in rates of suicide between patients hospitalized in a psychiatric facility (higher rates) compared to a medical facility. Overall, what is consistent is that the rates of mortality and suicide are significantly higher than in the general population.

The rates of parasuicidal behavior, which includes suicide attempts, self-injurious behavior and deliberate self-harm (cutting, burning, biting, hitting and choking) and intense suicidal ideation, differ across studies, as seen in Table 19-2. Males with EDs exhibited more than double the attempted suicide rate than females, and also were more frequently homosexual in their orientation (Bramon-Bosch, et al., 2000).

AN patients made significantly more suicide attempts than BN patients (Franko, et al., 2004). This too is consistent with completed suicides being more common in AN than BN as indicated in Table 19-2- in one report (Keel, et al., 2003). However, when suicide attempts and self-injurious behaviors were grouped together, then BN patients showed almost double the number.

At this time, therefore, there is inconsistency regarding ED subgroup diagnosis and the relationship to suicidal behaviors and completed suicides.

Some of the associated risk factors that have been identified with these parasuicidal behaviors in patients with EDs have been summarized in Table 19-2. The range of contributing variables includes: severity of depression, history of laxative abuse, anxiety, obsessive-compulsive behaviors, hostility, paranoid ideation, alcohol and drug abuse, antisocial behaviors and low cholesterol levels.

Does having experienced the traumatic event of sexual abuse contribute to the development of an ED? A review (Brewerton, 2005) of the relationship between traumatic experiences and the development of ED confirmed that childhood sexual abuse (CSA) to be a significant but non-specific risk factor, especially for the development of BN in adults and adolescents of both sexes. Of particular interest was one study that examined adolescents who experienced date violence, including date rape, and found that, for both girls and boys, they were more likely to have suicidal thoughts or attempts than their non-abused peers (Ackard & Neumark-Sztainer, 2002).

However, Brewerton (2005) concluded that the link between EDs and trauma-related comorbidity, such as PTSD, remains relatively un-researched in terms of long-term course, prognosis and treatment response.

Table 19. 1. Studies of suicide and eating disorders

Authors	Subjects: Location of Origin, Diagnosis, Age in Years	Suicide Rates	Findings
Sullivan (1995)	3,006 females: New Zealand, AN, age range = 15-24	27% of the deaths were due to suicide	The aggregate mortality rate was found to be much higher than the annual death rate due to all cause of death for females aged 15-24 years.
Emborg (1999)	2,526 females, 237 males: Denmark, AN or AN related ED, mean age admitted to psychiatric hospital = 23.2, mean age admitted to somatic hospital = 21.3	AN 2.2%	Patients admitted to a psychiatric hospital are more likely to commit suicide than patients admitted to a somatic hospital, who usually die of natural causes.
Pompili et al (2004)	1,536 patients: USA, Denmark, Germany, UK; AN, age range = 14-25	2.30%	Suicide among patients with AN is more frequent when compared to the general population.
Harris et al (1997)	1,300 females: Canada, England, USA, Sweden, Norway, Denmark, New Zealand; AN BN, mean age = 20	AN and BN 2.2%	Nearly all cases were referrals to medical or psychiatric departments. The suicide risk was 23 times the expected.
Moller-Madsen et al (1996)	790 females, 63 males, Denmark, AN , age range = 14-64.7	18 of 22 cases of unnatural death due to suicide	In females, the highest standardized mortality ratio is in those first hospitalized in their 20's. In males, the highest SMR is in those first hospitalized in their teens.
Herzog et al (1998)	246 females: Boston, USA, AN-R AN-BP BN, age range = 24-46	AN 2.2% BN 0%	AN population has a higher suicide rate than the non-AN population.
Keel et al (2003)	246 females:Boston, USA; AN BN, age range = 12-18	AN 4.1% BN 0.4%	The best preditor of fatality was the severity of alcohol use disorder. Standardized mortality ratios were elevated for causes of mortality and suicide in AN, but not for death in BN.
Korndorfer et al (2003)	193 females, 15 males, Minnesota, USA; AN, age range = 10-57	0.96%	Death certificates likely underestimate the frequency of AN as cause of death and as a comorbidity in cause of suicide.
Crisp et al (1992)	St. George (England) Cohort: 81 females: AN, mean age = 16.8 Aberdeen (England) Cohort: 63 females: AN, mean age = 19.1	St. George 1% Aberdeen 6%	Complications of AN and suicide are the two most common causes of death for this disorder.
Powers et al (1994)	15 females: Florida, USA: ED, mean age = 25.6 15 males: Florida, USA; ED, mean age = 25.8	females 0% males 6.7%	Clinical findings at the onset of treatment were very similar between males and females in terms of eating disorders symptoms.

Note:
AN = Anorexia Nervosa; AN-R = Restricting Anorexia Nervosa; AN -BP= Binge Purge Anorexia Nervosa; Nervosa;
BN = Bulimia nervosa; ED = Eating Disorder.

Table 19. 2. Studies of parasuicide and eating disorders

Authors	Subjects: Place of Origin, Diagnosis, Age in Years	Parasuicidal Behavior	Parasuicidal Rates	Associated Risk Factors	Findings
Miotto et al (2003)	1000 adolescents: rural Italy, AN BN EDNOS, age range = 15-19	Intense Suicidal Ideation	Males 5% Females 5%	Depression, anxiety , obsession-compulsion, hostility, paranoid ideation, interpersonal sensitivity	Both males and females reporting suicidal ideation achieved significantly higher scores on the ED inventories.
Johnson et al (2002)	717 adolescents: Northern NY State, USA, AN BN EDNOS, mean age = 13.8	Attempted Suicide	With ED 12.5%	Depression, anxiety, substance use	EDs during adolescence may be associated with an elevated risk for a broad range of physical/ mental health problems during early adulthood.
Favaro and Santonastaso (1996)	398 women: Italy, AN BN, age range = 20-27	Attempted Suicide	AN,BN-NP 2.7%, 5.7% AN,BN-P 20.0%,14.1% AN,BN laxatives 18.75%, 16.7%	Obsession-compulsion, depression, anxiety, hostility, phobic anxiety	Psychiatric symptoms were significantly more serious in purging compared to nonpurging groups.
Corcos et al (2002)	295 females: France, Switzerland, Belgium, AN BN, mean age = 25.3	Attempted Suicide	1st attempt before BN 15.9% ; After onset of BN 59.8%	Depression, impulsive disordered conducts	BN who had attempted suicide reported more suicidal ideation during adolescence. This suicidal group also reported more life events, such as family separation, prior or concomitant to the onset of their ED.
Milos et al (2004)	288 females: Switzerland, AN BN EDNOS, age range 17-30	Attempted Suicide	AN-R 10.5% AN-BP 34.7% BN-P 29.9% BN-NP 14.3%	Severe depression, vomiting, use of laxatives, fear of weight gain	Subjects with a purging type ED more frequently had a history of attempted suicide than subjects with a nonpurging type ED.
Franko et al (2004)	246 women: Boston, AN BN, mean age = 24.8	Attempted Suicide	AN 22.1% ; BN 10.9%	AN severity of depression BN history of laxative abuse	Significantly more AN subjects than BN subjects made a suicide attempt.

Authors	Subjects: Place of Origin, Diagnosis, Age in Years	Parasuicidal Behavior	Parasuicidal Rates	Associated Risk Factors	Findings
Loas et al (2005)	245 females: France and Switzerland, AN BN, age range = 15-50	Attempted suicide, suicidal ideation	Bulimic pts had a 1.89 fold higher risk of SA than anorectic pts.	depression, dependent personality, borderline personality	Excess dependency or dependent PD increase likelihood of SI or SA in BN pts.
Bulik et al (1999)	222 females: New Zealand, AN BN, age range = 17-48	Attempted suicide	BN 31%; AN 27%	temperament: high persistance; character dimensions: low self-directedness and high self-transcendence	Females with BN reported less severe intent to die compared to those with AN. In AN group, SA equally likely w/ or w/o comorbid MDD.
Youssef et al (2004)	152 females: France, AN BN, age range = 18-24	Attempted Suicide	AN 29.7%; BN 30.0%	Depression, antisocial practices, hysteria, psychopathic deviate, obsessiveness, anger/fears	Suicide attempts were most frequent in subjects with purging behavior. Those attempting suicide with EDs were mostly students.
Stein et al (2004)	145 females, 5 males: Pennsylvania, USA, AN BN EDNOS, age range = 17-45	Attempted Suicide, impulsive self-injurious behavior	21% with history of at least one suicide attempt, 11% with history of self-injury	bipolar disorder, depression, drug abuse	Parasuicidal AN patients had a later onset of their ED compared to non-suicidal patients.
Welch and Fairburn (1996)	102 women: England, BN, age range = 16-35	Deliberate Self-Harm	BN 30%	Overdose, cutting, burning, alcohol/drug abuse	BN cases used more drugs than control groups. BN cases also had a higher rate of deliberate self-harm than controls.
Favaro et al (1994)	74 females: Italy, AN, mean age = 23.6	Attempted Suicide, impulsive self-injurious behavior, suicidal ideation	AN 82.4% reported suicide attempts, self-injurious behavior or suicidal Ideation	Significantly lower cholesterol levels	Subjects who reported previous suicide attempts, impulsive self-injurious behavior, or current suicidal ideation showed significantly lower cholesterol levels than subjects without suicidality.

Table 19. 2. (Continued)

Authors	Subjects: Place of Origin, Diagnosis, Age in Years	Parasuicidal Behavior	Parasuicidal Rates	Associated Risk Factors	Findings
Bramon-Bosch et al (2000)	30 males, 30 females: England, AN BN EDNOS, mean age = 23.2, 18	Attempted Suicide	males 50% females 23%	Anxiety and depressive disorders	Suicidal behavior was more frequent among male patients. More homosexuality in males.
Wildman et al (2004)	54 females: Pennsylvania, USA, AN BN EDNOS, age range = 23-37	Attempted Suicide, cutting, burning, hitting, biting, choking	AN-R 18.5% AN-BP 29.6 BN 55.6%	Depression, anxiety, substance use	Onset of major depression occurred more often before the onset of an ED.
Yamaguchi et al (2000)	49 females, 2 males: Japan, AN BN EDNOS, age range = 14-36	Attempted suicide	45% made SA ; 69% of those by AN -BP	mood disorder, personality disorder (BP, OCPD, Histrionic)	High parental overprotection assoc with suicidal behavior in ED pts. More suicidal pts reported h/o child abuse than nonsuicidal pts.
Kent (1997)	48 women who overdosed, of which 4 met criteria for BN: South London, age range = 17-65	Suicide attempt by deliberate overdose	n/a	increased levels of internally directed irritability or impulsivity	Clinically significant level of ED behavior is found in women who present to the hospital following acts of deliberate self-poisoning.
Bryant-Waugh et al (1996)	22 children (16 female, 6 male): England, AN, mean age = 3.1	Suicidal Behavior	AN 13.6%	Suicidal Ideation	Clinical features of early onset AN were found with the majority of children presenting fear of fatness, distorted body image, and excessive exercising.

Note:

AN = Anorexia Nervosa; AN-BP = Binge Purge Anorexia Nervosa; AN-R = Restricting Anorexia Nervosa; BN = Bulimia Nervosa; BN-P = Purging Bulimia Nervosa;

BN -NP = Non purging Bulimia Nervosa; ED = Eating Disorder; EDNOS = Eating Disorder not otherwise specified.

Association of Eating Disorders, Suicide and Psychopathology

To care for individuals with an ED it is essential to understand the coexisting psychiatric disorders present in order to plan treatment effectively. Rarely do EDs occur as the sole form of psychopathology (Fornari, et al., 1992). Depressive and anxiety disorders, as well as substance abuse, are frequently encountered. Considerable attention has been given to the relationship between ED and affective disorder. The Axis I disorders most commonly occurring with AN and BN are depression, anxiety disorders and substance abuse (Douzinas, et al., 1994). The nature of the relationship between EDs and depression is complex and must be understood in the context of the psychological effects of starvation. The work of Keys and colleagues (1950) in the Minnesota Experiment, documented that malnutrition and emaciation can produce symptoms that can be indistinguishable from depression. Depression in an anorectic individual, however, is not always the result of malnutrition. In some instances, the mood disorder is premorbid to the ED. Data have been published on the prevalence of depression in anorectic patients who are no longer malnourished. In one study of psychiatric comorbidity of depression and ED, the lifetime rate of major depression was approximately 50% for the anorectic and bulimic individuals, but nearly 90% for those with the AN binge-purge subtype (Fornari, et al., 1992). Attempts to clarify the link between ED and anxiety disorders have centered on studying related traits in patients afflicted with these illnesses or in determining the frequency with which patients meet criteria for both illnesses. One study (Fornari, et al., 1992) found that depressive disorders were not more frequently encountered than anxiety disorders in an ED sample. No significant sub-group differences were found with the exception of the AN-BP subtype being significantly more likely to have a lifetime history of obsessive-compulsive disorder than the AN-R sub-group. A significant body of data suggests that EDs and substance abuse, especially alcoholism, are interrelated. The evidence for this association is particularly compelling in individuals with BN, in which a clear increase in the rates of substance abuse in both patients and their first-degree relatives has been demonstrated (Douzinas, et al., 1994). A number of considerations may contribute to the fact that nearly one-quarter of all eating disordered patients give a current or past history of substance abuse. Some may abuse amphetamines in their drive for thinness. Others become dependent on benzodiazepines in order to fall asleep. In one study, more than half of the female patients on a substance abuse unit in a psychiatric hospital met DSM IV criteria for an ED. As reported, EDs are associated with high rates of co-morbid psychopathology including mood disorders, anxiety disorders, substance abuse and personality disorders (Fornari, et al., 1992, Grillo, et al., 1996; Wonderlich & Mitchell, 1997) and in turn these illnesses have been associated with both suicidal and parasuicidal behaviors, as well as completed suicide.

The Management of Suicidal Behavior and Effective Treatment Planning

ED patients with serious co-morbid psychiatric conditions (Mann, et al., 2001), especially suicidal ideation or intractable depression, may not only require admission to an inpatient facility, but may be extremely challenging for mental health practitioners. As outlined in the

APA Practice Guidelines (2000), it is imperative to thoroughly evaluate and assess every patient who presents with AN, BN or ED-NOS, with a comprehensive psychiatric interview, especially covering any history of suicidal ideation, parasuicidal behavior, suicidal attempts and a family history of suicidal behavior and completed suicide. Also critical to consider are the ethical and legal issues surrounding treatment compliance and refusal by either the individual or the family of the individual with an ED. The need for the mental health practitioners to continue outpatient treatment or to hospitalize even against the patient's or the family's wishes when lives are at risk (Fornari, et al., 2001) remains a therapeutic challenge for clinicians. Understanding the family history of psychopathology and suicidal behavior is often critical to the proper clinical care of the individual with an ED.

CONCLUSION

It is clear that there is a strong relationship between suicidal behavior and completed suicide throughout the life span of individuals with EDs. Epidemiological surveys have confirmed the considerably high suicide rate as well as prevalent parasuicidal behaviors. As has been mentioned earlier, rarely do EDs present as the sole form of psychopathology. The associated comorbidity generally found in this population may likely be related to the increased risk of suicide.

Clinician awareness of the heightened risk of suicide in ED patients is critical during the assessment and the ongoing treatment of these individuals. Clinicians must monitor their own negative reactions with ED patients who are suicidal in order to maintain a hopeful stance for recovery. As chronicity sets in, clinicians often tire, as do their families, leading to hopelessness and despair. In order to try to prevent the patient's death, the clinician must monitor that hopelessness in the patient and the family. It is sometimes necessary to intervene against the wishes of both the patient and the family, who have given up hope of recovery. The legal capacity of the clinician to do so may vary from state to state and country to country, depending upon their mental health laws. When the clinical course reaches an impasse, obtaining outside consultation, such as a second opinion, may enhance the clinical care.

This chapter has reviewed studies regarding the relationship between EDs, suicide and suicidal behaviors around the world. The patients lived primarily in Western Europe, North America, New Zealand and Japan, representing many unique cultures. The course, treatment and outcome of an ED are surely impacted by the particular culture. In addition, suicide may have a different meaning in each country. The statistics do not tell the personal, familial and community effects of these deaths.

In conclusion, there is a strong relationship between suicide, suicidal behaviors and EDs. The rates cited likely reflect an underestimate of the true incidence of deaths by suicide in this population. Shame, stigma and inaccurate reporting all contribute to this phenomenon. The prevention of suicide in individuals with an ED remains a major challenge of clinical care. We call on all health professionals to come together to bring about change in the delivery of treatment to these individuals. It is hoped that further research will help reduce the significant mortality rates of these serious and prevalent illnesses.

ACKNOWLEDGMENTS

This chapter is a revised and updated version of an original article by Dancyger, I.F., Fornari, V.M. (2005) Eating disorders and suicide: Is there a relationship? In Suicidal Behavior in Adolescence (eds J. Merrick& G. Zalsman) pp. 143-155. London and Tel Aviv: Freund Publishing House Ltd. Reproduced by permission.

REFERENCES

Ackard, D. M., & Neumark-Sztainer, D. (2002). Date violence and date rape among adolescents: association with disordered eating behaviors and psychological health. *Child Abuse & Neglect*, 26, 455-473.

American Psychiatric Association. (2000). Practice guidelines for the treatment of patients with eating disorders. *American Journal of Psychiatry*, 157, Supplement, 1-29.

Bramon-Bosch, E., Troop, N., & Treasure, J. (2000). Eating disorders in males: a comparison with female patients. *European Eating Disorders Review*, 2000, 8, 321-328.

Brewerton, T. (2005). Psychological trauma and eating disorders. In S. Wonderlich, J. Mitchell et al. (Eds.) *Eating Disorders* Re*view, part 1*, pp. 137-154. Oxford, UK: Radcliffe Publishing

Bryant-Waugh, R., Hankins, M., Shafran, R., Lask, B., & Fosson, A. (1996). A prospective follow-up of children with anorexia nervosa. *Journal of Youth & Adolescence,* 25, 431-437.

Bulik, C. M., Sullivan, P. F., & Joyce, P. R. (1999). Temperament, character and suicide attempts in anorexia nervosa, bulimia nervosa, and major depression. *Acta Psychiatrica Scandinavica*, 100, 27-32.

Corcos, M., Taieb, O., Benoit-Lamy, S., Paterniti, S., Jeammet, P., & Flament, M. (2002). Suicide attempts in women with bulimia nervosa: frequency and characteristics. *Acta Psychiatrica Scandinavica*, 106, 381-386.

Crisp, A. H., Callendar, J. S., Halek, C., & Hsu, G. (1992). Long-term mortality in anorexia nervosa. *British Journal of Psychiatry*, 161, 197-214.

Dancyger, I. F., Fornari, V. M., & Katz, J. L. (2005). Day treatment in the spectrum of care for anorexia nervosa. In P. Swain (Ed.) *Trends in Eating Disorders Research*, pp 123-139. New York: Nova Science.

Douzinas, N., Fornari, V., Goodman, B., Sitnick, T., & Packman, L. (1994). Eating disorders and abuse. *Child & Adolescent Psychiatric Clinics of North America*, 3, 777-796.

Emborg, C. (1999). Mortality and causes of death in eating disorders in Denmark 1970–1993: a case register study. *International Journal of Eating Disorders*, 25, 234 -251.

Favaro, A., Caregaro, L., DiPascoli, L., Brambilla, F., & Santonastaso, P. (2004). Total serum cholesterol and suicidality in anorexia nervosa. *Psychosomatic Medicine*, 66, 548-552.

Favaro, A., & Santonastaso, P. (1996). Purging behaviors, suicide attempts, and psychiatric symptoms in 398 eating disordered subjects. *International Journal of Eating Disorders*, 20, 99-103.

Fornari, V., Dancyger, I., Schneider, M., Fisher, M., Goodman, B., & McCall, A. (2001). Parental medical neglect in the treatment of adolescents with anorexia nervosa. *International Journal of Eating Disorders*, 29, 358-362.

Fornari, V., Kaplan, M., Sandberg, D., Matthews, M., & Katz, J. (1992). The relationship between depression and anxiety disorders in anorexia nervosa and bulimia nervosa. *International Journal of Eating Disorders*, 12, 21-29.

Franko, D. L., Keel, P. K., Dorer, D. J., Blais, M., Delinsky, S., Eddy, K., & Herzog, D. (2004). What predicts suicide attempts in women with eating disorders? *Psychological Medicine*, 34, 843-853.

Grillo, C. M., Becker, D. F., Walker, M. L., Edell, W., & McGlashan, T. (1996). Gender differences in personality disorders in psychiatrically hospitalized young adults. *Journal of Nervous & Mental Disease*, 184, 754-757.

Harris, E. C, & Barraclough B. (1997). Suicide as an outcome for mental disorders. *British Journal of Psychiatry*, 170, 205-228.

Herzog, D., Greenwood, D. N., Dorer, D., Flores, A., Ekeblad, E., Richards, A., & Keller, M. (2000). Mortality in eating disorders: a descriptive study. *International Journal of Eating Disorders,* 28, 20-26.

Johnson, J., Cohen, P., Kasen, S., & Brook, J., (2002). Eating disorders during adolescence and the risk for physical and mental disorders during early adulthood. *Archives of General Psychiatry*, 59, 545-552.

Keel, P., Dorer, D., Eddy, K., Franko, D., Charatan, D. & Herzog, D. (2003). Predictors of mortality in eating disorders. *Archives of General Psychiatry,* 60, 179-183.

Kent, A., Goddard, K., van den Berk, P., Raphael, F., McCluskey, S., & Lacey, J. (1997). Eating disorder in women admitted to hospital following deliberate self-poisoning. *Acta Psychiatrica Scandinavica,* 95, 140-144.

Keys, A., Brozek, J., Henschel, A., Mickelsen, O., & Taylor, H. (1950). *The biology of human starvation*. Minneapolis: University of Minnesota Press.

Kornderfer, S., Lucas, A., Suman, V., Crowson, C., Krahn, L., & Melton, L. (2003). Long term survival of patients with anorexia nervosa: a population–based study in Rochester, Minn. *Mayo Clinic Proceedings*, 78, 278-284.

Loas, G. ,Guilbaud, O., Perez-Diaz, F. et al. (2005). Dependency and suicidality in addictive disorders. *Psychiatry Research*, 137, 103-111.

Mann, J., Brent, D., & Arango, V. (2001). The neurobiology and genetics of suicide and attempted suicide: a focus on the serotonergic system. *Neuropsychopharmacology,* 24, 467-477.

Milos, G., Spindler, A., Hepp, U., & Schnyder, U. (2004). Suicide attempts and suicidal ideation: links with psychiatric comorbidity in eating disorder subjects. *General Hospital Psychiatry*, 26, 129-135.

Miotto, P., De Coppi, M., Frezza, M., & Preti, A. (2003). Eating disorders and suicide risk factors in adolescents: an Italian community-based study. *Journal of Nervous & Mental Disease,* 191, 437-443.

Moller-Madsen, S., Nystrup, J., & Nielsen, S. (1996). Mortality in anorexia nervosa in Denmark during the period 1970 -1987. *Acta Psychiatra Scandinavica*, 94, 454-459.

Pompili, M., Mancinelli, I., Girardi, P., Ruberto, A. & Tatarelli, R. (2004), Suicide in anorexia nervosa: a meta-analysis. *International Journal of Eating Disorders*, 36, 99-103.

Powers, P. S., & Spratt, E. G. (1994). Males and females with eating disorders. *Eating Disorders*, 2, 197-214.

Stein, D., Lilenfeld, L., Wildman, P., & Marcus, M. (2004). Attempted suicide and self-injury in patients diagnosed with eating disorders. *Comprehensive Psychiatry*, 45, 447-451.

Sullivan, P. (1995). Mortality in anorexia nervosa. *American Journal of Psychiatry,* 152, 1073-1074.

Welch, S., & Fairburn, C. G. (1996). Impulsivity or comorbidity in bulimia nervosa: a controlled study of deliberate self-harm and alcohol and drug misuse in a community sample. *British Journal of Psychiatry*, 169, 451-458.

Wildman, P., Lilenfeld, L., & Marcus, M. (2004). Axis I comorbidity onset and parasuicide in women with eating disorders. *International Journal of Eating Disorders*, 35, 190-197.

Wonderlich, S. A., & Mitchell, J. E. (1997). Eating disorders and comorbidity: empirical, conceptual, and clinical implications. *Psychopharmacology Bulletin*, 33, 381-390.

Yamaguchi, N., Kobayashi, & J. Hirokazu, T. (2000). Parental representation in eating disorder patients with suicide. *Journal of Psychosomatic Research*, 49, 131-136.

Youssef, G., Plancherel, B., Laget, J., Corcos, M., Flament, M., & Halfon, O. (2004). Personality trait risk factors for attempted suicide among young women with eating disorders. *European Psychiatry,* 19, 131-139.

In: Suicide from a Global Perspective: Psychiatric Approaches ISBN: 978-1-61942-267-4
Editors: A. Shrivastava, M. Kimbrell, and D. Lester © 2012 Nova Science Publishers, Inc.

Chapter 20

Chronic Suicidal Ideation in Borderline Personality Disorder

Randy A. Sansone and Melinda G. Fierros

Introduction

Borderline personality disorder (BPD) is a complex and intriguing personality dysfunction that is characterized by a reasonably intact social façade in conjunction with chronic self-regulation difficulties and recurrent self-destructive behavior. Self-regulation problems may manifest as eating disorders (e.g., anorexia or bulimia nervosa, binge eating disorder and obesity), alcohol and substance abuse or dependence including prescription misuse, promiscuity, difficulties regulating money (e.g., gambling difficulties, bankruptcies and overspending on credit cards), and chronic pain syndromes. Self-destructive behavior may manifest as graphic or subtle disfigurement of oneself (e.g., self-mutilation through scratching, cutting or burning oneself), suicide gestures and attempts, relationships with abusive partners, high-risk behaviors (e.g., having unprotected sexual relationships with HIV-positive individuals, jogging in dangerous parks at night and frequenting treacherous bars), and high-risk hobbies (e.g., bungee jumping and mountain climbing). To emphasize the relevance of self-harm behavior, Mack (1975) described this particular feature as the "behavioral specialty" of those with BPD.

The Diagnosis of BPD

In the DSM-IV-TR (American Psychiatric Association, 2000), BPD is classified as a Cluster B personality disorder. This personality disorder grouping is highlighted by dramatic, emotional and erratic characteristics as opposed to Cluster A personality disorders, which are characterized by odd and eccentric features, or Cluster C personality disorders, which are characterized by fearful and anxious features. According to the DSM-IV-TR, the diagnostic criteria for BPD are: (a) frantic efforts to avoid abandonment; (b) a history of unstable and intense relationships with others; (c) identity disturbance; (d) impulsivity in at least two functional areas such as spending, sex, substance use, eating or driving; (e) recurrent suicidal threats or behaviors as well as self-mutilation; (f) affective instability with marked reactivity of mood; (g) chronic feelings of emptiness; (h) inappropriate and intense anger or difficulty controlling anger; and (i) transient stress-induced paranoid ideation or severe dissociative symptoms. Using the DSM-IV-TR approach, five of the preceding criteria are required for diagnosis.

THE EPIDEMIOLOGY OF BPD

In the American population, the prevalence of BPD is estimated to be around 2% (American Psychiatric Association, 2000). As expected, the prevalence of this disorder is much higher in mental health settings (Quigley, 2005). For example, we found that nearly 50% of study participants in an American urban inpatient sample met the criteria for BPD on semi-structured interview (Sansone, et al., 2001).

Likewise, in a retrospective review of psychiatric records in a resident-provider outpatient psychiatric clinic, we found that 22% of the patients were diagnosed with BPD traits or disorder (Sansone, et al., 2003). As for primary care settings, Gross, et al. (2002) found a prevalence rate of 6.4% among American outpatients in an internal medicine setting.

As for the prevalence of BPD in other countries, Paris (1996) asserts that the disorder is more likely to be encountered in Western cultures. However, actual data appear to be somewhat conflicting. For example, BPD appears to be relatively infrequent in Norway (Torgersen, et al., 2001) in comparison to high rates of the disorder (i.e., between 10% and 18%) found among French high school students (Chabrol, et al., 2001).

Although probably less common, BPD has been described in developing as well as non-Western countries (Paris, 1996), including Turkey (Senol, et al., 1997), Korea (Hong, et al., 1998), India (Pinto, et al., 2000), and Argentina (Corsaro, 2000). According to research, the psychodynamic and behavioral characteristics of the disorder appear to be fairly similar regardless of country (Ikuta, et al., 1994; Pinto, et al., 2000).

If differences in the prevalence rates of BPD truly exist across the globe, what might explain this? It is possible that there are disparate rates from country to country because some societies may have inherent features that protect against the postulated causes of BPD (i.e., genetic predisposition, repetitive childhood trauma, parental psychopathology and family dysfunction) (Sansone, et al., 2007).

In part, genetic vulnerability may vary across the globe. Likewise, closely knit extended families and communities may potentially moderate the deleterious effects of childhood trauma, parental psychopathology and family dysfunction.

In addition to varying rates of prevalence across the globe, it may be that the symptoms of BPD manifest differently in various cultures (Sansone, et al., 2007). For example, while self-mutilation is fairly common and socially tolerated in the United States, such behavior may be perceived within Indian society as more pathological and less tolerated. In addition, in many countries, suicide gestures and attempts may be strictly religiously proscribed. Therefore, individuals in other cultures may manifest BPD symptoms in more culturally adaptive ways, such as through somatic preoccupation (Sansone, et al., 2007).

SUICIDAL BEHAVIOR IN BPD

One fundamental and highly discriminating feature of BPD is *chronic* self-harm behavior (Sansone, et al., 1998). As noted previously, this may manifest as suicide gestures, attempts and completions. According to empirical data, at least three-quarters of patients with BPD attempt suicide (Black, et al., 2004). In addition to suicide gestures and attempts, a significant minority of individuals with BPD complete suicide. According to follow-up studies over 27 years, approximately 10% of patients with BPD eventually complete suicide (Paris, 2002). This statistic is probably artificially lower than the actual percentage because of the difficulty in differentiating genuine suicide completions from staged "accidents."

Acute Versus Chronic Suicidal Ideation

In our view, suicidal ideation may be classified as either acute or chronic in nature (Fine, et al., 1990; Sansone, 2004; Sansone, et al., 2007). Acute suicidal ideation is typically: (a) an emergent and uncharacteristic response by the individual to stress, (b) precipitated by an acute and overwhelming psychosocial stressor, and (c) more likely to be associated with an Axis I disorder such as major depression. In contrast, chronic suicidal ideation is likely to: (a) represent a chronic and maladaptive interpersonal style, (b) be precipitated by interpersonal events that are highlighted by themes of perceived or genuine abandonment or rejection, and (c) be more likely to be associated with an Axis II disorder, commonly BPD.

Because these two types of suicidal ideation are distinctly different, the best clinical approaches to management would seem to differ as well. For acute suicidal ideation, temporary or short-term psychiatric hospitalization, whether voluntary or enforced, would appear beneficial and useful as the individual's preoccupation with suicide is usually acute, atypical, and likely to be time-limited. In addition, temporary confinement is realistic and practical.

In contrast, for chronic suicidal ideation, short-term psychiatric hospitalization appears to be of minimal benefit. First, there is no known *acute* treatment for chronic suicidal ideation. Long-term outpatient psychotherapy is the recommended treatment, with an emphasis on restructuring the individual's maladaptive responses to interpersonal stressors (Sansone, 2004). Second, there appear to be distinct risks with the short-term hospitalization of patients with BPD (Sansone, et al., 2007). These risks include: (a) in-hospital regression, which tends to develop within about three to four days and is highlighted by the worsening of the patient's symptoms; (b) contagion phenomenon, in which naïve patients with BPD assimilate the behaviors of seasoned self-harmers whom they observe in hospital settings; and (c) in-hospital conflict among the staff, which generally results in the erosion of the psychological treatment of the patient due to disharmony and dissension among treatment providers. Indeed, if patients with chronic suicidal ideation were to be hospitalized, what would be the appropriate endpoint of inpatient treatment? The recession of chronic suicidal ideation may take years.

It might be argued that patients with BPD experience acute suicidal ideation that is superimposed on chronic suicidal ideation. Therefore, the task would be to differentiate acute versus chronic suicidal ideation. However, we would argue that, again, despite the *acute* emergence of suicidal symptoms, the dynamic derivatives are the same - chronic and persistent maladaptive responses to interpersonal events.

Likewise, it might be argued that individuals with BPD who are suicidal should be admitted to hospital to protect professionals against possible litigation. However, we believe that such reflexive behavior by professionals is ultimately destructive for the patient. Again, there is no acute treatment for chronic suicidal ideation and, in addition, there are distinct risks with the hospitalization of patients with BPD (e.g., symptom worsening with confinement). To curtail potential legal ramifications, we suggest that professionals document in the medical record the patient's diagnosis, along with rationales for disposition, in order to justify the appropriate re-direction of the individual to outpatient treatment.

While the long-term psychotherapy treatment of suicidal ideation in patients with BPD and the corresponding relationship issues that precipitate such events is beyond the scope of this chapter, suffice it to say that there are a variety of approaches. Many of these approaches are eclectic, individualized by clinicians, and entail contracting (Sansone, et al., 2006) as well as predominant psychodynamic and cognitive-behavioral elements (Levitt, 2006). A few approaches are highly structured, systematized, and time-limited with robust cognitive-behavioral components. Examples of these focused programs are Dialectical Behavior Therapy (Linehan, 1993) and Systems Training for Emotional Predictability and Problem Solving (Blum, et al., 2002).

While none of the preceding eclectic or systematized approaches has extensive empirical validation, they appear to be clinically promising (Linehan, et al., 2006). In support of this observation, research indicates that the majority of patients with BPD improve in their symptomatology over periods as brief as six years (Zanarini, et al., 2004) and up to ten years (Zanarini, et al., 2006).

Conclusion

BPD is a personality disorder characterized by self-harm behavior including suicide attempts. The prevalence of the disorder in the USA is around 2%. While possibly more common in Western countries, BPD exists across the world. Global variation may be the result of genetics, culture, or some combination of the two. While suicide gestures and attempts are fairly common in individuals with BPD, the rate of completed suicide is far less frequent, at around 10%. While this represents a minority of patients, it remains a substantial percentage.

In terms of treatment, suicidal ideation may be classified as acute or chronic in nature. Acute suicidal ideation is typically an emergent event that is associated with an acute psychosocial stressor and a comorbid Axis I disorder. In contrast, chronic suicidal ideation is generally a long-standing interpersonal process that is related to maladaptive patterns in relationships with others and a comorbid Axis II disorder, typically BPD. For acute suicidal ideation, the treatment in most cases would consist of temporary psychiatric hospitalization to provide support and stabilize the patient, which is feasible and realistic. For chronic suicidal ideation, the proposed treatment is long-term outpatient psychotherapy, with an emphasis on restructuring relationship processes. In most circumstances (there may be exceptions), to hospitalize individuals with chronic suicidal ideation is counter-therapeutic and may result in in-hospital regression, the assimilation of new self-harm behaviors from other hospitalized patients, and divisive conflict in the hospital staff. While very little empirical data exist on the effectiveness of psychotherapy treatments with regard to chronic suicidal ideation, such treatments appear promising, particularly given follow-up studies that indicate significant symptom resolution.

REFERENCES

American Psychiatric Association. (2000). *The Diagnostic and Statistical Manual of Mental Disorder* (4th edn- text revision) (DSM-IV-TR). Washington, DC: APA.

Black, D. W., Blum, N., Pfohl, B., et al. (2004). Suicidal behavior in borderline personality disorder: prevalence, risk factors, prediction, and prevention. *Journal of Personality Disorders*, 18, 226-239.

Blum, N., Pfohl, B., St. John, D., et al. (2002). STEPPS: a cognitive-behavioral systems-based group treatment for outpatients with borderline personality: preliminary report. *Comprehensive Psychiatry*, 43, 301-310.

Chabrol, H., Montovany, A., Chouicha, K., et al. (2001). Frequency of borderline personality disorder in a sample of French high school students. *Canadian Journal of Psychiatry*, 46, 847-849.

Corsaro, B. (2000). Characteristics of borderline patients in Argentina. *Psicologia Contemporanea*, 7, 86-91.

Fine, M. A., & Sansone, R. A. (1990). Dilemmas in the management of suicidal behavior in individuals with borderline personality disorder. *American Journal of Psychotherapy*, 44, 160-171.

Gross, R., Olfson, M., Gameroff, M., et al. (2002). Borderline personality in primary care. *Archives of Internal Medicine*, 162, 53-60.

Hong, S. H., & Kim, Y. H. (1998). A validation study of the Borderline Personality Disorder Scale in Korean university students. *Korean Journal of Clinical Psychology*, 17, 259-271.

Ikuta, N., Zanarini, M. C., Minakawa, K., et al. (1994). Comparison of American and Japanese outpatients with borderline personality disorder. *Comprehensive Psychiatry*, 35, 382-385.

Levitt, J. L. (2006) A self-regulation approach for the patient with an eating disorder and borderline personality disorder. In R. A. Sansone & J. L. Levitt (Eds.) *Personality disorders and eating disorders: Exploring the frontier*, pp. 183-196. New York: Routledge.

Linehan, M. M. (1993). *Cognitive-behavioral treatment of borderline personality disorder*. New York: Guilford.

Linehan, M. M., Comtois, K. A., Murray, A. M., et al. (2006). Two-year randomized controlled trial and follow-up of Dialectical Behavior Therapy vs therapy by experts for suicidal behaviors and borderline personality disorder. *Archives of General Psychiatry*, 63, 757-766.

Mack, J. (1975). Borderline states: An historical perspective. In J. E. Mack (Ed.) *Borderline states in psychiatry*, pp. 1-27. New York: Grune & Stratton.

Paris, J. (1996). Cultural factors in the emergence of borderline pathology. *Psychiatry*, 59, 185-192.

Paris, J. (2002). Implications of long-term outcome research for the management of patients with borderline personality disorder. *Harvard Review of Psychiatry*, 10, 315-323.

Pinto, C., Dhavale, H. S., Nair, S., et al. (2000). Borderline personality disorder exists in India. *Journal of Nervous & Mental Disease*, 188, 386-388.

Quigley, B. D. (2005). Diagnostic relapse in borderline personality: risk and protective factors. *Dissertation Abstracts International*, 65, 3721B.

Sansone, R. A. (2004). Chronic suicidality and borderline personality. *Journal of Personality Disorders*, 18, 215-225.

Sansone, R. A., Rytwinski, D., & Gaither, G. A. (2003). Borderline personality and psychotropic medication prescription in an outpatient psychiatry clinic. *Comprehensive Psychiatry*, 44, 454-458.

Sansone, R. A., & Sansone, L. A. (2006). Borderline personality and eating disorders: an eclectic approach. In R. A. Sansone & J. L. Levitt (Eds.) *Personality disorders and eating disorders: Exploring the frontier*, pp. 197-212. New York: Routledge.

Sansone, R. A., & Sansone, L. A. (2007). *Borderline personality disorder in the medical setting: Unmasking and managing the difficult patient.* Hauppauge, NY: Nova Science.

Sansone, R. A., Songer, D. A., & Gaither, G. A. (2001). Diagnostic approaches to borderline personality and their relationship to self-harm behavior. *International Journal of Psychiatry in Clinical Practice*, 5, 273-277.

Sansone, R. A., Wiederman, M. W., & Sansone, L. A. (1998). The Self-Harm Inventory (SHI): development of a scale for identifying self-destructive behaviors and borderline personality disorder. *Journal of Clinical Psychology*, 54, 973-983.

Senol, S., Dereboy, C., & Yuksel, N. (1997). Borderline disorder in Turkey: a 2- to 4-year follow-up. *Social Psychiatry & Psychiatric Epidemiology*, 32, 109-112.

Torgersen, S., Kringlen, E., & Cramer, V. (2001). The prevalence of personality disorders in a community sample. *Archives of General Psychiatry*, 58, 590-596.

Zanarini, M. C., Frankenburg, F. R., Hennen, J., et al. (2004). Axis I comorbidity in patients with borderline personality disorder: 6-year follow-up and prediction of time to remission. *American Journal of Psychiatry*, 161, 2108-2114.

Zanarini, M. C., Frankenburg, F. R., Hennen, J., et al. (2006). Prediction of the 10-year course of borderline personality disorder. *American Journal of Psychiatry*, 163, 827-832.

In: Suicide from a Global Perspective: Psychiatric Approaches ISBN: 978-1-61942-267-4
Editors: A. Shrivastava, M. Kimbrell, and D. Lester © 2012 Nova Science Publishers, Inc.

Chapter 21

ALCOHOL AS A SUICIDE RISK FACTOR

Danuta Wasserman and Airi Värnik

INTRODUCTION

Dramatic socio-political and economic changes in the former USSR during Gorbachov´s "perestroika" (restructuring) followed by strict restrictions in alcohol production, sale and consumption during 1985-1990 turned out to a "natural experiment" allowing to explore the influence of alcohol use to suicide mortality. On aggregate level, during the 3 first years of "perestroika" alcohol consumption fell in all the republics of the USSR by 33%–53%, simultaneously there was a 40% decline in suicide rates for men, particularly those of working age, as compared to a 3% decline in 22 European countries during the same period. For males, alcohol appears to explain more than 50% of suicides (the attributable fraction), for females - 27%. On individual level, a case-control, psychological autopsy study revealed that 61% of the suicides (68% among males and 29% among females) were alcohol abusers or alcohol-dependent. Also, post-mortem blood alcohol concentration measurements in individuals who committed suicide revealed that for the fall of suicide rates during alcohol restrictions were responsible mainly individuals with alcohol in blood found at autopsy. Consequently, reducing alcohol availability may be an effective way of reducing suicide, especially in men. Alcohol restrictions appear to have the greatest impact on suicide mortality among those whose alcohol consumption is high.

The World Health Organization ranks alcohol as the third most serious preventable risk factor for premature death in developed nations. The rising trend of alcohol problems in developing countries is alarming from the suicide prevention point of view. Several aspects of the association between alcohol and suicide mortality have been studied extensively.

Studies using time-series analysis at aggregate level have demonstrated a positive correlation between per capita alcohol consumption and suicide rates (Norström, 1988; Gruenewald, et al., 1995; Lester, 1995; Wasserman & Varnik, 1998a, 1988b, 2001; Wasserman, et al., 1994, Varnik & Eklund, 1998; Norstrom & Skog, 2001; Ramstedt, 2001; Nemtsov, 2003). There are substantial regional variations, a result of marked cultural disparities in drinking habits (Gruenewald, et al., 1995; Lester, 1995).

The suicide rate falls at the following estimated rates when alcohol consumption decreases by 1 litre per capita per year: approximately 2.5% in Denmark (Skog, 1993) and 5% in Sweden, Norway and Hungary (Norström, 1988; Skog & Elekes, 1993).

Alcohol is known from clinical studies to be a key factor in suicidal behavior. Reports on case series have shown alcohol-dependence rates of 15%–47% among suicides (Arato, et al., 1988; Barraclough, et al., 1974; Cheng, 1995; Foster, et al., 1997; Rich, et al., 1988; Vijayakumar & Rajkumar, 1999). Depression is common among alcoholics, and alcohol dependence also produces depressive symptoms. (Barraclough, et al., 1974; Cheng, 1995; Henriksson, et al., 1993; Inskip, et al., 1998).

Psychiatric epidemiological studies have demonstrated elevated suicide mortality among alcoholics. In longitudinal cohort studies of alcoholics, lifetime suicide risk is estimated at 7% for alcohol dependence (Wasserman 2001).

The association between acute alcohol intoxication and suicide has been less thoroughly explored. Cherpitel, et al. (2004) reviewed 37 studies of acute alcohol use and suicidal behavior published between 1991 and 2001, studies with varying methodology and results. The range of cases with alcohol present in pos-mortem samples ranged from 10% to 69%.

A major anti-alcohol campaign in the USSR, a huge country with a population of almost 300 million, provided a unique experience from which evidence-based conclusions can be drawn. The campaign, launched on June 1st 1985, included strict restrictions on alcohol production, sale and consumption, with punishments for those who did not follow the rules, and also improvements in treatment and rehabilitation (Värnik, 1997; Wasserman & Värnik, 1998a; Nemtsov, 2003; Värnik, et al., 2007). The present chapter reviews the results of a series of studies by the Wasserman-Värnik group concerning the association between alcohol and suicide at the aggregate level. The group studied the correlation between per capita alcohol consumption with rates of death from external causes, such as suicide, death from alcohol poisoning and death from undetermined causes of death. This was studied by gender between 1970 and 1990, and particularly during the major anti-alcohol campaign in 1985–1989, in the former Soviet Union republics. The figures were also studied at individual level, identifying cases of alcohol abuse and dependence among those who committed suicide and examining blood alcohol to find out the role of alcohol in the sharp fall in suicide rates during the period when availability of alcohol was restricted.

Material and Methods

For studies at aggregate level, the figures for deaths from external causes provided by the All-Union Statistical Committee in Moscow were used. The figures for suicide, undetermined death and death from alcohol poisoning were separated by gender in order to calculate death rates per 100,000 inhabitants per year. The data were compared with the data kept by local statistical committees and in available published materials. The reliability and validity of the statistical data were considered to be good (Leon, et al., 1997; Wasserman & Varnik, 1998b).

Besides the trends for the whole period studied, 1970–1990, suicide for the years 1984 (the last year of the so-called period of stagnation during the Brezhnev era, before restructuring during Gorbachov´s perestroika), 1986 (the height of restrictions on alcohol production, sale and consumption), 1988 (the continuing anti-alcohol campaign and aspirations for spiritual liberation and democracy) and 1990 (the year when the anti-alcohol campaign came to an end) were analysed specifically (Wasserman & Varnik, 1998a, 1998b).

Moreover, an in-depth study of 427 suicides, using a case-control, retrospective, psychological autopsy study design, for one year in Estonia was performed. Both controls and suicides were matched by region, gender, age and nationality. A diagnosis of alcohol abuse and dependence (AAD) according to DSM-IV was based on interviews with the relatives of persons who had committed suicide and with controls (Kõlves, et al., 2006).

A total of 5,054 suicide cases registered by the Estonian Statistical Office and tested for blood alcohol (ethanol) by the Estonian Bureau of Forensic Medicine were studied for the years before the period of alcohol restrictions (1981–1984), during the period when alcohol restrictions were in force (1986–1988, the 'intervention period'), and after the period of the major anti-alcohol campaign (1989–1992). Data for 1985 were excluded because the anti-alcohol campaign began on June 1st 1985. Autopsy rates were high: 95% for males and 88% for females. Suicide cases were divided into three levels in terms of the per mill (‰) of alcohol in blood: 0.5–1.49, 1.5–2.49 and >2.5 (Värnik, et al., 2007).

Blood alcohol concentration (BAC) in samples collected by forensic pathologists during the medical autopsies was assessed by head-space chromatography and reported in per mill (‰). One per mill (1.0‰) is equivalent to 100mg/100ml and 21.7 mmol/l. BAC over 0.5‰ was termed 'inebriation' and denoted as BAC(+) (Värnik, et al., 2007).

Figures for alcohol consumption in the general population of the former USSR republics for the years 1984, 1986 and 1988 were obtained from official sources (Statistics, 1989) and for 1990 (the Soviet Union's last year of existence) through statistical estimation since state statistical indicators were unavailable for that year (Wasserman, et al., 1994).

RESULTS AND DISCUSSION

Aggregate Level

High alcohol consumption in the Slavic and Baltic republics, ranging from 9.8 to 11.6 litres of pure alcohol per capita per annum in 1984, coincided with high suicide rates in these regions. Low alcohol consumption was associated with low suicide rates, particularly in the Caucasian republics. Between 1984 and 1988, alcohol consumption fell in all the republics of the USSR by 33%–53% of the 1984 consumption rate. Simultaneously, there was a 40% decline in suicide rates for men, particularly those of working age (Wasserman & Värnik, 2001), as compared to a 3% decline in 22 European countries during the same period (Värnik, et al., 1998).

Regression analysis, with alcohol consumption as an independent variable and suicide rates and the whole category of deaths from external causes as dependent variables, revealed a positive correlation with alcohol consumption for both males and females. For males in most republics, alcohol appears to explain more than 50% of suicides (the attributable fraction) (Wasserman, et al., 1994). For females, alcohol appears to be of lower explanatory value since the attributable fraction of alcohol for suicides was estimated at 27% (Wasserman, et al., 1998, 1994)

However, studies at the aggregate level run the risk of the ecological fallacy. We therefore continued with our studies at an individual level.

Individual Level

The Proportion of Alcohol Misusers in Suicide Cases

A case-control, psychological autopsy study of 427 suicide cases indicated, according to DSM-IV diagnoses, that 61% of the suicides (68% among males and 29% among females) were alcohol abusers or alcohol-dependent. These figures are considerably higher than those found in other psychological autopsy studies where unselected suicide cases in different countries were analysed (Arato, et al., 1988; Barraclough, et al., 1974; Beskow, et al., 1990; Cheng, 1995; Foster, et al., 1997; Henriksson, et al., 1993; Rich, et al., 1988; Vijayakumar & Rajkumar, 1999). Individuals who committed suicide in Estonia showed higher rates of alcohol abuse and alcohol dependence than matched controls from general practitioner lists (OR=11.4, 95% CI 7.1–18.5).

Among the suicides diagnosed as alcohol-dependent according to the research protocol, only 29% received clinical diagnoses during their lifetimes, according to their clinical records. This finding indicates that general practitioners and clinicians markedly underdiagnosed alcohol dependence, and that there is a need to improve diagnosis and treatment of alcohol abusers and those who are alcohol dependent (Kõlves, et al., 2006).

Alcohol-Positive Suicides

During 1981–1992, post-mortem blood alcohol concentration (BAC) measurements in individuals who committed suicide revealed that alcohol was drunk prior to the act in 42.3% of cases. During the period of alcohol restrictions, suicide fell by 39%, with the largest fall occurring for those with the highest BAC (2.5‰). This decrease was observed in both sexes. There was only a modest decrease in suicide in those with low BAC.

These results strongly suggest that the anti-alcohol restrictions had the biggest impact on persons who were heavy alcohol abusers. Suicide rates started to rise again when the anti-alcohol campaign came to an end. This result is similar to that from other suicide prevention activities. When they stop, the preventive effects also cease.

Conclusion

Alcohol consumption is closely correlated with suicide, and reducing alcohol availability may, therefore, be an effective way of reducing suicide. Alcohol reduction seems to be effective in diminishing suicide rates in both sexes, but especially in men. Alcohol restrictions appear to have the greatest impact on suicide mortality among those whose alcohol consumption is high (Värnik, et al., 2007).

References

Arato, M., Demeter, E., Rihmer, Z., et al. (1988). Retrospective psychiatric assessment of 200 suicides in Budapest. *Acta Psychiatrica Scandinavica*, 77, 454–456.

Barraclough, B., Bunch, J., Nelson, B., et al. (1974). A hundred cases of suicide: clinical aspects. *British Journal of Psychiatry*, 125, 355–373.

Cheng, A. T. (1995). Mental illness and suicide: a case-control study in east Taiwan. *Archives of General Psychiatry*, 52, 594–603.

Cherpitel, C. J., Borges, G. L., & Wilcox, H. C. (2004). Acute alcohol use and suicidal behavior: a review of the literature. *Alcoholism: Clinical & Experimental Research*, 28, 18S–28S.

Foster, T., Gillespie, K., & McClelland, R. (1997). Mental disorders and suicide in Northern Ireland. *British Journal of Psychiatry*, 170, 447–452.

Gruenewald, P., Ponicki, W. & Mitchell, P. (1995). Suicide rates and alcohol consumption in the United States, 1970–89. *Addiction*, 90, 1063–1076.

Henriksson, M. M., Aro, H. M., Marttunen, M. J., et al. (1993). Mental disorders and comorbidity in suicide. *American Journal of Psychiatry*, 150, 935–940.

Inskip, H. M., Harris, E. C., & Barraclough, B. (1998). Lifetime risk of suicide for affective disorder, alcoholism and schizophrenia. *British Journal of Psychiatry*, 172, 35–37.

Kõlves, K., Värnik, A., Tooding, L. M., & Wasserman, D. (2006). The role of alcohol in suicide: a case-control psychological autopsy study. *Psychological Medicine*, 36, 923–930.

Leon, D. A., Chenet, L., Shkolnikov, V. M., et al. (1997). Huge variation in Russian mortality rates 1984–94: artefact, alcohol, or what? *Lancet*, 350, 383–388.

Lester, D. (1995). The association between alcohol consumption and suicide and homicide rates: a study of 13 nations. *Alcohol & Alcoholism*, 30, 465–468.

Nemtsov, A. (2003). Suicides and alcohol consumption in Russia, 1965–1999. *Drug & Alcohol Dependence*, 71, 161–168.

Norstrom, T., & Skog, O. J. (2001). Alcohol and mortality: methodological and analytical issues in aggregate analyses. *Addiction*, 96(Supplement 1), S5–S17.

Norström, T. (1988). Alcohol and suicide in Scandinavia. *British Journal of Addiction*, 83, 553–559.

Ramstedt, M. (2001). Alcohol and suicide in 14 European countries. *Addiction,* 96, 59–75.

Rich, C. L., Ricketts, J. E., Fowler, R. C., et al. (1988). Some differences between men and women who commit suicide. *American Journal of Psychiatry*, 145, 718–722.

Skog, O. J., & Elekes, Z. (1993). Alcohol and the 1950–90 Hungarian suicide trend: is there a causal connection? *Acta Sociologica*, 36, 33–46.

Skog, O. J. (1993). Alcohol and suicide in Denmark, 1911–24: experiences from a 'natural experiment.' *Addiction*, 88, 1189–1193.

Statistics, USSR (1989). *O potreblenii alkogolnih izdelii i sotsialnih posledstvii pjanstva i alkogolizma* (Alcohol consumption and consequences of alcohol abuse and alcoholism).

Wasserman, D. (2001). Alcoholism and other psychoactive substance abuse. In D. Wasserman (Ed.) *Suicide: An unnecessary death*. London, UK: Martin Dunitz Publishing House.

Wasserman, D., & Varnik, A. (1998a). Reliability of statistics on violent death and suicide in the former USSR, 1970–1990. *Acta Psychiatrica Scandinavica, Supplement* 394, 34–41.

Wasserman, D., & Värnik, A. (1998b). Suicide-preventive effects of perestroika in the former USSR: the role of alcohol restriction. *Acta Psychiatrica Scandinavica, Supplement* 394, 1–44.

Wasserman, D., & Värnik, A. (2001). Perestroika in the former USSR: history's most effective suicide preventive programme for men. In D. Wasserman (Ed.) *Suicide: An unnecessary death*, pp. 253–258. London, UK: Martin Dunitz.

Wasserman, D., Värnik, A., & Eklund, G. (1994). Male suicides and alcohol consumption in the former USSR. *Acta Psychiatrica Scandinavica*, 89, 306–313.

Wasserman, D., Varnik, A., & Eklund, G. (1998). Female suicides and alcohol consumption during *perestroika* in the former USSR. *Acta Psychiatrica Scandinavica, Supplement* 394, 26–33.

Vijayakumar, L.. & Rajkumar, S. (1999). Are risk factors for suicide universal? A case-control study in India. *Acta Psychiatrica Scandinavica*, 99, 407–411.

Värnik, A. (1997). *Suicide in the Baltic Countries and in the former republics of the USSR.* Stockholm, Sweden: Karolinska Institute.

Värnik, A., Kõlves, K., Väli, M., Tooding, L-M., & Wasserman, D., (2007). Do alcohol restrictions reduce suicide mortality? *Addiction*, 251–256.

Värnik, A., Wasserman, D., Dankowicz, M., et al. (1998), Age-specific suicide rates in the Slavic and Baltic regions of the former USSR during *perestroika*, in comparison with 22 European countries. *Acta Psychiatrica Scandinavica, Supplement* 394, 20–25.

INDEX

A

B

C

D

E

F

G

H

I

J

K

L

M

Q

R

S

T

U

V

W

Y